Gram Panchayat Planning

About the Author

Dr. Amitava Mukherjee specializes in participatory methods, micro-level planning, monitoring and evaluation. He held the Chair in Economics and Planning at the Lal Bahadur Shastri National Academy of Administration, Mussoorie; he was Head UN Centre for Agricultural Engineering and Machinery Beijing; Head UN Centre for Poverty Alleviation through Alternative Crops, Bogor, Indonesia and Senior Expert, United Nations Economic and Social Commission for Asia and the Pacific, Bangkok. He has written extensively on micro-level planning, poverty alleviation and food security comprising over 40 books and numerous papers, and has lectured across the continents. See for further details <amitavamukherjee.org>

Gram Panchayat Planning

Essays in Honour of B.N. Yugandhar

Former Secretary to Prime Minister of India and
Member, Planning Commission of India

Amitava Mukherjee

CONCEPT PUBLISHING COMPANY PVT. LTD.
NEW DELHI-110059

ISBN-13: 978-93-88937-88-7

First Published 2021

Published and Printed by

Concept Since 1974

Concept Publishing Company Pvt. Ltd.
A/15-16, Commercial Block, Mohan Garden,
New Delhi-110059 (INDIA)
T : 91 11 25351460, 91 11 25351794
E : publishing@conceptpub.com; *W* : www.conceptpub.com

Cataloging in Publication Data--Courtesy: D.K. Agencies (P) Ltd. <docinfo@dkagencies.com>

Mukherjee, Amitava, 1951- **author.**
Gram panchayat planning : essays in honour of B.N. Yugandhar / Amitava Mukherjee.
pages cm
Includes bibliographical references and index.
ISBN 9789388937887

1. Panchayat—India. 2. Political planning—India. I. Yugandhar, B. N., 1937- honouree. II. Title.

LCC JS7009.M85 2021 | DDC 320.84 23

Preface

Most in the villages in India live with limited means of livelihood. Poverty, illiteracy, unemployment, morbidity, poor infrastructure and communication problems are still real issues. The lack of primary health care facilities, lack of primary education along with gender disparity, high incidence of infant mortality, poor maternal health, child undernourishment are additional issues for the villages especially the women.

Projects and programmes aiming to have sectoral approach to development like the Swatch Bharat Abhiyan or MNREGA as well as an integrated approach towards development of the village and Panchayats (sometimes with special focus on areas like healthcare and mother and child development, sanitation and drinking water, women empowerment, vocational training for rural youth, sensitizing the use of green energy and environment to have a model village etc.) have been implemented over decades[1] to tackle the above problems. Various improvements have been affected from time to time, to fine tune the various programmes. However, there is a long way to go.

One of the makers of modern India, Gandhi, envisaged an India where villages would be independent entities, supporting themselves by harmonizing human needs with local resources pretty much like the "Sufficiency Economy Philosophy (SEP)" framework philosophy propagated in Thailand from the 1980s by His Majesty the late King Bhumibol Adulyadej of Thailand[2]. "Sufficiency Economy Philosophy (SEP)" lays stress on responsible consumption, awareness, reasonableness and resilience, and a more balanced, holistic and sustainable approach to development. Today, driven by the monster of over-exploitation and the alarming diminution of natural resources, development experts are anxiously trying to find ways and means to realize the Mahatma's vision by making the village ecosystem sustainable in India and ratchet up the "Sufficiency Economy Philosophy (SEP)".

But modern trends of what some may call manipulative development often tends to belie any such hope. Garrett Hardin[3] used to recount a tale of how a group of competing farmers grazed cattle on a common pasture, where each farmer found that it is more profitable in the short run to graze more cattle notwithstanding what the pasture could stand. In the long run it led to the eventual destruction of the pasture and with that the destruction of the farmers' livelihood as well. The allegory elucidates aptly the relentless need for better use of resources by India and the consequences of muddled use of resources[4]. And this is possible through better planning, owned by the people whose lives matter.

India dreadfully needs to increase productivity of all the components of the village systems and sub-systems, starting from agricultural to social and institutional systems and in a sustainable way. Current rural development efforts are often disjointed in that they focus mostly on one sector say agriculture or social development. And these efforts are often inconsistent and counter-productive. For example, villagers who dig irrigation tanks do not want to do anything about building infrastructure for optimal use of the tank water or do anything about appropriate land-use to protect the catchment of these tanks. Those rearing Bovine wealth or are engaged in supply of milk to the nearby markets, pay scant attention to augmenting supply of fodder.

The wayout could be to promote integrated village planning, for development and/or betterment of social infrastructure, the enhancement of the total resource base of the village ecosystem, the provision of basic needs, production of basic biomass needs of the village and the equitable distribution of resources. The social power-status structure of the village is very important and hence they must be factored in the village plans. Some sections of the population may depend more on free provision of social services in the village while others may depend more on common property resources[5]. The access and the rights to use these services and resources must be clearly defined and safeguarded. This assumes even more importance as experience has revealed that government is more effective where it allows the common people and local community to generate and implement generation and development programmes.

The widely diverse nature of village economy and its social, human and ecosystems in India and varying power structures in different parts of the country make village planning truly complicated. It is thus long been recognized that it is difficult — even impossible — to envisage any one plan being effective for every village developed on a national level. An effective plan has to take into account particulars at the village, community and ecosystem-specific levels.

This has been recognized by the Government from time to time and guidelines for development of Village plans have been issued. For example, on October 11, 2014, the Government of India launched an ambitious scheme for village development, namely, the **Saansad Aadarsh Gram Yojana** (SAGY). The scheme requires 'Saansads' or elected MPs to convert 3 villages in their constituency into 'Adarsh Grams' or model villages worthy of replication elsewhere in the country. It endorses an integrated approach towards development that includes better and improved physical infrastructure in the villages, along with building community spirit. It aims for better governance (transparency, accountability and integrity), active people's participation (mutual cooperation, self-help & self-reliance and improved standard of living & quality of life), and environmental consciousness that can be replicated. It hopes to use the resources from existing schemes for furthering the cause of these villages. The **Saansad Aadarsh Gram Yojana**, enjoined village level plans. But many of the guidelines issued and programmes outlined depended on the ability of the cutting edge level development workers' ability and ingenuity to develop participatory plans at the village level[6]. As a result a whole body of materials has been generated which provided valuable insights into the characteristics, contents and problems of our village economy but fall short of being plans that can be operationalized.

It is widely recognized that women play a vital role in the affairs of village communities. Women take an active interest in programmes designed to improve the conditions of the village especially the micro-environments, natural resources and ecology because of their culturally determined role as collectors of food, non-timber forest produce, fuel, fodder and water. But because women seldom participate in any institution dominated by men, special provision should be made for women's participation in the development of the Gram Panchayat plans and their implementation.

This Book has been designed to be a comprehensive guide to

Village and Gram Panchayat Planning, being cognizant of all the factors mentioned above. There are five Chapters in the Book.

Chapter-1 is on the Conceptual Specifications for Gram Panchayat Planning. In planning for development, combining available human, social, institutional, ecological, environmental and physical resources for the well-being of the community may be seen as key to planning at Village and Gram Panchayat levels. The key issues are: (i) whether communities and governments can jointly and severally create new livelihoods, employment opportunities, develop human capabilities (providing primary health care and elementary education) and increase productivity (of factors of production). And (ii) at what cost of planning, zoning, and environmental considerations is these livelihood, employment and productivity objectives to be pursued? These questions which are not easy to answer and there are conceptual, policy, and operational difficulties, whose solution provides the rationale for Village or Gram Panchayat-level economic development. Hence Chapter-1 deals with the Conceptual Specifications for Gram Panchayat Planning. This will help the readers to search for answers to the fundamental rhetorical questions since antiquity, namely, Why? How? What? When? For whom? By whom and where?[7]

Chapter-2 deals with the principles of Gram Panchayat Planning. At the core of Gram Panchayat Planning process is *decentralization* involving the sharing of planning functions at different levels, devising mechanisms and procedures for the effective intra-area and inter-area flows of information and interaction *per se*. It has to be ensured that interactive participation and iterative dialogue and interface with the people take place. These are germane to making the Gram Panchayat planning process a harmonious, inter-dependent and participatory in character and content. These taken one with the other make the Gram Panchayat Plans themselves geographically relevant, economically authentic and administratively implementable. For these to happen adherence to certain guide posts is imperative. These guideposts are provided by definitive principles, where principles are pre-made decisions. The most important principles of Gram Panchayat planning are discussed in Chapter 2. They will act as guideposts and touchstones while preparing and implementing the Village or Gram Panchayat Plans.

Having outlined the conceptual specifications and principles of Gram Panchayat Planning, Chapter 3 is on how to prepare a Village and Gram Panchayat Plan. There are four components of Village and

Gram Panchayat Plans, as genre of micro-level planning, has to encompass four dimensions of development: physical plan, financial plan, resource (financial resources, human resources, social resources or social capital, natural resources and financial resources) plan and a spatial plan. In this Chapter it should be underscored that in this manual the discussion relates to areas where participatory methods are used. This Chapter provides the nuts and bolts of village and Gram Panchayat Planning on the above four aspects. It basically the answers the question of "How" of village and Gram Panchayat Planning and takes the reader through the steps involved in the formulation of a village or Gram Panchayat Plan.

Chapter 4 is on ways and means to apply participatory methods in village and Gram Panchayat Planning. Making planning at the grassroots level participatory involves four intertwined elements: tools, methods, processes and sharing. This Chapter provides details of all the four elements. It is important to get all four right otherwise we may end up with sub-optimal results.

Chapter 5 is on capacity building. This Book in the first four Chapters deals with the preparation of village and Gram Panchayat Planning. But village Gram Panchayat Planning is a facilitated process. It is not an autonomous process. Thus it has to be facilitated by those who know the people, their aspirations, local conditions and resources as also the techniques and methods of planning. Hence planning at the village and Gram Panchayat cannot be either be facilitated nor plans developed by people who are not properly trained in the skill sets required to prepare and facilitate Gram Panchayat plan. Capacity-building of all functionaries involved directly in Gram Panchayat Development planning and in facilitating such planning is of utmost important. This assumes even greater importance in view of the fact that many of the elected functionaries of the Panchayats are neo-literates. Training such people in the village and Gram Panchayat planning is very important. And such training should be a continuous process as under Article 243D of the Constitution "not less than one-third (including the number of seats reserved for women belonging to the Scheduled Castes and the Scheduled Tribes) of the total number of seats to be filled by direct election in every Panchayat shall be reserved for women and such seats may be allotted by rotation to different constituencies in a Panchayat." So after every election new members would be elected who needs training in skills, knowledge and attitude and behaviour for planning.

There are several treatises on the subject but most are either too detailed to be used at only the village and Gram Panchayat level[8] or are not directly related to village and Gram Panchayat planning per se or deal with only one aspect of the Gram Panchayat Plans. Thus Chapter 5 is, thus, an indicative way of imparting a set of functional skills for facilitating Gram Panchayat planning as is necessary for initiating community development through praxis. The Chapter is designed to train people and sensitize them to the philosophy of the people-centred development and stakeholder participation in the Gram Panchayat planning. The seeds of the future involvement of stakeholders are sown at the planning stage. The Chapter thus attempts to build the Capability Spectrum in terms of knowledge, skills and attitudes and hence behaviour that the Gram Panchayat planning team must necessarily possess for facilitating the process of Gram Panchayat planning in their communities.

New Delhi, August 2019 **Amitava Mukherjee**

Notes

1. Some of the Schemes/programmes are: 1. Deen Dayal Upadhyay Grameen Kaushal Yojna, 2. Roshni: Skill Development Scheme for Tribals, 3. Swachchh Bharat Mission, 4. Sansad Adarsh Gram Yojna, 5. Heritage Development and Augmentation Yojna (HRIDAY), 6. Mahatma Gandhi National Rural Employment Guarantee Scheme (MGNREGS), 7. National Rural Livelihood Mission, 8. Pradhan Mantri Gram Sadak Yojna, 9. Training to Rural Youth for Self Employment (TRYSEM), 10. Antyodaya Anna Yojna (AAY), 11. Village Grain Bank Scheme, 12. National Rural Health Mission, 13. Aam Aadmi Bima Yojna, and 14. Kutir Jyoti Programme 15. Sarva Siksha Abhiyan.
2. **King Bhumibol Adulyadej's "Sufficiency Economy Philosophy (SEP)",** *http://newdelhi.thaiembassy.org/en/2019/01/king-bhumibol-adulyadejs-sufficiency-economy-philosophy-sep-translated-hindi/.*
3. Sanchari Pal: "15 Progressive Indian Villages That Will Make You Want to Ditch Your City Life Right Away!", **The Better India**. https://www.thebetterindia.com/85354/inspiring-indian-villages-sustainable-development/accessed on 10th August 2019.
4. Take the case of a village ecosystem. If too many trees are rampantly cut for fuel or fodder or timber, or population pressure forces the expansion of croplands and habitats, thus reducing forests and grazing pastures, the fallouts can be shattering. Confronted with shortage of firewood, villagers

would take progressively use, for example, cow dung as fuel. This in turn would dispossess soil of vital organic soil nutrients. That would adversely affect productivity of land. Vanishing pastures would reduce livestock, leading to a shortage of animal manure. And, the vicious circle would continue.

5. Studies from different states of India have found that CPRs contribute, 1.1 per cent to 29 per cent of the income of poorer households. The average contribution at the state level is 0.1 per cent to 22 per cent, 10 per cent, 22 per cent to 27 per cent and 19 per cent to 29 per cent in Gujarat, Karnataka, Punjab and West Bengal respectively. These figures for non-poor/cultivating households are 0.1 per cent to 11.4 per cent, 6.2 per cent, 22 per cent and 0.13 per cent to 5.62 per cent. https://shodhganga. inflibnet. ac.in/bitstream/10603/121041/9/09_chapter%203.pdf. Also see N.S. Jodha: "Some places again: a 'restricted' revisit to dry regions of India", in Rucha Ghate, Jodha, N.S. and Mukhopadhyay (eds.): **Promise, Trust and Evolution: Managing the Commons of South Asia**, New York: Oxford University Press, 2008, pp. 1651-69. N. S. Jodha: "Common property resources and the rural poor", **Economic and Political Weekly**, 21, 1169-1181, 1986.
6. ActionAid: **Village Book Training Manual : Community Led and Planning Process,** Myanmar, 2014.
7. Even though the classical origin of these questions as situated in ethics had long been lost, they have been a standard way of formulating or analyzing rhetorical questions since antiquity. The *rhetor Hermagoras of Temnos*, as quoted in pseudo-Augustine's De Rhetorica, applied Aristotle's "elements of circumstances" as the loci of an issue:
   Quis, quid, quando, ubi, cur, quem ad modum, quibus adminiculis.[Robertson, D.W., Jr (1946). "A Note on the Classical Origin of "Circumstances" in the Medieval Confessional". **Studies in Philology,** Vol. 43, No. 1, pp. 6–14. (Who, what, when, where, why, in what way, by what means)
   St. Thomas Aquinas [See Thomas Aquinas and Daniel J. Sullivan (eds.): **The Summa Theologica. Great Books of the Western World.** 19, translated by Fathers of the English Dominican Province in **Encyclopedia Britannica**. pp. Q7. Art. 3. Obj. 3. 1952] also refers to the elements as used by Cicero in **De Inventione** (Chap. 24 DD1, 104) as: Quis, quid, ubi, quibus auxiliis, cur, quomodo, quando.[**Ibid**]
8. See for example: Government of Haryana: **Guidelines for the preparation of Gram Panchayat Development Plan, HAMARI YOJANA – HAMARA VIKAS,** Development and Panchayats Department, Government of Haryana, Chandigarh (undated); D. Bandyopadhyay, Amitava Mukherjee, Mitali Sen Gavai: **Empowering Panchayats: Handbook for Master Trainers: Using Participatory Approach**, New Delhi: Concept Publishing Company (2003) and **Empowering Women Panchayat Members: Handbook for Master Trainers Using Participatory Approach**, New Delhi: Concept Publishing Company (2006).

Acknowledgements

In the preparation of this work, I have received the help, guidance and support of many people, over a fairly long period of time. To them I am very grateful, even if I don't mention their names specifically as the list is too long to be paraded here without boring you.

I am grateful to three stalwarts in development work from Hyderabad: Late Sri B.N. Yugandhar, Former Secretary to Prime Minister of India for initiating me to the nuances of planning; the Late S.R. Shankaran, Former Secretary to Government of India who had an inexhaustible yarn of insights into rural development and the Late C.H. Hanumantha Rao, Former Member of the Planning Commission, who guided the work of the District Panning Unit, LBS National Academy of Administration, Mussoorie, where I started working on grassroots planning.

I am especially thankful to Sri S.M. Vijayanand (IAS), the then Secretary, Ministry of Rural Development, Government of India at whose initiation I undertook this work; Dr. Ramesh Chand, Member Niti Ayog, New Delhi; Sri Amitabh Kundu, Professor JNU, New Delhi: Smt. Gyan Mudra, Professor and Head, Centre for Good Governance and Policy Analysis, NIRDPR, Hyderabad; Sri Somesh Kumar (IAS), Chief Secretary, Government of Telangana; Sri Vijay Raghavan, Country Director, Johanniter International Assistance, Afghanistan; Sri Janardana Rao, of Concern International, Afghanistan; Sri Bishnu Parida, Chief Operating Office, Jharkhand State Rural Livelihood Mission, Ranchi; Sri Sumantra Patra, State Project Manager, Jharkhand State Rural Livelihood Mission, Ranchi; Sri T. Vijay Kumar (IAS), the then Mission Director, National Rural Livelihood Mission, New Delhi; Sri Debraj Behera, World Bank Group & Food and Agriculture Organization of the United Nations; Prof. Satosh Mehrotra, Professor of Economics, Centre for Informal Sector and Labour

Studies, School of Social Sciences, Jawaharlal Nehru University, New Delhi; Sandip Chachra, Country Director, ActionAid, India; Sri Indu Prakash Singh, City Makers, New Delhi; Sri Hari Govind Singh and Arthik Anusandhan Kendra, Allahabad and Halia, Mirzapur; Sri Baldev Singh, Block President, Nauni Majgaon, Himachal Pradesh; Sri Vinay Raj, International Federation of Red Cross and Red Crescent, Bangalore; Sri Upendra Choragudi, Myanmar.

I thank Sri Ashok Mittal ji and Concept Publishing Company Pvt. Ltd., New Delhi, who agreed to have the book published painstakingly. They have been our lifelong friend and publisher. I thank my son Taponeel Mukherjee for his unending encouragement and to Poornima for always questioning me: "When is your book coming out". She should be happy it is here now.

My thanks are due to the librarians of the CENTRAL LIBRARY, University of Delhi, Delhi; National Institute of Rural Development and Panchayati Raj, Hyderabad; Lal Bahadur Shastri National Academy of Administration, Mussoorie; United Nations Libraray, Lodhi Road, New Delhi and Library of the India International Centre, New Delhi.

Contents

List of Figures

1

Conceptual Specifications for Gram Panchayat Planning

Introduction

It is being increasingly recognized that, irrespective of national economic strategies pursued to stimulate the economy, economies at the sub-national level particularly at the gram panchayat and district levels, in a diversified economy cannot depend upon only national economic strategies. Motivations of the private sector do not coincide with the needs or interests of local communities, workers, or weaker sections of society. In free economies, communities are market places too, and therefore, communities must be able to deploy resources placed at their disposal efficiently and gain competitive advantages to create new livelihoods, new employment, increase productivity and maintain their existing economic base. That is, people at grassroots (read village and Gram Panchayat-levels) level must combine their available human, social, institutional, and physical resources to build a system for the well-being of the community.

Combining their available human, social, institutional, and physical resources for the well-being of the community may be seen as either a new approach or the reformulation of the failed "trickle down" policies of the past. The key issues are: (i) whether communities and governments working together or separately, can create new livelihoods, employment opportunities, develop human capabilities (providing primary health care and elementary education) and increase productivity (of natural resources); and (ii) at what cost of planning, zoning, and environmental considerations are these livelihoods, employment and productivity objectives, being pursued? These are difficult issues to decide and there are conceptual, policy, and operational difficulties, whose solution provides the rationale for village or Gram Panchayat-level economic development.

Community-based Socio-Economic Development

Community based socio-economic development is a process by which government, development institutions and the community manage their existing resources, and resources placed at their disposal, and enter into new social contract with the various stakeholders in the local economy to improve delivery of social services, create new livelihood and employment opportunities, increase productivity and stimulate economic activity in a defined area (say Gram Panchayat or even a village). The key element in community-based economic development is "endogenous development" using more effectively the potential of community's own financial, human, natural, institutional, and physical resources. This new orientation leads to a focus on taking community-based initiatives in the development process to create new and better livelihood and employment opportunities and increased productivity of natural resources as well as improve delivery of basic services especially of primary health care, elementary education and drinking water. The reasons are not far to seek:

> *[Previous economic development theories and programme efforts]... have relied too heavily on a belief that the benefits of economic growth and expansion will "trickle down" to improve conditions of the poor.... They have separated and distinct camps and... they have focused almost exclusively on trying to remedy perceived 'defects' in the poor inadequate education of skills, weak community supports, lack of motivation and ignored the very real, potent barriers in the structure of opportunities the poor confront on the "demand" side of the labour market equation.*[1]

Economic development at the micro-level, is process oriented involving, *inter alia*, the formation of new institutions, the development of alternative livelihood options, the improvement in the employment generating capacity of existing employers to produce better products, the identification of new markets, the transfer of knowledge, and the nurturing of new enterprises. As Williams, writing for the OECD, puts it,

> *When you move beyond importing [jobs]... and start a strategy of creative innovation and adaptation, then [local] "innovation" becomes an economic, social, and a local [development] preoccupation, rather than just a technical one.*[2]

Irrespective of form, community-based economic development has one primary goal, which is to improve the well-being of the community, and in so doing bureaucracy, local governments, people, institutions and voluntary organizations must take on an initiating, rather than a passive, role.

In essence, the community, bureaucracy and government at the local levels, using the resources of existing community-based institutions (where they exist and possess economic potential)—is required to assess the potentials and marshal the necessary resources to develop the local economy. Private decisions and public economic activity are intimately related and affect livelihood and employment opportunities and well-being of the whole community. There is a need to take a new and different perspective towards backwardness of the local economy. No matter how poor or well-off the local economy may be, bureaucracy, local level government institutions, and the private initiatives are essential partners in the socio-economic development process, and will have to work as a cohesive whole.

It may be of interest to note that Gram Panchayats are primarily concerned with rural sector of a group of villages and a Gram Panchayat also partakes the nature of a region.[3] The country as a whole can be conceived of as the macro-region; the states can be conceived of as macro-meso-regions; the districts, can be conceived of as micro-regions and the blocks or Gram Panchayats (a cluster of villages) may be conceived of as super-micro-regions. Without complicating too much, a four-tier planning hierarchy and levels is indicated in Fig. 1.1.

A Priori Justification for Community-based Planning such as Gram Panchayat Planning

For the developing countries, like India, with serious inter-regional disparities in development and a complex heterogeneous social structure, the spectra of poverty is highly "location specific" and "group specific". The sensitive issues pertaining to poverty of such

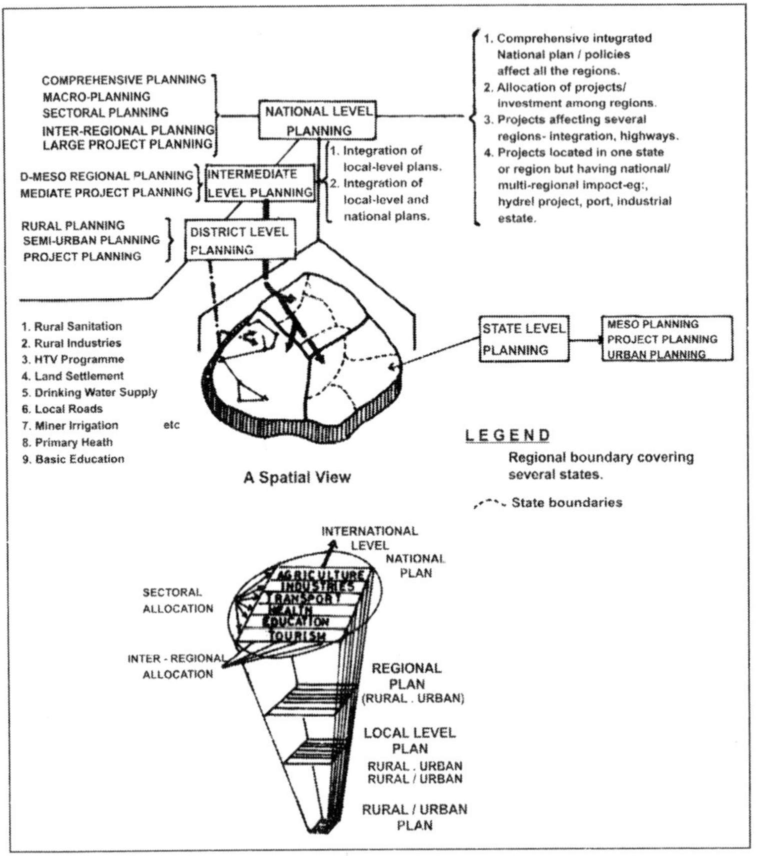

Fig. 1.1: A Hierarchical View

dimension and location can be best dealt with, not from a central place, but from the scene of action itself. This warrants a community-based approach to planning for socio-economic development, so that, the process can be sensitive to local perceptions and immediate requirements.

In a democratic society, the process of planning should also be democratic, in tune with the political framework of the country, at least to ensure participative plan formulation at appropriate levels according to the felt needs of the people and involve the community generally, in the process of plan implementation. The masses would only then be partners in socio-economic development. After all the process of socio-economic development is an adventure in which the people must participate for the development impulses to be long lasting and pervasive.

The extent of poverty in a developing country, like India, automatically mirrors the scarcity element of investible resources and requires optimization in investment decisions. Because community-based planning, like Gram Panchayat Planning, ensures better spatial convergence and sequencing of inter-related activities, optimal deployment of investible funds is likely to be better ensured in a community-based planning framework than in centralized decision-making systems.

Optimality in investment decision also requires detailed knowledge of the area of planning, across different levels and sectors. Resource endowments, physical features, geographical relief, hydrological system, geomorphologic characteristics, habits, customs, usage, practice, local problems, and on and on, on a growing list of traits, are varied and as diverse between regions as it could be. Realistic planning would require marshalling of these divergent informations as building blocks for the planning exercise at the local level (read community level). There is no gainsaying that community-based planning such as Gram Panchayat Planning provides a much efficient way of so doing than what would be possible under a centralized decision system.

These brief observations as justification for community-based planning also provide a glimpse at the complexity of the community-based planning process. Community based planning is not tantamount to mere knocking down the citadel of central planning into smaller units, but is a process that involves ensuring "complementarities", "consistencies", "flows" and closing of "gaps". In a sense, the community-based planning represents what is now fashionable to call, "systems approach" to the planning process, that presupposes the existence of sub-systems within the system itself and where the sub-systems will have a cluster of activities grounded on inter-dependent and inter-related activities. Like the systems approach, community-based planning presupposes inclusion of as complete a segmentation of the task involved as possible, in "managerial commands". Thus, the sub-systems (community-based planning, planning at the state, district or block level) are relatively independent systems but are also parts of an inter-dependent whole. While delineating sub-systems (community-based planning like Gram Panchayat Plans, State Plans,

District Plans or Block Level Plans) the edifice of the planning process will have to be built upon the three principles of: (a) activity differentiation, (b) inter-dependency, and (c) small external effects.

Typology of Planning and Approaches to Gram Panchayat Planning

Within the broad classification of Centralized *vis-à-vis* Community-based Planning there could be substantial diversity. A quick review of the classificatory frame of planning, conceived from different perspectives, would be of interest.

(a) Community-based Planning could be *comprehensive* or *partial,* former connoting planning for the totality of the local area and the latter signifying planning for a part of the local area. Comprehensive planning takes stock of the aggregate resources and aggregate targets for the entire local area. In an open systems where planning is used as either a countervailing instrument or alternatively as corrective action for market failures, planning revolves around public investments. This is a case of partial planning. Thus, partial planning partakes the nature of planning for a particular segment in the local area, like public water and sanitation, and its consequence on the local economy as a whole is left to be taken note of in national accounting and statistical analysis. Additionally in countries like India where the economy can be conceptually divided between three broad sectors (the public sector, the private sector and the joint venture sector) partial planning could also imply planning for a sector. While in most countries the public sector would normally include social overheads, transport, communication, education, public health and education, much depends upon the ideological indoctrination of the political milieu about the extent and area of State participation in economic activity. Thus, the distinction between comprehensive planning and partial planning, is a difference based on the substance and scope of planning for socio-economic development.

(b) A distinction between *imperative planning* and *indicative planning* as they relate to community-based planning is a distinction, not substance, but *methodology of planning.* For example, an imperative Gram Panchayat planning will enjoin that the Panchayats as the third-tier in governance will formulate the plans, ensure execution and initiate monitoring it such that the plans are instruments of only authorization. An Imperative Gram Panchayat Plan will really be a document of authorization that will tell each stakeholder what it must produce and how much it may invest.

Indicative Gram Panchayat planning will, on the contrary, be a system where the plan will only laydown the broad parameters of objectives and perspectives, whose attainment is left to the individual initiative of participating agencies and institutions. The Indicative Gram Panchayat Planning, in contradistinction to imperative planning, will "indicate expectations, aspirations and intentions but not binding commitments" of the Gram Panchayat. Such a plan document will authorize nothing. The element of coercion of an Imperative Gram Panchayat Plan will be non-existent and the concept of foisting decisions of a few will be missing. Indicative Gram Panchayat Planning would thus be perceived as a co-operative harmonious and natural process, built fundamentally upon induced participation of community of the Gram Panchayat area. However, experts are of the view that there could really be no Gram Panchayat Planning that is totally indicative in essence, because some controls and regulatory devices have to be pressed into operation for the implementation and success of any plan, and even some experts maintain that indicative Gram Panchayat Planning will not be planning at all as the plan will look into the future without any effort to change the same.

The fact remains that indicative planning at the Gram Panchayat-level will admit of greater flexibility and more individual and community initiatives than in case of Imperative Gram Panchayat Planning. The concept of indicative Gram Panchayat Planning will be rooted in the theory of demand expectations which enjoins that the rate of growth that can be achieved is, within limits, partly a matter of the growth rates that the relevant bodies in society (particularly entrepreneurs) expect to be achieved.

This variation in the content of the degree of freedom allowed for community and individual actions and initiative, in an Imperative Gram Panchayat Planning and in an Indicative Gram Panchayat Planning, explains the genesis of the appellations *"planning by compulsions"* and *"planning by inducements"* applied to these two types of planning respectively. One could argue and justifiably so, that the distinction between types of planning is *based on the techniques* deployed in ensuring achievement of plan objectives than their contents.

(c) The planning processes can be differentiated between *centralized* and *decentralized* planning, based on territorial levels where they are sought to be operationalized. In centralized planning the entire plan is conceived, implemented and monitored from a central location, despite existence of a hierarchy of economic planning regions and administrative delineation. In a decentralized planning framework, on the contrary, planning at several levels for the relative level of planning region or administrative boundary, is conceived, executed and evaluated. *Gram Panchayat Planning is essentially a variant of decentralized planning.* Centralized and decentralized planning are often referred to as "single level" or "multi-level" planning, and the appellations reveal the character and concept involved in these planning phenomena.

(d) Our discussion in Section II had generated the broad concepts of macro-economic planning region, meso-economic planning region and micro-economic planning region. Conforming to these regions, planning could be *macro-level* planning at national level.[4] *Meso-level* planning (State or group of States), *Micro-level* Planning (at District or Block level) and of course, *Local-level* planning (Gram Panchayat, Block or Village level). These variants are planning essentially by territorial space sized in descending order of magnitude. Our concern on the book is with Community-based Gram Panchayat Planning only, which is essentially a local level planning. However, since, we have abolished national-level planning, we consider Gram Panchayat Plan as a *micro-level* plan.[5]

(e) If time element is injected in differentiating types of community-based planning (read Gram Panchayat Planning), there could be three types of planning, depending on the time profile: the short-term Gram Panchayat Planning, Medium term Gram Panchayat Planning and the Long-term Gram Panchayat Planning. Short-term Gram Panchayat Plans will be directed to tackle situations requiring only small scale variations in social development or production and employment pursuits, as against Long-term Gram Panchayat Plans that would deal with institutional and structural changes for long-term socio-economic development of the gram panchayat. Viewed in that perspective the distinction between Short-term and Long-term Gram Panchayat Plans is grounded more on *operational* time than on *clock time*.

However, there are writers who would seek to distinguish between *short-run* and *long-run* planning based on clock time also.

A *short-run* Gram Panchayat Plan could be a plan spanning over a year or two, and a *Long-run* Gram Panchayat Plan could be in respect of ten or fifteen years. The choice of the number of years, for temporal distinction of planning process between *short-run* and *long-run,* is decidedly arbitrary, and there could be several variations of it. For instance a *Short-run* Gram Panchayat Plan could relate to a year, or two or three years, and a *Long-run* Gram Panchayat Plan could relate to ten fifteen or even twenty years. No rational limits can be laid down for making such distinctions with exactitude. That also explains why one could also talk about a *medium range* Gram Panchayat Plan, as an intermediary concept between *short-run* and *long-run* Gram Panchayat Plans, say a plan covering five years or so. Adhering to this scheme, a classification of our Annual Plans, Five Year Plans and Perspective Plans as *short-run,* medium range and *long-run* Gram Panchayat Plans respectively, would seem to be acceptable.

All planning, it needs to be underscored, should ideally be a continuous process and impact of developmental efforts should be allowed sufficient time to fructify. Objectives of Gram Panchayat planning, like sustained improvement in livelihood and standard of living, sustained development of backward villages (of *Dalits, Adivasis*, Manual Scavengers), uninterrupted improvement in the availability of food, nutrition, and shelter, all require uninterrupted and uninterruptible efforts extended over considerable periods of time, despite Keynes' warning that in the *long-run* "we are all dead". Gram Panchayat Planning whatever the form, has to, therefore, grapple with current situation, and then work out concrete programme of action, several years in advance. There lies the need, as some would argue, for having a set of several Gram-Panchayat Plans: a long-range view of trends and directions, in a *perspective plan;* an *intermediate plan,* providing a coherent set of programmes on which effort and attention can be concentrated and *an annual* plan that would provide operational content of the plans as finite steps, where the annual plan is integrated with annual budget. This set of Gram Panchayat Plans (containing perspective plans, intermediate plans and annual plans) would provide continuity to planning, for linking up past achievements with present activities and future directions of the Gram Panchayats.

Let it be underscored that the demarcation between *medium* range Gram Panchayat Plans and *intermediate* Gram Panchayat Plans; and *short-run* Gram Panchayat Plans and *annual plan* is blurred and the lines demarcating these are very thin. Indeed there is no basic difference, between the two sets, in content and character: the differences are more of semantics than of substance. However, the difference between *long-run* Gram Panchayat Plans and *perspective* Gram Panchayat Plans should be clearly recognized. A perspective Gram Panchayat Plan will set the direction and the final goals of planning: *long-run* Gram Panchayat Plan is a means to achieve the direction and final objectives set by *perspective plan.*

(f) Whether it is a *long-run* or a *short-run* plan, Gram Panchayat planning must relate to resource endowment of the area, which is why it may be fashionable to define Plans as being either *physical* or *financial* especially in community-based planning like Gram Panchayat Planning being discussed here. In physical planning, the factors of production, namely land, labour, capital, raw materials etc. available will the subject of Gram Panchayat Planning both during the process and period of planning. Based on an assessment and audit of such resources, physical targets will be determined in the Gram Panchayat plan with regard to, for instance, agricultural and industrial production, consumption levels, primary health care services and indeed with regard to all of the physical target variables taken into reckoning in the Gram Panchayat Plan. Attempts are to be made to inter-relate these physical target variables, make them mutually consistent, and through appropriate balancing of sorts, situations of either excess or shortages are to be eliminated. It is possible, however, that since physical target variables may not admit of balancing within a short-period of time, say five years or so, Gram Panchayat Physical planning may strictly speaking relate to the domain of long-term perspective plan.

Conceptually *financial planning*, as the connotation implies, relates to planning of financial resources, emanating from various sources like taxation, borrowing, deficit financing, foreign aid, public debt and the entire spectrum of sources. For Gram Panchayat Planning the availability of resources is mostly restricted to statutory grants from the State and small levies. Borrowing, deficit financing, foreign aid and public debt are not available. Nevertheless, in a Gram Panchayat Plan the availability of financial resources has to be matched against the needs of the physical plan.[6] Because, the financial part of the planning is concerned with the financial provisions for carrying out the physical programmes of the plans, physical planning and financial planning complement each other, and must be part of any Gram Panchayat Plan.

(g) Strategy could also be a basis for generating a class in planning. Planning cannot be isolated at levels of aggregates of output, income and employment. Conceptually, just as an economy can be broken down into the primary sector (covering agriculture, and allied activities), the secondary sector (consisting of manufacturing industries) and the tertiary sector (comprising trade, commerce, insurance, banking, transportation etc.), so can Gram Panchayat Plans be made to have a bearing on and in relation to these sectors separately. Gram Panchayat Planning pertaining to the various sectors of the local area economy, each as a constituent unit of the area, may be called *Sectoral* Gram Panchayat *Planning* or just *Sectoral Planning.*

A blind approach to sectoral planning can lead to several pitfalls. When it comes to operationalizing the sectoral plans, it tends to become technocratic and normative, and therefore, its efficacy in our system, with institutional framework for plan implementation and development work somewhat weak, becomes very limited. Secondly, sectoral planning ignores spatial factors and treats an area and an economy as a mere point, because by its very nature sectoral planning is a sectoral process only. Data with regard to potentials and non-ubiquitous character of physical, social and economic space is either non-existent or is dispensed with, if available. Sectoral planning, therefore, is likely to fail to bring about functional cohesion to the process of socio-economic development.

(h) There exists a close interdependence between development on the one hand, and the structure and evolution of the spatial pattern of human activities on the other in an area. A Gram Panchayat Plan has to have regard for the need to change the Spatial structure of these activities, if the basic social, economic, ecological and environmental objectives of planning are to be adequately achieved and if a move forward in one sector alone is not to retard progress in other sector or sectors. This will be the core of Gram Panchayat Spatial Planning. "The order in the process of development is not... confined to functional sub-systems; it is equally profound in the Spatial incidence and spread of economic development and manifests itself in the formation of Spatial sub-systems or regions".[7] This is the contribution of *Spatial planning* for development. There is an increasing recognition now that consideration of full and integrated development of resources, social justice founded on fair dispersal of plan activity and advantages of optimum location, embodied in spatial planning effort, provide validation for adoption of Spatial planning for sustainable development.

Incidentally Spatial planning could be either *adaptive* or *developmental:* the former depending upon a recognition of the influence of general pattern of development on the Spatial system; the latter is conceived of as a response to the pressures and requirements of socio-economic development. "The task of adaptive planning is then to streamline the process of spatial evolution so as to achieve at any point in time on Spatial structure which matches the needs of industry for efficiency and growth. Developmental or active *Spatial planning* on the other hand sets itself a more ambitious task. Based on the recognition of the interplay and feedback relations between economic development and spatial evolution, it seeks to identify and achieve within a dynamic and historical context a pattern of evolution of the Spatial structure that at any point in time is judged to be most efficient from the point of view of promoting a sustained process of rapid economic development. In this way, the Spatial organization of the economic and socio-cultural activities is conceived as a means to promote long-term development...[8] "In the context of Gram Panchayat Planning the focus should be on *developmental spatial planning.*

It was also fashionable to define planning from the point of view of programme content. Thus, one can have the classification of Gram Panchayat Planning as *economic planning* and *developmental planning.* Economic planning, *prima facie*, is more fashionable in developed economies, where social capital and infrastructure essential for the required quantitative expansion and structured adjustment of the economy already exists. Development planning is more suited for developing countries like ours, where the necessary social capital and infrastructural facilities are inadequate or non-existent to start and sustain economic development. By its very nature, development planning is experimental and involves both economic and social factors as elements to be planned for.

In a broader sense, Gram Panchayat Development Planning will mean planning for human transformation, a task which is much more arduous, much more intriguing and at once, comprehensive than that of accelerating growth in a growing economy—the task of Gram Panchayat Economic Planning. It is likely, therefore, that in formulating and implementing development plans at the Gram

Panchayat-level as at the State level, objectives and techniques may have, often, to be subjugated to social policy. It is in this sense that that Gram Panchayat Development Planning may be regarded as far more comprehensive than Gram Panchayat Economic Planning and that its design will generate structural changes in the local economy to facilitate the growth of the economy. Gram Panchayat Development Planning in one of its articulate forms may be best suited in India, which is marked by persistent social and institutional rigidities, institutional barriers to change, low labour productivity, low levels of income and a pattern of attitude towards work and performance that is inimical to overall development.

(i) The planning process at the Gram Panchayat-level, whether sectoral or spatial, whether economic or development can, partake the nature of either *normative* or *systems*. As the word indicates, normative Gram Panchayat Planning will enjoin a search for the best possible results with regard to the objectives set. A normative approach to Gram Panchayat Planning will normally take into reckoning five groups of problems:

(a) the procedure for defining goals and objectives;
(b) the phasing of the plan and defining of sequences and linkages;
(c) inter-linking and integrating sectoral and functional elements of the plan;
(d) inter-linking and integrating other area plans, and finally; and
(e) determining the contribution that specialists can put into the system and co-ordination of the specialist's activities.

A Gram Panchayat Physical Planning will provide a classic example of normative approach, where the Gram Panchayat Planning team is converted into experts, analysts, surveyors, model makers and operators all moulded into one, quite unconcerned about what would be the fate of the plan, were the environment, in which the planner operates, to undergo change and transformation, or even turn hostile. Since, the Gram Panchayat Planning team is "coolly rational and antiseptic", its role is limited to the mere formulation of the plan for the best possible results in relation to the established goal, leaving the implementation part to the executive embodied in the politicians and to the elements that make the politico-administrative structure of the day. The Gram Panchayat Plan, designed to achieve best results for the established objectives, in a dynamic world will be bereft of flexibilities which are essential to make it meaningfully operational. The very conceptualization of the planning team operating in a highly stochastic world in deterministic terms will make the plan somewhat removed from reality.

The *systems approach to planning* in contrast will deem the exercise of Gram Panchayat Planning a social process operating in a highly stochastic world and in the context of a varying and varied socio-technical content. The planning system will be conceived of as an institution, formed by constituent elements of values, goals, roles, factors of production, organization and their clientele, rules, norms, regulations and the inter-relationship between individual and collective participants of planning.

If one were to analyze this conception of planning, the elements of a *systems approach* to Gram Panchayat Planning could be clearly discerned as under:

(a) values, ideologies and goals;
(b) execution of the developmental task; tasks to be undertaken by the planning team;
(c) organizational framework by which the development tasks are to be executed;
(d) the executives, specialists and professionals participating in planning; and
(e) the accepted norms and set rules that regulate the inter-relationship between individual stakeholders and individual organizational units and roles of the executors.

(j) If environmental phenomenon is taken as one of the bases for classification, there could be differentiation of planning as *rural, urban* and *general planning*. Rural planning would obviously enough be concerned with planning for rural areas. It has become very fashionable currently to talk about rural development or integrated rural development. A plan that relates to such development is a rural plan. Urban plan similarly relates to plan for the urban areas. The plan that encompasses both a rural and an urban territory without having regard to either its urban or rural bias, is the *general plan*. An urban or a rural plan seems to have more operational significance when the economy is demarcated as urban or rural, as the case may be.[9] A Gram Panchayat Plan is essentially a rural plan[10].

(k) One can also classify planning based on availability of investment resources, as being *Fresh-End Gram Planning* and *Diagnostic Gram Planning.* If Gram Panchayat Planning has to be resorted to, like that of geonomic space, a new start with adequate finances is to be made one would call *Fresh-End Gram Panchayat Planning*. It is akin to Zero-based Budgeting in budgetary exercises where the new budget is prepared on a clean slate without having any regard for the past budget. In contrast, if within the structure of long standing spatial organization of the local area (Panchayat), planning is to be adopted, given that resources are limited, it would be what is known as *Diagnostic Gram Panchayat Planning*. The word "diagnosis" is of crucial importance, for it is indicative of the elements of search in the Gram Panchayat Planning Team's job: search for the segments that requires resources most and search for resources that are extremely scarce. And once this search is complete, the Planning Team's will be called upon to tackle the traditional problem of economics: that of matching scarce economic resources to unlimited alternative uses.

NOTES AND REFERENCES

1. Corporation for Enterprise Development: *Investing in Poor Communities,* Washington DC: Corporation for Enterprise Development, 1992.
2. Williams S. Rt. Hon: 1986. *Local Employment Generation: The Need for Innovation, Information and Suitable Technology* Paris: OECD, p. 1.
3. This notwithstanding the fact that the concept of such regionalization when judged against the principles of regionalization, may be open to question.
4. We are not considering international level plan, although a macro-economic planning region could involve more than one country.
5. Thus, *macro-level* planning will be State or group of States' Plan. *meso-level* plan will be District/Block level plan.
6. "The essence of financial planning is to ensure that demands and supplies are matched in a manner which exploits physical potentialities as fully as possible without major and unplanned changes in the price structure...the outlay is fixed in terms of money and the estimates are made on the basis of various hypotheses regarding the growth of national income, consumption, imports etc., to cover this outlay by taxation, savings and the increase in cash holdings".

7. Hermansen, T. (1971). *Spatial Organization and Economic Development*, being Development Studies No. 1, Mysore: Institute of Development Studies.
8. Misra, R.P. House. *et al.*, 1976. *Regional Development Planning in India*, New Delhi: Vikas Publishing Co.
9. Following from the above, one could also talk about planning designated on the basis of nodality of locations of major settlements. There could, thus, be *hinterland, planning, inlands planning* and *areal planning.*
10. See Article 243ZD of the constitution of India.

2

The Basic Principles of Gram Panchayat Planning

Being a Genre of Decentralized Planning

Introduction

The heart of the Gram Panchayat Planning process is the issue of decentralization involving the sharing of planning functions at different levels, devising mechanisms and setting out procedures for the effective intra-area and inter-area flows of information and intra-area and inter-area interaction between and among the areas. It has to be ensured, additionally, that meaningful participation, dialogue and interface with the people take place, making the Gram Panchayat planning process a harmonious whole, inter-dependent and participatory in character and content, making the plans themselves geographically relevant, economically authentic and administratively implementable. This implies adherence to certain specified principles and the following are amongst the most important principles of Gram Panchayat planning.

(i) The Principles of Functional Decentralization and Non-Concurrency.
(ii) The Principle of Financial Decentralization.
(iii) The Principle of Mobilization of Local Resources.
(iv) The Principle of Planning Localism.
(v) The Principle of Decentralized Administration.
(vi) The Principle of Public Participation.
(vii) The Iteration Principle (The Relay-Re-Relay Process).

The Seven Principles of Gram Panchayat Planning

The Principle of Functional Decentralization

Gram Panchayat Planning has to be a harmonious whole with unity in purpose (livelihood generation, employment generation, income generation, social development or whatever) but diversity in means. It can be effective only when the partners in Gram Panchayat Planning process have a clear vision about their functions and agree to perform these in terms a non-competing, non-overlapping and mutually supporting system. Among the first steps in the Gram Panchayat Planning process is, therefore, the division with precision and clarity, of the total planning functions among the various levels of the territorial hierarchy, namely, at the village level, at the Gram Panchayat Level, at the Zilla Parishad level and so on. That is, assigning planning activities amongst the various territorial levels, for their effective and efficient performance. Developmental functions have different geographic scope and are hence best performed at levels where they are most relevant. It is quite true that developmental activity cannot be performed within neat watertight compartments. But it is as much true that it is possible to identify developmental functions which are best implemented at a particular territorial level and assign it to that level, taking into account their linkages with the developmental

Box 2.1: M Eleventh Schedule (Article 243-G): Functions of Panchayat

1. Agriculture including agricultural extension, 2. Land improvement, implementation of land reforms, land consolidation and soil conservation, 3. Minor irrigation, water management and watershed development, 4. Animal husbandry, dairying and poultry, 5. Fisheries, 6. Social forestry and farm forestry, 7. Minor forest produce, 8. Small scale industries including food processing industries, 9. Khadi, village and cottage industries, 10. Rural housing, 11. Drinking water, 12. Fuel and fodder, 13. Roads, culverts, bridges, ferries, waterways and other means of communication, 14. Rural electrification including distribution of electricity, 15. Non-conventional energy sources, 16. Poverty alleviation programmes, 17. Education including primary and secondary school, 18. Technical training and vocational education, 19. Adult and non-formal education, 20. Libraries, 21. Cultural activities, 22. Markets and fairs, 23. Health and sanitation including hospitals, primary health centres and dispensaries, 24. Family welfare, 25. Women and child development, 26. Social welfare including welfare of the handicapped and mentally retarded, 27. Welfare of the weaker sections, and in particular, of the Scheduled Castes and the Scheduled Tribes, 28. Public distribution system, and 29. Maintenance of community assets.

functions at the other territorial-tiers involved in the process of planning. Gram Panchayat Planning will be best where an inter-linked and interdependent multi-tier planning process has been established. The identification of the planning functions that are non-concurrent, to be performed at the different planning levels, with each tier having a harmonious link with the other sub-national level tiers, is the cornerstone of the arch of functional decentralization.

The Principle of Financial Decentralization

Government of India has the powers to raise resources far exceeding any other tier of government such as the States and the Districts. Unlike in an unitary system the entire resources are mobilised by the Central Government and then funds are made to devolve down to lower-tiers, in India all tiers of Government are invested with powers, to raise resources but these powers of exaction diminishes as we move down the various tiers.

Gram Panchayats which are called upon to discharge particular functions must have the financial capacity to do so and hence allocation of financial resources required to perform those functions efficiently should be available. In the context of multi-level planning system as in India (States, Districts and Gram Panchayats) this implies that the funds required for the implementation of the projects in the various planning tiers are to devolve to the tier, responsible for planning at that level. This implies that for Gram Panchayat Planning the establishment of appropriate financial disaggregation procedures, of suitable budgeting methods and of re-appropriation procedures ought to have high priority.

Financial decentralization includes disaggregation of financial resources from the Centre to the State, District and Gram Panchayats, which are responsible for planning at their respective levels. And in so doing it must be borne in mind that in the allocation of resources to the States, Districts and Gram Panchayats weightages must be given to regional disparities, imbalances in area development and other features of backwardness. Countries that have experimented with methods of financial decentralization initially determined the amount of divisible outlays allocable to sub-national levels from the total development resources available nationally and then a breakdown for the various sectors and sub-sectors has been attempted by adopting a formula assigning weightage to different indicators of development.

The principle of financial decentralization when applied to any particular sector, requires the key question for determination should revolve around the issue of the nature and number of planning functions which will be invested to lower territorial-tiers and planning tier, namely the States, Districts and Gram Panchayats. In general, the transfer of resources from the Centre to States, Districts and Gram Panchayats ought to be based on set principles which would subserve the development objectives of the country as a whole, such as "growth", employment generation, improved sanitation and removal of regional disparities etc.

The Principle of Mobilization of Local Resources

For a successful Gram Panchayat Planning System, the village community must be encouraged to generate a portion of the required resources locally, for at least two reasons: one, it would imbibe in the community a sense of participation among the people; and two, motivate the masses to achieve self-reliance, at least partially. It has to be realized, however, that mobilization of resources at the Gram Panchayat/Village Level is not autonomous to begin with and therefore, incentives may be required at the initial stages. This incentive can be in-built in the resource transfer mechanism itself, like earmarking a part of the resources to devolve down, for a matching contribution by the community. Gujarat's scheme is an example in point.

The Principle of Planning Localism

The philosophy of Gram Panchayat Planning, has ingrained in it, the concept of enlarging the scope of local-level decision-making, and therefore, in allocating functions to States, Districts and Gram Panchayats and in allocating resources down the line, it is essential that the scope of local-level decision-making is enlarged. It has been the experience in many states earlier that a very large portion of the resources that devolve down from higher to lower-tiers of planning, are exhausted by on-going projects and programmes. This has to be avoided and one way to do so is to have a provision of what has come to be known in India, as "untied funds", placed at the disposal of the District Planning boards or Zilla Parishad or Gram Panchayats. Such measures have their own relevance in as much as they foster a sense of responsibility and increase the capability of the Gram Panchayat planners. The decentralized budget in Sri Lanka is a block grant that partakes the nature of untied funds, harnessing greater involvement at lower levels of planning in the utilizing the resources.

The Principle of Decentralized Administration

Gram Panchayat Planning to be truly functional must be accompanied by the delegation of adequate powers and responsibilities so as to enable them to perform the designated functions efficiently. This is administrative decentralization or 'deconcentration', as it is sometimes called. The extent of command to be retained at the Centre and the extent of powers to be delegated to the States, Districts and Gram Panchayats in the decentralized superstructure of India has been decided taking into account factors peculiar to each situation. No hard and fast rule can be laid down in this regard but it could be emphasized that changes in rules of procedures for giving administrative and technical sanctions, for release of funds, for inter-sectoral transfers and powers of re-appropriation are critical for a truly good Gram Panchayat Planning. Transfer of functions and personnel are vital in making Gram Panchayat Planning efficient[1].

The Principle of Community Participation

The one great advantage of decentralized planning of which Gram Panchayat Planning is a leading species, lies in its ability to have interface with people and harness their participation in developmental efforts. There are two views on community participation: One, the "mobilizing" views, which envisions participation as mobilization of the community for the success of development projects and two, the "empowering" view which enjoins empowering the community to make its own choice. It is this latter view of community participation, of empowering the community, which is relevant in Gram Panchayat Planning because the key concept of planning at the Gram Panchayat is that it is based on felt needs of the people, perceived through interaction with the community for whom plans are formulated. This participatory strategy enables the majority of the community members suffering from low incomes, low levels of education, poor health and sanitation and restricted or non-existent opportunities to make their voices heard in the planning process, to articulate their needs and remedies. This paves the way for their further participation.

The participation of the community in Gram Panchayat Planning will not be generated automatically: it has to be facilitated by suitably changing the existing institutional framework, often dominated by those elements of society who adjure changes and embrace *status quo*. At the higher levels of planning (District or State-levels) participation will be more indirect because it is impossible for the planners located away from the "scene of action" to have interface with people spread all over the district or state, particularly so where the States or Districts in the country are as larger as they are. Only at the Gram Panchayat, participation of the people will be direct and it is the only level where one could have meaningful community participation. Hence, it should be seriously harnessed. And since at the Gram Panchayats, community participation would be for "decision-making" and should be conceived of both as a means and a goal of development; only then that it can serve as a medium of social transformation and as a pre-condition for authentic development, based fundamentally within the under developed areas at the sub-national level.

The Principle of Iteration

Community participation is anathema to single stroke planning: it is a relay and re-relay process where the Gram Panchayats, through a repetitive process of interaction, seek continuously inputs from the community in Gram Panchayat Planning and plan implementation. The various planning levels, who are engaged in the planning for their respective levels, have to act and interact repeatedly, till a harmonious planning is achieved. This iterative interaction is achieved through vigorous and continuous flows of information, both from the community to the Gram Panchayat Planning Team and *vice versa*. The flows of information, to the community from the Gram Panchayat Planning Team would largely consist of information pertaining to policies, priorities, targets, guidelines for planning, budgetary information, coordination directives, reviews of monitoring and evaluation of projects and suggestions for re-scheduling plans and re-planning (where the original course of action for the territorial-tier pursued has been found wanting). This is box number 3 (hidden box) of Johari's window. The flows of information, both from the community to the Gram Panchayat Planning Team consists of data, information on local needs and preferences, area priorities, area targets and problems and constraints faced at the local level. This is box number 2 (Blind box) of Johari's window. A hypothetical system with levels, flows and interaction is Fig. 2.1. This iterative process of Gram Panchayat Planning, in the manner envisaged here, requires an interactive adjustment mechanism capable of constantly aligning the Gram Panchayat Plans with resource availability and at each round of implementation.

This interactive adjustment mechanism ideally would consist of an appropriate planning machinery at Gram Panchayat-level at least. The structure and composition of this planning machinery is crucial to the success of Gram Panchayat planning process, because it is the basic tool with which to prepare the plans and organise both the upward and downward flows and interactions. The efficiency of this planning apparatus makes or mars the success of Gram Panchayat planning process at various stages. In this regard it is also very important to upgrade the Gram Panchayat Planning Team;[2] they should be trained and briefed with all latest changes, and as the work load of the machinery increases it has to be expanded, so that, it can be efficient and responsive to the needs of good planning, plan implementation and plan monitoring.

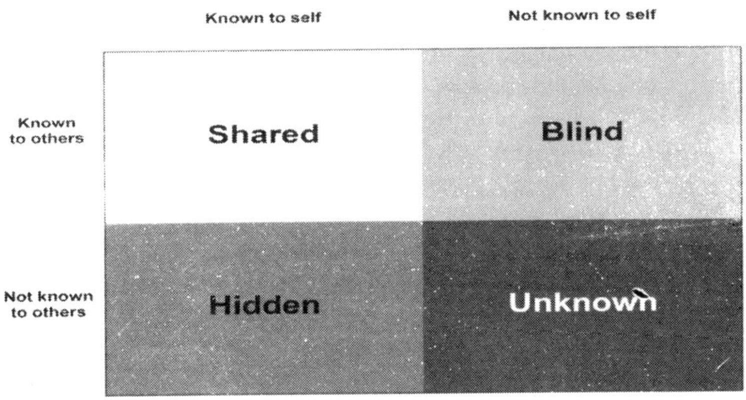

Fig. 2.1: Johari's Window

Actions Needed for Establishing a Gram Panchayat Planning System

Gram Panchayat Planning by all accounts is a demanding operation and its effective operationalization is a function of several parameters. The various actions required may be summed up as follows:

- Defining the appropriate planning and decision-making functions for Gram Panchayats in the hierarchy of planning (Block, District and State-levels), so that, there are no overlapping of areas in planning among the three levels.
- Matching planning functions with adequate allocation of financial resources to the Gram Panchayat so as to enable the performance of plans in an effective manner.
- Equipping each Gram Panchayat with properly staffed planning machinery to discharge the designated planning and decision-making functions effectively. A professional planning machinery at this level is imperative.
- Training the planning and development personnel in the tasks of development planning especially participatory methods and development *per se*, at the Gram Panchayat level.
- Development of an appropriate data base and information system at Gram Panchayat level to support the planning and decision-making activities.
- Establishing suitable organizational structures for coordination as part of the overall mechanism for planning.
- Establishing appropriate linkages downward (i.e. sector/component projects linkage), horizontal (i.e. sector linkage) and vertical (i.e. sectoral hierarchy linkage) linkages for integrated development of a Gram Panchayat.
- Establishing an effective two-way communications network through hierarchical, expert group, status group and other group consultations for exchange of information, between the various stakeholders in Gram Panchayat Planning, quickly and efficiently.
- Instituting regular information flows from Gram Panchayat Planning Team (for policies/priorities, targets, guidelines, finances, reviews, evaluation and the like) and from the community (for data on local needs and preferences, area priorities, area targets, feedback on the implementation of

projects and local-level perception relating to problems and constraints and the like), which are inescapable for the efficient functioning the planning system.

- Delegating various administrative powers and authority, to the Gram Panchayats for quicker decision-making, nearer to the scene of action.
- Organizing and monitoring of the planning process, on a continuous basis with evaluation being conceived as a learning process and as an occasion for reflection.
- Finally, organizing interface with the people at various levels through formal and informal methods so that the felt needs and aspirations of the people are assimilated in the planning process.

Dynamics of Gram Panchayat Planning

A Gram Panchayat planning system is essentially a dynamic, interacting and integrating phenomenon, where a relay/re-relay process of information operating both from outsiders (the GP Planning Team) to the insiders (community members) and from the insiders to the outsiders provide the circulatory life-blood for the system, and facilitates the process of continuous ongoing revision and adjustment of plans to align them with the changing situations and circumstances. Ideally the Gram Panchayat Planning units should, therefore, have to be a two-way role to play: one, in organizing the planning function within its jurisdiction, and two, in inter-weaving their plans and integrating the Gram Panchayat plans into the plans at the District and State levels whenever warranted, through a process of a staged and sequential procedure involving successive approximations, interactions and interfaces. This is what the dynamics of the Gram Panchayat planning process is all-about.

NOTES AND REFERENCES

1. See Sudhir Krishna: "Restructuring the Institutional Arrangements to Strengthen the Panchayats" in Amitava Mukherjee (ed.) *Panchayats in the Nineties*, New Delhi: Vikash Publishing House, Private Ltd. 1944.
2. D. Bandopathyay *et al.* (eds.): *Empowering Panchayats, Handbook for Master Trainers, Using Participatory Approach,* New Delhi, Concept Publishing Company, 2003.

3

Manual on Gram Panchayat Planning using PLA Methods

MICRO-LEVEL PLANNING USING PLA METHODS

The Four Components of Micro-level Plans

Micro-level planning, has to encompass four dimensions of development.

(i) It must be a ***physical plan***. The plan must outline what physical facilities will be included in the plan, such as the number of schools to be established, number of water harvesting structures to be created, the length of the "milk roads" to be laid out, and so on.

(ii) A micro-level plan must give an idea of the quantum of resources required to carry out the physical plan suggested. A micro-level plan must, therefore, be a ***resource plan*** (financial resources, human resources, social resources or social capital, and natural resources).

(iii) A Micro-plan must have a time-frame. The various components of the plan will be implemented within a time-frame and at various points in time within that larger time-frame.

(iv) A micro-level plan, must also have a ***spatial plan***. It should indicate the places where physical facilities will be built.

In this manual the discussion is restricted to areas where participatory methods are used.

Role of Attitudes in the Application of PLA in Micro-Planning

The real crunch is the availability of the right kind of orientation to the different actors especially the Gram Panchayat Development Planning (GP-DP) Team, in the preparation of a micro-plan based on PLA techniques. There are two problems that are basic to it. The first one relates to reorienting the understanding of the various actors in the GP-DP Team about respecting and utilizing the intelligence and knowledge of the common man. It has been proved that the common man is intelligent and knowledgeable about what is good for the community. The success of GP-DP using participatory methods will require that the orientation of all their actors in GP planning from the Gram Panchayat-level to the Zilla Parishad or District-level functionaries (both officials and elected), changes from one of a benefactor providing solutions to what they perceive as the people's problems, to one of listening to the people and paying heed to their advise and ideas. The orientation has to change from the "lecturing mode" to the "Learning mode". It is only then that the use of participatory micro-level planning be successful.

The second problem would be to inculcate in the GP-DP Team involved in GP planning, the ability to empathise with the people. The GP-DP Team have not only to accept that the common man deserves to be respected for his intelligence and knowledge, but they should have the ability to look at the problems from a people's perspective. For instance, if the GP-DP Team is involved in understanding the extent of poverty in a Gram Panchayat, the criterion for judging poverty should be a criterion which local people perceive as correctly reflecting the extent of poverty in the area under reference. That is, those involved in GP-DP and the potential users have to schew the reluctance to use people's wisdom and local knowledge.

The Steps of Micro-Level Plans

The various steps in a micro-level planning exercise are as under:

Pre-Planning

Step-1: Preparation.
Step-2: Developing the facilitator's vision.
Step-3: Sensitizing the Community.

Content Planning

Step-4: Determining the shared Vision of the community.
Step-5: Situation analysis.
Step-6: Problem identification.
Step-7: Prioritization of the problems: generating the objectives of the plan.
Step-8: Finding Solutions: generates activities or projects.
Step-9: Deciding on locations: Spatial planning.

Details of Steps Using Participatory Methods in Micro-Level Planning

Step-1: Preparation Step

In the preparation step, the first step is creation of a database. In the Indian context, a huge mass of data is generated by a well-organized Governmental system for generating data. Data available from the Population Census operations especially the Village and Town Directory generated by it, the Agricultural Census operation and the Livestock Census operation are very useful. The data collected by the Central Statistical Organization (CSO) could also prove useful. The District Credit Plans developed by the Lead Bank of the area and in some cases the District Plans prepared by the district administration (often by the District Planning Officer/District Statistical Officer) come in very handy. There are several private agencies, which also generate data, though much of it is macro-data. The data base required is illustrated at ***Annexure I*** [which esssentially is ***Annexure II*** in the Sansad Adarsh Gram Yojana (SAGY) guidelines].

Before Fieldwork

There are some steps which GP-DP Team needs to take togather and analyze reliable and precise information. These steps before fieldwork are as follows:

Selection of Interdisciplinary Team

GP-DP Team should be diverse. For example, as far as possible, for the GP-DP Team select people:

- who know agriculture and irrigation,
- who know dairy farming,
- who know about fisheries,
- who know about forestry,
- who know education,
- who know water, sanitation and health issues,
- who know watershed management,
- who know livelihoods, and
- who knows about civil, road construction and water supply.

They could be drawn from the Government Institutions, local NGOs, Schools, and Colleges and may be in some cases local Universities. Human resource available from Companies under their CSR is also an option. It may also be possible to identify a person who may have domain knowledge in more than one area but related ones.

Collation of Secondary Information

Before the fieldwork GP-DP Team to study the secondary data of the area for which GP-DP exercise is being undertaken. It will provide the background information and basic "assumptions" of fact and information that the people will provide. It may be helpful in developing topics, sub-topics or checklists to be used in acquiring information for the GP-DP. The GP-DP Team must know why they are in a village? They must know what kind of plan they will facilitate and what kind of village they are going to? What kind of people to expect?

Brainstorming for Developing Sub-topics

Have a venue fixed. A class-room in a village school itself is ideal.

Generally, a brainstorming session may be organized for developing topics or sub-topics around which GP-DPs are to be facilitated. Ideally, a number of experienced people, not necessarily team members, may be invited in the session to generate specific issues on a particular area. A large number of issues will generally be raised in respect of the GP. The GP-DP Team must allow a free flow of discussion and information but clearly clarify that the issues raised brainstorming session are important, but all of them may not be covered by the GP-DP, otherwise false expectations will be raised. Record the issues raised in a flip chart or on the black-board, depending on the availability. The issues are repeatedly discussed in the session relating to the practical situation and are finalized as a guide for collecting required information using PLA. GP-DP Team may focus on a variety of issues as given below:

For Poverty Reduction

(a) Identifying patterns of poverty in the GP.
(b) How different schemes and programmes implemented?
(c) How to prioritise of the basic services for poor groups and localities?
(d) How to ensure that the entitlements provided under different laws, programmes and schemes are accessed (PESA rights, forest rights, social security, food security, education, health, nutrition)?
(e) How to improving livelihoods particularly through MGNREGS and the institutions of the poor created under NRLM?

Human Development

(a) How to provide literacy and education including skill development?
(b) How to provide delivery of health services, especially public health?
(c) How to promote food and nutrition?
(d) How to better child sex-ratio?
(e) Ways and means to improving quality of human development services particularly through *anganwadis*, schools, hospitals, enhancing access to them.
(f) Upgradation of related infrastructure.

Social Development

Ways and means to improve the well-being of vulnerable and marginalised groups like:

(a) SCs, STs, including particularly Vulnerable Tribal Groups and Minorities.
(b) Persons with disabilities.
(c) Elderly people.
(d) Women especially deserted women.

(e) Children.

(f) Vulnerable groups like bonded labourers, child labourers, de-notified tribes and nomads, distress-migrants, manual scavengers, transgenders, victims of trafficking etc.

(g) How to improve the social determinants affecting the status of the groups mentioned above?

Economic Development

(a) What activities to promote which would increase local production and productivity, increase employment and employability?

(b) Improve market access and marketability of the local produce.

(c) Promote value addition, create productive infrastructure like markets, ponds, fisheries, livestock development, horticulture development, land development, minor irrigation facilities, dug wells, irrigation tanks etc.

(d) While focusing on agriculture and allied sectors, how to promote local manufacturing especially traditional industries and services?

(e) And how to promote financial inclusion.

Ecological Development

(a) What are the ways and means for maintenance and upgradation of various eco-systems like water bodies, pastures, grass lands, catchments and local forests?

(b) What are the ways and means for conservation of biological resources and their sustainable use like non-timber forest produce, firewood, fodder, medicinal plants etc.?

(c) How to promote integrated watershed management while conserving biological resources and promoting their sustainable use?

Activities taken up under GP-DP should be environment-friendly and bio-diversity enhancing.

Public Service Delivery

(a) Streamlining delivery of services like issuance of certificates, registration of birth and death, Streamlining the issuance of licences/permits and welfare services like pensions (old age pension, widow pension etc.).

(b) Ways and means to migrate to electronic delivery of services.

(c) How to improve the quality of service delivery?

(d) How to ensure proper upkeep and use of existing assets?

(e) What strategies to adopt for maximising local development through measures which require zero or minimal investment?

Good Governance

(a) How to adopt processes and systems relating to
- participation, particularly of the marginalised groups,
- transparency and proactive disclosures,
- community-based monitoring, and
- due processes in budget and expenditure.

(b) How to promote close partnership with institutions of the poor, particularly SHGs and women?

This calls for a 'Good Governance' plan for each GP including a Citizens' charter.

Enter into a Team Agreement

In the GP-DP Team agree on how to carry out fieldwork, especially participatory tools to be applied for collecting the required data. Generally, the choice of tools depends on topics and expected output. In the GP-DP Team consider the situation and select the tools which fit better for collecting reliable and precise data. Therefore, in the GP-DP Team decide which tools and techniques fit better for a particular Gram Panchayat.

During Fieldwork

Rapport Building

Rapport building is an important task for the GP-DP Team for facilitating a GP-DP we have discussed this earlier but given its importance, usually be done to develop communications and to establish working relationships with the people living in the Gram Panchayat, it is again stressed here. Generally, initiate rapport building immediately as the GP-DP Team enters a village. The GP-DP Team could follow the following steps suggested in facilitating a GP-DP using participatory methods:

- Talk to the people in their local language whenever they are met, such as on the trail, agricultural fields, tea shops, homes etc.
- Learn a local trait by doing it (Learning by Doing) like ploughing the field, "driving" a bullock cart, harvesting crops and the like.
- Treat and respect people as per their local custom.
- Ask the knowledgeable people about a subject or area in a village.
- Try to meet with traditional village/GP leaders before starting work in the field and enlist their support.
- Clearly explain reasons for coming to the GP.
- Show genuine interest in the local issues.
- Choose time and venue that are convenient for the people.

Maintaining Protocols

In the GP-DP Team maintain protocols (as a set of rules governing how people act in a given situation, a code of conduct) in the team. In GP-DP using participatory methods, protocols are rules of interpersonal behaviour by which GP-DP Team agrees to operate. The followings are the protocols suggested for GP-DP Team for GP-DP using participatory methods:

- A facilitator (from the team) controls the total process by singling start, filling gaps etc.;
- Each team member pursues a sub-topic, following one's own line of enquiry and reasoning;
- The order of facilitating a participatory method is sequenced and adhered to (who starts, who follows, who finishes);
- Predetermined members take notes during each other's turn;
- Unanticipated questions that arise out of turn are held for later;
- Unwanted people (e.g. drunken people, trouble makers etc.) are politely diverted by a team member; and

- After each day's sessions, debrief as a group, discuss findings to verify and record incomplete information for recollection.

Data Collection by Applying Tools and Techniques

It is important to flag certain aspects of developing a GP-DP using participatory methods/techniques.

The collection of data and information will be by applying appropriate participatory tools/techniques once the rapport is developed in a village, like Social Mapping or Resource Mapping. But these Maps (and all PLA Methods) once completed needs to be interviewed by applying "probing" and "iterating techniques" for collecting more in-depth insight and for cross checking (also called Triangulation) the information collected using participatory methods. Some techniques for interviewing outputs from participatory Sessions are given below:

Semi-Structured Interviewing (SSI)

Semi-structured interviewing is conducted using the sub-topics to guide the specific questions decided by GP-DP Team. Often conducting SSI with key informants, who have good knowledge about the GP and its resources, has been found rewarding. Here, create actual questions during the interview. Make the questions precise and easy to understand. Avoid ***leading*** questions while conducting SSI.

Iteration

Use Iteration as one of the techniques for cross-checking information gathered for GP-DP using participatory methods. In this technique, the same question is repeatedly asked in different situations, or different set of people, or different tools for confirming the given information. GP-DP Team should use the flexibility of the participatory methodology through iteration as it provides an opportunity to reform questions and formulate new questions, especially during the use of the same participatory tool.

Probing

The main function of a probe is to encourage the respondent to answer more fully and accurately. Furthermore, it also helps the GP-DP Team to structure the respondent's answer and make sure that all topics of interest are covered. To establish the basic situation always start questions with the 'seven helpers':

- who,
- what,
- why,
- when,
- where,
- whom,
- and how.

Direct Observation

One can use Direct Observation especially in GP-DP for social development. In Direct Observation, relevant indicators are actually viewed in the field to verify the collected information or to generate questions. For example, if providing relief to women from smoke while cooking is an issue, the use animal dung for cooking or the making of animal dung cakes/their drying can be directly observed and the scarcity of firewood in the area can be seen.

Step-2: GP-DP Team's Vision

On that basis of the secondary data, the GP-DP Team must form an idea (a vision) for the GP: where will GP-DP Team like the GP to move on in 5 or 10 years down the line; how should the people in the GP look like ten years down the line etc. That is the GP-DP Team should have a vision for the GP and its area, to successfully facilitate a good GP plan.

Step-3: Sensitizing the Community

Sensitizing the Community is a composite of several Steps. If the GP being worked with is new to the GP-DP Team, the obvious thing to do first is to "build rapport". A large number of methods have been invented and used by development practitioners to build rapport with the community, beginning with "meet and greet" using their custom, talking to them in their language, walking through the area where the community lives, "Joint Walks", giving a helping hand, "doing it yourself" or learning by doing or simply just listening to their stories.

An integral part of the sensitization process is telling the people in the GP, the purpose of the planning exercise, its scope, limitations and the parameters within which the GP-DP must be prepared (including the size of the budget), implementability, what is expected of the community in implementing the plan and the chances of its success. GP-DP using PLA methods should have an open and transparent beginning.

The sensitization should also ensure managing the community's expectation. GP-DP using PLA methods builds the community's expectation, often disproportionate to what could possibly be done. GP-DP Team should moderate unrealistic expectations. While expectations act as an motivator for community action (because a hopeless community rarely acts !), it must be realistic.

Involve the Gram Panchayat in the sensitization. Some of the activities which could be considered are:

(a) Interaction (*charcha*) with the Gram Sabha, Mahila Sabha, and Bal Sabha.
(b) Interaction (*charcha*) with occupational groups and local organizations, including youth clubs.
(c) Organization of cultural and sport events.
(d) Wall writings, *Shivirs*, *Padayatras*, *Nukkad naataks* etc.
(e) Painting and Literary Competitions on how the village could be made a model one.
(f) Demonstration of videos of best practices in village development.

These activities would result in a broad collective vision of what the village should be like and kindle the enthusiasm of the villagers.

Step-4: Collective Vision: Determining the Community's Vision

Understand the collective vision. It is fundamental to facilitate a good GP-DP. What changes does the people see as signalling their development, which must be achieved: better education, improved health care, improved social capital, sustainable livelihoods, better agriculture, higher income or whatever. It is generally expected that the sensitization process would yield collective vision. Record this collective vision. Should there be a need to further explore the community vision, methods like *Dream Mapping* and *Semi-Structured Interviews* (SSI) come in handy. Facilitation of the dream map may require a current mapping first and then moving on to draw the future scenario. The current map may be a new map or an existing map if one exists.

Slep-5: Situation Analysis

There are five kinds of analysis that are possible in situational analysis.[1] In this exercise we need to only facilitate Social Mapping and Resource Mapping and Scoring/Ranking which are sufficient for GP-DP.

Social Map

A ***Social Map*** is a visual depiction of all man-made structures in a village or area (and could include the status of human capital like the health status and educational attainment though the latter are subject of Thematic Social Map discussed below). It shows human habitation, the location and nature of housing, infrastructure such as roads, drains, schools, health outlets, drinking-water facilities, water channels and places of worship, settlement patterns including location houses of marginalized groups. Women headed households, status of houses (*kuccha*, *pucca*, IAY Houses) and social status of the head of the household can be depicted using suitable symbols.

A Social Map is prepared by the community members and is not drawn to scale. It reflects the perceptions of community.

Ideally Social Mapping should be at two levels:

(i) The first level of social mapping exercise should be to generate a General Social Map (called just Social Map) which depicts the overall social situation of the village including, but not restricted to what is mentioned in the foregoing paragraph.

(ii) The second level social mapping exercise should generate Thematic Social Maps depicting the state of literacy in the Village (A Literacy Map), the state of health of the villagers (Health Map), and the state of social overheads (Institution Map) and so on. They are also called "Thematic Social".

While the Social Map will capture the general social picture, the Thematic Social Maps will provide detailed information on the specific determinants of social development: education, health and institutions.

Key Components of a Social Map

- Availability of social and economic infrastructure such as roads, bridges, schools, health outlets, places of worship etc., community centre, electricity poles, solar power, hand pumps, wells, shops, ration shops etc.) in an area or community.
- *Status* of social and economic infrastructure (such as gravel roads, broken roads, good roads, culverts or iron bridges etc.), in an area or community.
- Habitation pattern of the people such as houses, kinds of houses (Thatched, *Kucca*, *Pucca*) as well as concentration of particular class or kind of people (like STs, SCs, Blacksmiths etc.) in any part of the area or community under discussion.
- Thematic Social Maps provide information regarding the human resource situation of households like their health status or literacy status and their living condition in the village.

A Social Map of a village in Egypt is shown below:

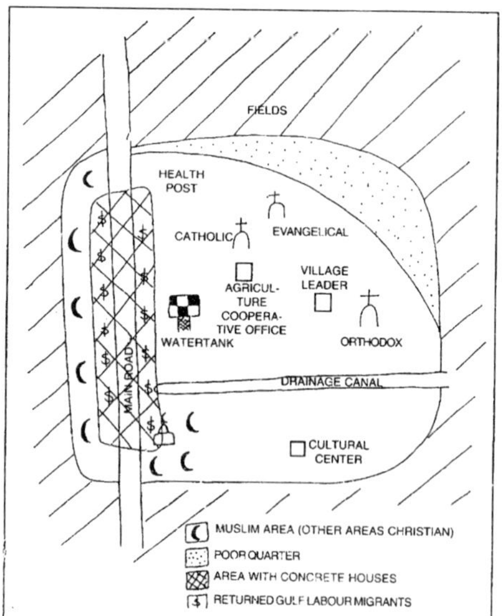

Fig. 3.1: Social Mapping of Village in Egypt.

Use of Social Map

- In developing a vision for the GP about the future of a community or village, i.e. developing a perspective for a area or village or community.
- In developing a situation analysis for micro-level plan (in our case GP-DP).
- In ascertaining the location of dwellings of marginalized people or households.
- In finding out the existence and status of delivery of basic services.
- To learn about the households and their location in the village/ hamlet/ward.
- To learn about the socio-economic pattern in the village.
- The social, economic, gender and ability related status of the households.
- In identifying vulnerable households.
- In finding out common areas like places for bazaars, holding community events, cremation/burial etc.
- To compare the status of a community or village at two or more points in time in respect of development issues like social infrastructure, demographics etc.
- To discuss Government Programmes like National Social Assistance Programme (NSAP), MNREGS and Indira Awaas Yojana (IAY).
- To discuss the list of beneficiaries of various Government programmes and list of people who are excluded.
- To examine the list of people who do not get their entitlements.

Use of Earlier Social Map(s)

Before initiating a social map, GP-DP Team needs to ascertain, if there is any social map that exists for that GP. If one exists, there is no need to facilitate a fresh social Map, then such map and data should be validated and updated through participatory process, instead of facilitating the entire map afresh.

Steps in Social Mapping

- Fix the location. Ensure that the location/venue has enough room to accommodate the expected number of people. See if it is in a central place in the village and accessible to all. Be sure that it is convenient and comfortable for everyone in the community/village. There should be enough shade for the participants. In case you decide to have the map drawn on the ground, make sure the surface fairly smooth for the exercise.

Box 3.1: Principles for Participatory Gram Panchayat Development Planning

- Timing and place should be governed by local context of separate sections of the community.
- Recognize diversity: different groups, as defined locally by age, gender, well-being, ethnicity, religion, caste, language etc. have different perspectives.
- Knowledge and experience of the community should be respected.
- GP-DP Team should use the process of GP Planning as an opportunity to learning not lecture.
- Be open, honest and transparent about the objectives of the GP-DP planning process with all sections of the community.
- Do not interrupt.
- Do not lecture.
- Be a good active learner.
- Be a good listener.
- Always hand over the "pen", that is, pass the initiatives and responsibility to community members.
- The community can do it. They have a lot of capabilities.
- Respect the information generated by the community. Don't stand on them!
- Never alter the diagrams or instruments created by the community: it is their property.
- Seek the community's permission to take photographs especially of women and poverty.
- Seek the community's permission to record, remove and use information they provide.
- The original diagrams and copies of reports should be preserved in the community as far as possible.

- Avoid the venue for mapping being in a religious place as there may be sensitivities involved.
- Fix a time for the exercise in consultation with the local people.
- Invite them for the mapping exercise.

- Reconsider where you will facilitate the Social Map: On the floor/ground or on Chart Paper. Both have their advantages and limitations.
- If the Map is facilitated on Charts Papers, ensure that more than one chart paper is joined together so that the people are not constrained by space to draw the map.
- Ensure you have the required material for mapping (apart from local material) like Rangoli powder, chalks, Chart Papers, Marker Pens, flash cards etc. in adequate quantity.
- Once at the venue, clearly explain the purpose of Social Mapping to the people at the start of the process.
- Leave it to the people to use whatever materials they choose.
- "Handover the Stick" or better still "Handover the Pen" to the people. Empower them and let the people have total control and initiative.
- Suggest to the people to begin by marking the directions as they deem fit. Deviating from geographer's mapping they may indicate the side from which sun rises as the East and mark it as such in the paper/ground.
- Facilitate so that people may start by drawing the prominent features of the area/village such as a Railway Track or the main road, or the Temple/a Church/Mosque or the School Building or an Old Big Tree or whatever. Most of the time people start by drawing the main road or a landmark and then move on to add other details.
- Drawing of the landmarks is important as it provides the community a sense of direction. For example people are often seen to say that the SC colony is to the east of the School and so on.
- The houses start appearing after the landmarks are delineated. Generally, the houses are shown mirroring the actual reality: in terms of size, design, kind of the materials used for roofing (like concrete, tiled, thatched etc.).
- Watch who all are actively involved, and who all are being left out. Take proactive steps to involve the left out group in the process.
- Once the mapping is over, ask some people present there to identify their houses in the map.
- Always number the households. It will be essential for finding out their entitlements and deprivation.

- Ask them to depict the household details that are particularly necessary for the planning: like women headed households, households with communicable diseases, households with people who are differently-abled and so on.
- Interview the map with open ended questions. Clarify those aspects which are not clearly shown and request for more information, if necessary. Remember there is no second chance!

  Note: If the facilitator has something to add or clarify, he/she must wait for the right moment and not disrupt the process.
- Have the map copied on to chart papers if the map was drawn on the floor or the ground. Ensure accuracy in copying!
- Triangulate the information generated with others in the locality.
- Display the Map at a prominent place where all people have free access so that if any errors have crept in those can be pointed out.
- Facilitate corrections of the errors in the map should any be found.

Interview the Social Map with open ended questions, at least covering the key questions mentioned above. Refer to section (p. 34). on "Data collection by applying tools and techniques" discussed above. Clarify those aspects which are not clearly shown and request for more information, if necessary. Facilitate the process so that the needs around the issues covered by the Social Map are clearly spelt out. Remember there is no second chance!

The GP-DP Team should be aware that the outsiders' role is limited to facilitation and they should intervene only when necessary, like when the process is not progressing well or some people are left out or a disruptive person enters the group. See box given below on "Difficult People".

Analysis of a Social Map

Once a Social Map is prepared, it has to be analyzed. The following is a non-exhaustive list of issues/ideas to look for in an analysis of the Social Map:

Box 3.2: Difficult People

The Angry Person: Always aggressive and angry.
The Sniper: The Sniper likes to always make sarcastic, rude remarks and enjoys hurting others.
The Know-It-All: They have lots to offer, are generally competent. They can not stand to be contradicted or corrected but they will go out of their way to correct others.
The Think They Know It All: A cocksure attitude often fools people into believing their phony "facts".
The Grenade: Grenades tend to explode into uncontrolled ranting all the time.
The Yes Person: Someone who wants to please others so much that she never says no.
The Maybe Person: Does not make choices that will hurt feelings, he avoids decisions, causing frustration.
The Nothing Person: This person offers only a blank stare, no verbal or non-verbal signals.
The Negative Person: Always says no whenever any new ideas arise, or even when old ones are recycled.
The Whiner: Whiners feel helpless most of the time. They want things to be perfect, but nothing seems to go right.
The Gate Keeper: Would not allow others to talk.
The Shy Person: Does not open his mouth.
The Destructive Person: A person who demolishes everything.

- Number of households (HH) in the village and where are they located.
- Is the number of households growing or shrinking?
- Number of HH which have job cards.
- Number of days of employment per HH received over the past one year.
- Institutions and facilities (community hall, schools, MCH Centre, Anganwadi Centre, community wells etc.) are found in the village, their number and locations.
- Note if the facilities are located in any particular area. If yes why so?
- Note any specific area of the village where marginalized groups (such as SCs, STs, OBCs, Others and Minorities) live.
- Identify and count the vulnerable households like—
  - Those which are the landless households.
  - Those which are the small/marginal farmer households.
  - Those which are the wage labour dependent households.
  - Those families resort to cyclical migration and distress-migration regularly.

  - Those HHs which are the female-headed households.
  - Households with PwDs, old age, homeless.
  - Households from which bonded labourers, child labourers come.
  - Households of de-notified tribes and nomads.
  - Households of manual scavengers, transgenders, victims of trafficking etc.
  - Households with chronically ill people.
- Location and number of households which have inhabitants who are chronically ill like suffering from cancer, leprosy, HIV/AIDs etc.
- Location and number of households where the majority of the children in the household are illiterate or out of school especially the girl children.
- Location and number of households where there are more than 2 children.
- Location and number of households where assets have been previously created under Government Programmes.
- Location and number of houses that are *kuccha*/*pucca*/semi-*pucca*.
- Location and number of houses that have been built under IAY.
- Location and number of Households which have young people between the ages 18-35 living there.
- Location and number of Households that have pension beneficiaries.
- The approximate boundaries of the village with regard to social interaction and social services.
- What are the social structures and institutions found in the village? And their number?
- What religious groups are found in the village? And their number?
- What ethnic groups are found in the village? And their number?
- Any other issue that the Gram Panchayat Planning Team may deem necessary.

Interview the Social Map with open ended questions (as discussed in section (p. 34) on "Data collection by applying tools and techniques"), at least covering the key questions mentioned above. Clarify those aspects which are not clearly shown and request for more information, if necessary.

Facilitate the process so that the needs for social development in the GP are clearly spelt out.

Remember There is no Second Chance!

It needs to be underscored that a social map drawn by women may be different from a social map drawn by men for the same village. This is because the reality of women is different from the reality of men. Remember "whose Reality Counts". Two examples below will illustrate the issue.

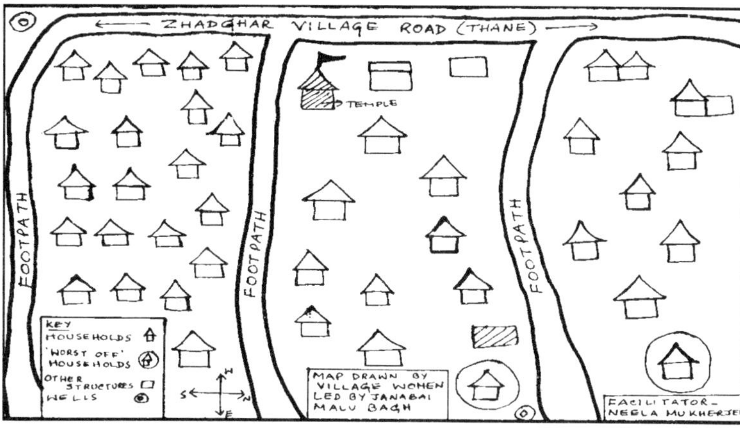

Fig. 3.2: Zhadghar Village Road (Thane).

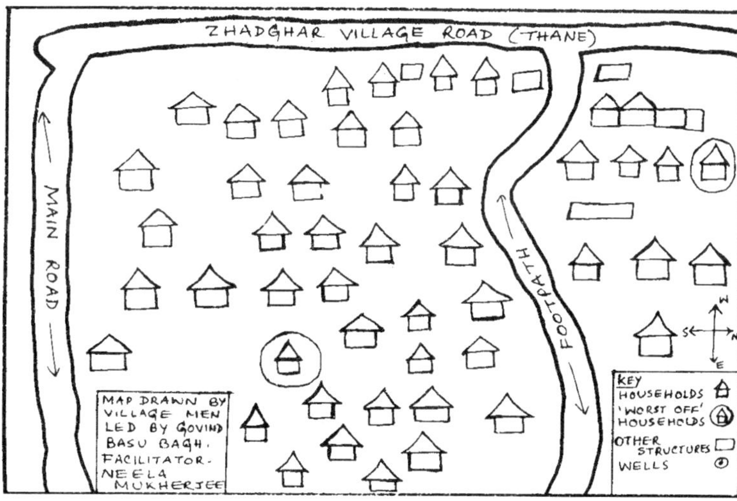

Fig. 3.3: Zhadghar Village Road (Thane).

The GP-DP Team must take a call if there is a need to facilitate Social Map separately for men and women. In some cases it is useful to have Social Maps drawn separately for men and women as a means of cross checking (Triangulation).

Inference from a Social Map

After a Social Map is analyzed, the next step is to draw inferences. It is difficult to indicate what could be the inferences drawn from a Social Map but some examples may be helpful.

- For example if the GP-DP is for Social Development, and if the houses of manual scavengers are located in one corner of the village, the inference will be untouchability persists in the village. The need is for social mobilization and "information, education and communication" on the subject.
- If the number of children is high in several households, then the inference may be that either women have poor access to reproductive health facilities or people are unwilling to adopt family welfare measures. The need is to provide better education to women, more information on family welfare and improve primary health care (like better MCH).
- If there are a large number of households with people having disabilities, the inference could be that child immunization is poor. There is a need to improve immunization and introduce care for people with disabilities.
- If there are a large number of households which have people who take advantage of Government Programmes, then the inference is that the level of deprivation is low.

These are some examples only of how inferences can be drawn. Each situation is unique and what the inference will be depends on each case.

Material Needed as per Need

- *Drawing on soft ground*: Coloured powders, sticks and other local material.

- *Drawing on cemented/hard floor*: Coloured chalks, and other local material.
- *Drawing on Chart Paper*: Large Sized Chart Paper, Pencils, Permanent Markers, Sketch Pens, Bindis, and other materials as appropriate.
- List of vulnerable households in the SECC with automatic inclusion and deprivation criteria.
- List of beneficiaries of various pension schemes.
- List of IAY beneficiaries.
- List of Job Card holders.

Finally, the approved Social Map may be painted on the wall or put up on public place for community to access in future.

Thematic Social Maps

In Thematic Social Maps, the steps for facilitating the Maps are similar to those for facilitating the General Social Map. The difference is that the Thematic Social Maps focus on the theme: literacy, health, housing and institutions. In some cases there can be one Map which serves as both the Generalized Social Map and Thematic Map if the community is small and the variables limited as shown below:

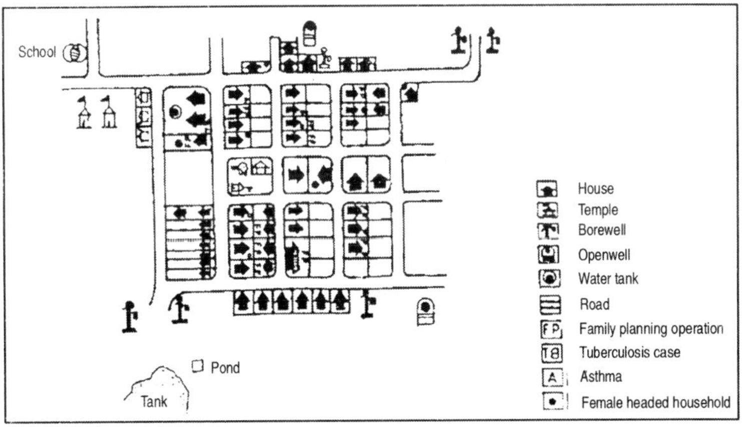

Fig. 3.4: Social Mapping: The map was drawn by villagers of Ramenahally Village.

Source: "Forest, Trees and People", *Newsletter*, Number 15/16.

However, for GP-DP let us discuss the Thematic Social Maps separately. We will discuss how to facilitate two Thematic Social Maps here: Literacy and Health. Let us discuss first how to facilitate a Literacy Map.

What is a Literacy Map?

Literacy Map is a visual depiction of the status of human capital with regard to educational attainment of the residents in a village. In planning for social development, it is very useful and can help identify gender discrimination, if any. An example of a Literacy Map is given below.

Steps in a Literacy Map

- Take the generalized social map.
- Request the people and facilitate a process where they can identify the kinds of educational attainments of the people in the village: illiterate, school drop-outs, class-8 pass, matriculates, college pass, University pass.
- Request the people to use symbols to denote each of these categories of literates. For example an illiterate person could be a "0". A Class 8 pass could be "(8)". A School Pass can

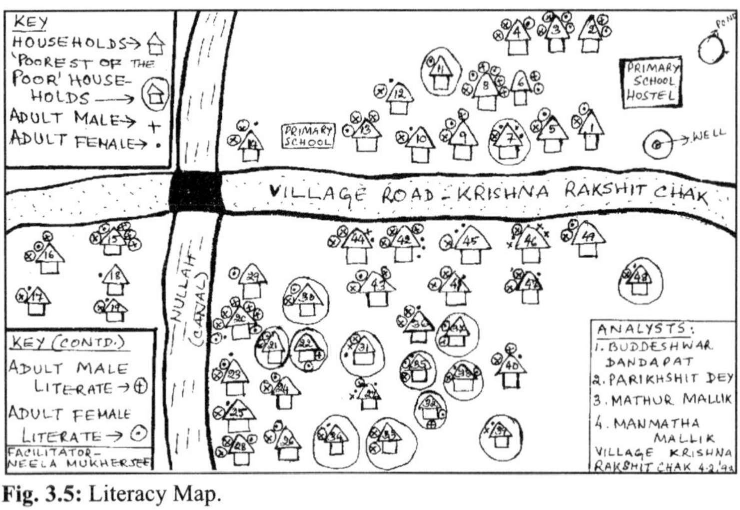

Fig. 3.5: Literacy Map.

be "(+)". A College Graduate could be "(++)". A University graduate can be shown as "(***)". A household without school children may be marked with (–).

- Request them to write down the symbols and what they represent on a chart paper.
- Now, request them to put the appropriate mark beside each house depending on the literacy level of their ***adult*** members.
- If one house has more than one adult member there should be more than one mark. For example, the same house can have an adult who is class 8 pass and one adult matriculate. Then that house should have (8) marking and a (+) marking.
- Ensure that markings have been completed for all the Houses.
- Now, count the number of marks under each category, that is, how many "0", "(8)", "(+)", "(++)" and "(***)" as well as (–) markings are there.
- Record the number of people who are illiterate, Class 8 pass, School Pass, College and University graduate.
- This will give you the state of literacy level in each household and in each category.

Interview the Literacy Map with open ended questions [as discussed in section (p. 34) on "Data collection by applying tools and techniques"], at least covering the key questions mentioned above. Clarify those aspects which are not clearly shown and request for more information, if necessary facilitate the process so that the needs for improving literacy in the GP are clearly spelt out. Remember there is no second chance!

Analysis of a Literacy Map

Now, analyze the Literacy Map using the points mentioned in Section (p. 34) on ***Probing*** above. Analysis of a Literacy Map will vary depending upon each situation. It depends on the capability of the GP-DP Team. However, some illustrations may be given as under:

- Number of households (HH) in the village with each category of literacy: illiterates, Class 8 pass etc.
- Is the number of households with school and college graduate growing or shrinking?
- Number of HH which have out of school children.

- Educational institutions and facilities found in the village, their number and role in the state of literacy.
- Note any specific level of educational attainment of marginalized groups (such as SCs, STs, OBCs, Others and Minorities).
- Identify and count the illiterate and out of school children in:
  - The landless households.
  - The small/marginal farmer households.
  - The wage labour dependent households.
  - Those families which resort to cyclical migration and distress-migration regularly.
  - HHs which are the female-headed households.
  - Households from which bonded labourers, child labourers come.
  - Households of de-notified tribes and nomads.
  - Households of manual scavengers, transgenders, victims of trafficking etc.
  - Households of large farmers.
  - Households belonging to upper castes.
- Location and number of households where the majority of the children in the household are illiterate or out of school especially the girl children.
- Location and number of houses that are *kuccha*/*pucca*/semi-*pucca*.
- Location and number of houses that have been built under IAY.
- Location and number of households that have pension beneficiaries.
- What are the social structures and institutions found in the village which promote literacy?
- And their number?
- The state of illiteracy in households of minority religious groups found in the village and their number.
- Whether ethnic groups found in the village have a larger share of illiterates and out of school children.
- Identify and count the graduates and University graduate in upper caste, large land-owning household.
- Note if the facilities are located in any particular area. If yes why so?

- Request information on the quality of the services provided from different facilities.
- Any other issue that the Gram Panchayat Planning Team may deem necessary.

Draw Inference from the Literacy Map

Record the inferences drawn. Some illustrations as under can help.

- Suppose the number of illiterate and out of school girl children are found uniformly in all classes of households then, the inference will be that education is not imparted for non-economic causes, like early child marriage or social barriers to girl children going to school. The need is social mobilization and information, education and communication.
- Suppose households of manual scavengers, transgenders, and victims of trafficking have relatively more illiterate and out of school children, one needs to investigate if social discrimination is a barrier to education. The need may be is to train teachers on ways and means to integrate such children in mainstream education.
- Suppose households from which bonded labourers come have a large number of out of school and or literate children, then the possibility is that children from the family of bonded labourers are child labourers and even bonded child labourer. The need is to galvanize the law enforcement agencies and work for the rehabilitation of the child labourers and even bonded child labourers.

Display the inferences in public.

Material Needed as per Need

- *Drawing on soft ground*: Coloured powders, sticks and other local material.
- *Drawing on cemented/hard floor*: Coloured Chalks, and other local material.
- *Drawing on Chart Paper*: Large Sized Chart Papers, Pencils, Permanent Markers, Sketch Pens, *Bindis*, and other material as appropriate.

Health Map

Health Map is a visual depiction of the status of human capital with regard to health of the residents in a village. In planning for social development, like the Literacy Map, it is very useful and can help identify gender discrimination, if any. An example of a Health Map is given below.

Steps in Facilitating a Health Map

- As in case of Literacy Map, the generalized social map is the starting point.
- Request the people and facilitate a process where they can identify the kinds of disease that the people in the village suffer from: diarrhoea, polio, tuberculosis, leprosy, asthma, people with disabilities, women suffering from multiple miscarriage etc.
- Request the people to use symbols to denote each of these diseases by a symbol. For example a person suffering from frequent diarrhoea could be a "(*)". A household which has polio affected people could be marked by "(P)". A household which has Leprosy affected people could be marked by "(+)". A Household with people with disabilities "(++)". Similarly, for other diseases.
- Request them to write down the symbols and what disease they represent on a chart paper.

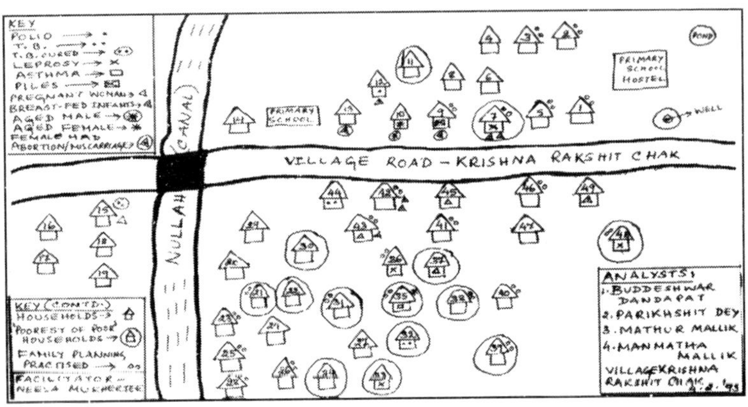

Fig. 3.6: Health Map.

- Hang or paste the Chart Paper of Symbols on the wall or board.
- Now, request them to put the appropriate mark beside each house depending on the disease members of the household may suffer.
- The same house can have several markings depending on the number of diseases they suffer from.
- Ensure that markings have been completed for all the Houses.
- Now, count the number of marks under each category, that is, how many "(*)", "(P)", "(+)" etc. markings are there.
- Record the number of people who suffer from each of the diseases identified by the community.
- This will give you the state of health level in each household and in each kind of disease.

Interview the Health Map as in case of Literacy Map with open ended questions, at least covering the key questions mentioned above. Clarify those aspects which are not clearly shown and request for more information, if necessary. *Facilitate the process so that the needs on the issues covered by the Health Map are clearly spelt out.*

Remember there is no second chance!

Once the Social Mapping is completed, the issues of social development in the GP should be apparent. Record these issues separately and display them on a prominent place in the Panchayat Bhawan.

Analysis of a Health Map

Now, analyse the Health Map using the points mentioned in Section (p. 34) *on **Probing*** above. This analysis will vary from place to place and depend upon the uniqueness of each situation. Some indications may be given as under:

- Number of households (HH) in the village with each of the diseases identified.
- Is the number of households suffering from incidence of diseases growing or shrinking?
- Number of HH which have people with disabilities.
- Health outlets/institutions and facilities (especially trained birth attendants and Multipurpose Health Worker (Female)

or Auxiliary Nurse Midwife, the (ANM), found in the village, their number and role in the state of health.

- Do people follow the systems of traditional medicines (Ayurveda, Siddha and Unani)?
- Note any specific disease affecting households of marginalized groups (such as SCs, STs, OBCs, Others and Minorities).
- Identify and count the number of people (separately for women and men) suffering from diseases in:
  - The landless households.
  - The small/marginal farmer households.
  - The wage labour dependent households.
  - Those families which resort to cyclical migration and distress-migration regularly.
  - Households which are the female-headed households.
  - Households from which bonded labourers, child labourers come.
  - Households of de-notified tribes and nomads.
  - Households of manual scavengers, transgenders, victims of trafficking etc.
  - Households of large farmers.
  - Households belonging to upper castes.
- Location and number of households where the majority of the people in the household suffer from diseases especially the women and the girl children.
- What are the social structures and institutions found in the village which promote good health? And their number?
- The state of health in households of minority religious groups and their number.
- Whether ethnic groups found in the village have a larger share of diseases and people with disabilities.
- Any other issue that the Gram Panchayat Planning Team may deem necessary.

Draw Inference from the Health Map

There is no one way of drawing inferences. Some examples are given below as an indicative way of drawing inference.

- Suppose there are a large number of households (especially the migrants) with people having disabilities, then it is possible that many of the inhabitants are employed in hazardous tasks and medical facilities dealing with disabilities are absent/ inadequate the immunization programme leaves something to be desired. The need may be to set-up medical facilities for dealing with disabilities and better the immunization campaign.

- If the a larger number of women suffer from diseases and a larger number of girl children are affected by polio it is possible that women's access to health services is lower than men's and/or here is discrimination against women/female child. The need may be to improve women's access to health services and posting of female para-medics in the relevant Health Centre.

The inferences are then recorded and displayed in a public place for inputs from the community.

Material Needed as per Need

- *Drawing on soft ground*: Coloured powders, sticks and other local material.
- *Drawing on cemented/hard floor*: Coloured Chalks, and other local material.
- *Drawing on Chart Paper*: Large Sized Chart Papers, Pencils, Permanent Markers, Sketch Pens, *Bindis*, and other material as appropriate.

Resource Mapping

Meaning of Resource Map

A *Resource Map* is a visual depiction of all natural endowments in a GP. As a corollary to Social Map, one can say Resource Map depicts the "nature made structures" in a village or area. Thus, a resource map depicts all the natural resources—land, water, forests, flora, fauna, hills, vegetative cover, fields, grazing lands, common property resources etc. In essence Resource Map for a Gram Panchayat reflects the natural capital base for a Gram Panchayat Plan.

Prior to initiating the participatory natural resource mapping the following needs to be done:

- GP-DP Team needs to ascertain, if an earlier map is available in the village. If one exists, then revisit such map, and update the data and information through participatory process.
- GP-DP Team needs to have a copy of the Cadastral map, a revenue village map available with a *Patwari*. This is a resource map of the Gram Panchayat that has been drawn over the cadastral map of the village.
- GP-DP Team needs to have a copy of the Toposheets to know contours in a water shed area. Contour line is a line joining point of the same elevation. Toposheets are handy in drawing watershed area from map.

Ideally there should be two Resource Maps

(i) A General Resource Map showing different resources available, and their condition in the GP and which the community can access in varying degrees and control. Thus, there could be resources that come under open access to common property to private.

(ii) A Specific Resource Map showing ownerships (disaggregated by gender if possible) of resources, land-use pattern (such as land-used for agricultural production, horticulture, pasture, silviculture etc., fallow, culturable wasteland), common property resources, like forests, pastures, peramboke, woodlots for fuel etc.

Resource Mapping is, thus, Undertaken to

- Map out (i) types, (ii) status, (iii) quantity, (iv) access and (v) distribution of natural resources in the GP like forests and trees, land, water and water bodies, micro-environments and common property resources.
- Understand the manner in which various resources are being accessed, utilized and managed by the community.
- Understand the availability, status and extent of natural resources available at the village(s) which can be used for the GP-DP which is especially useful in both developing natural resource-based livelihoods and planning for sustainable use of these resources.

- Categorize agricultural land, orchards, forest, grazing land and other local land categories and their ownership and control.
- Classify water bodies as ponds, percolation tank, irrigation tanks, tanks for fisheries, streams, canals, open wells, private wells, bore wells etc.
- Demarcate physical formations such as ridge lines and drainage pattern and categorize land as upland, low land etc.
- Determine the nature of control over the resources by the community members (disaggregated by gender) and/or GP.
- Identification of ongoing and incomplete works under various government programmes. Such works should also be identified.
- Classification of ongoing and incomplete work between those whose completion is of value to the community and those which are of no value to the community and best aborted.

It is underscored that a Resource Map using participatory method is, like a Social Map, not drawn to scale, because a Resource Map reflects people's perceptions (and not precisely measured) of natural resources of the community/village.

Key components of a Resource Map

A Resource Map for a Gram Panchayat depicts different aspects of natural resource endowment and management, of a community/area/ village including:

- Topography, terrain and slopes and natural drainage system of a Gram Panchayat habitation/village.
- A forest, scrub land, vegetation and tree cover and species available in the Gram Panchayat/village.
- Soil-type, fertility, erosion and depth of erosion in the Gram Panchayat.
- Land and land-use including land-used for agriculture, grazing land, community land etc.
- Command area, tenure, boundaries and ownership of land.
- Availability of water, rivers and their catchment area.
- Natural drainage system and watersheds/micro-watersheds.
- Availability of other water bodies and natural drainage system, watersheds etc.

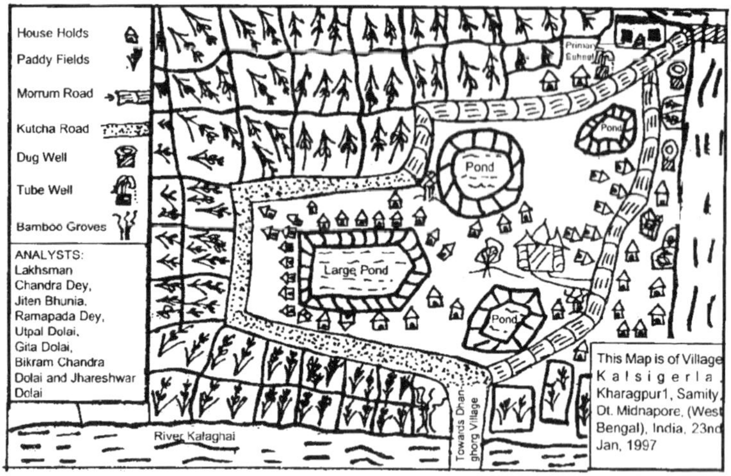

Fig. 3.7: General Resource Map.

Source: Neela Mukherjee: *Participatory Rural Appraisal: Methodology and Application*, (Concept, New Delhi), 1997.

- Various soil and water conservation measures.
- Various denuded areas, environmentally damaged areas.
- Availability of various sources of water and irrigation.

Use of Resource Map

A Resource Map is particularly useful because they provide a focused spatial structure for discussion and analysis of the natural resources.

A Resource Map helps in creating a common understanding amongst the community about their natural resource base.

Resource Maps have been found particularly useful for analysis of problems, looking at solutions and planning for action.

Resource Maps have been used to generate discussions among the participants about natural resources, their entitlement and utilization, problems related to deforestation and soil erosion etc. The focus gradually shifts from the identification and prioritization of problems related to the natural resources, to planning for intervention.

Some Key Questions for Resource Map

- What resources are abundant?
- What resources are scarce?

- Does everyone have equal access to resources: land, water, forests, fruits etc.?
- Do women have access to resources: land, water, forests, fruits etc.?
- Do the poor have access to resources: land, water, forests, fruits etc.?
- Do the SCs/STs/OBCs have access to resources: land, water, forests, fruits etc.?
- Do the SCs/STs/OBCs have access to common property resources: pasture land, forests, and fruits in CPRs?
- Who makes decision on land allocation?
- Where do people go to collect water?
- Who collects water?
- Where do people go to collect firewood?
- Who collects firewood?
- Where do people go to graze livestock?
- What kind of natural resource-based developmental activities does the community carry out as a whole community? Where?
- Which of the available resources are most valued by the community?
- Which resources does the community have the most problem with?

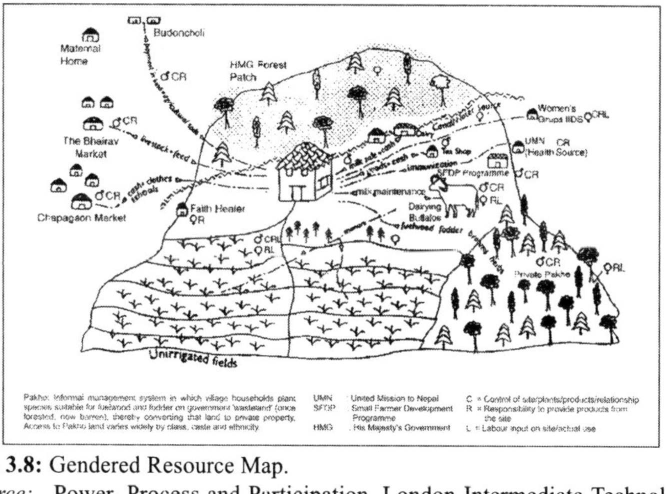

Fig. 3.8: Gendered Resource Map.

Source: Power, Process and Participation, London Intermediate Technology Press, 1996.

- Which of the available resources are most degraded?
- Do men and women have the same responsibility in resource management?
- Who controls the resources, women or men?

Steps in Resource Mapping

- Fix the location. Ensure that the location/venue has enough room to accommodate the expected number of people. See if it is in a central place in the village and accessible to all. Be sure that it is convenient and comfortable for everyone in the community/village. There should be enough shade for the participants. In case you decide to have the map drawn on the ground, make sure the surface fairly smooth for the exercise.
- Avoid the venue for mapping being in a religious place as there could be sensitivities involved.
- Fix a time for the exercise in consultation with the local people.
- Invite them for the mapping exercise.
- Reconsider where you will facilitate the Resource Map: on the floor/ground or on Chart Paper. Both have their advantages and limitations.
- If the Resource Map is facilitated on Chart Papers, ensure that more than one chart paper is joined together so that the people are not constrained by space to draw the map.
- Ensure you have the required material for mapping (apart from local material) like *Rangoli* powder, chalks, Chart papers, Marker pens, flash cards etc. in adequate quantity.
- Once at the venue, clearly explain the purpose of Resource Mapping to the people at the start of the process.
- Leave it to the people to use whatever materials they choose, including the ones you have brought along.
- "Handover the Stick" or better still "Handover the Pen" to the people.
- Empower them and let the people have total control and initiative in the Resource Mapping exercise.
- Suggest to the people to begin by marking the directions as they deem fit. Deviating from conventional mapping they may indicate the side from which sun rises as the East and mark it as such on the paper/ground.

- Facilitate so that people may start by drawing the prominent natural features of the area/village such as the main tank/ pond, or the river, if there is one or a Old Big Tree or whatever, even the main road. Most of the time people start by drawing a landmark (or water mark) and then move on to add other details. The fields and forest start appearing later.
- Watch who all are actively involved, and who all are being left out. Take proactive steps to involve the left out group in the process.
- Once the mapping is over, ask some people present there to identify their fields in the map.
- Request the participants then to depict the field and other details that are particularly necessary for the planning: like the crops that are grown in the fields; women headed households owning the fields; the kinds of trees in the village and the adjoining forests if there are any; common property resources like grazing land, fish ponds, natural sources of drinking water and irrigation water, tanks and so on.
- Villagers would generally identify areas of land by local names (like the deity they worship, name of big land owner in that plot, name of an adjoining natural water course). Request people to divide the village revenue land into such commonly termed patch names. Generally, villagers divide these patches by their common characteristics like type of soil/slope, crops being cultivated their etc.
- Facilitate a classification of the village into areas of different types, may be three types: better-off, medium and inferior patches. Generally, better-off areas would have irrigated double/triple cropped land, mostly owned by better-off people from the villages. Medium areas are not degraded and there is potential to improve yield with small investments in land and water management. These areas would usually be owned by people belonging to "middle" class. And inferior areas (for example called *"baad" khet* or *tanr* land in some parts of the country like in Jharkhand) would generally be owned by poor people. It needs lot of investment to make these areas yield good output.
- Interview the map with open ended questions, at least covering the key questions mentioned above. Clarify those aspects which are not clearly shown and request for more

information, if necessary. *Facilitate the process so that the needs of the GP on the issue covered by the Resource Map are clearly spelt out.* Remember there is no second chance!

- During the course of the interview discuss what ideas the community has to best develop the common property resources and assets, lands, water and vegetation to meet community's needs (of food and nutrition, fuel, fodder, wood and the like) by improving these lands, diversifying land-use or reducing vulnerability of these lands. Discuss especially how to help small and marginal farmers particularly vulnerable HHs. Facilitate so that they are able to identify and prioritize the interventions to be undertaken through Government Programmes.
- Note that if the facilitator has something to add or clarify, he/she must wait for the right moment and not disrupt the process.
- Have the map copied on to chart paper(s) if the map was drawn on the floor or the ground. Ensure accuracy in copying!
- Triangulate the information generated with others in the locality.
- Display the Map at a prominent place where all people have free access so that if any error has crept in map can be pointed out.
- Facilitate correction of the errors in the map should any be found by the community.

As in case of the Social Map, the GP-DP Team's role is limited to facilitation and they should intervene only when necessary, like when the process is not progressing well or some people are left out.

A Resource Map can be painted permanently on walls where they are visible to everyone. The maps prove handy for monitoring the progress. Use of the maps for discussions helps to increase awareness among the villagers, thereby improving transparency. Painted at a public place, such maps are available to the people at any point in time.

Analysis of a Resource Map

Once a Resource Map is prepared, it has to be analysed as in the case of the Social Map. The range of issues that can be analysed emerges from "Some Key Questions for Resource Map" (Section, p. 58). In addition the following issues should be explored:

- Number of households (HH) in the village which has land.
- Is the number of households with land growing or shrinking?
- Is the number of households who has land holdings, growing or shrinking.
- Number of HH which have water bodies (ponds, tanks, wells etc.).
- Institutions and facilities found in the village, their number and locations.
- Note if HHs belonging to marginalized groups (such as SCs, STs, OBCs, Others and Minorities) have land.
- Note if HHs belonging to marginalized groups (such as SCs, STs, OBCs, Others and Minorities) have access to irrigation water.
- Identify and analyse the special issues vulnerable households like:
  - ➢ If HHs who are the small/marginal farmer have access to water for irrigation.
  - ➢ If households of de-notified tribes and nomads, have land and access to water and forests, if any.
  - ➢ If HHs belonging to ethnic groups, if found in the village, have land and access to water and forests, if any.
  - ➢ If households of manual scavengers, transgenders, victims of trafficking etc. have access to land and water and forests, if any.
  - ➢ How HHs who resort to cyclical migration and distress-migration regularly manage their resources?
  - ➢ How HHs who are the female-headed households manage their resources?
  - ➢ How households with PwDs, old age, homeless manages their resources?
- Note any micro-watershed that may be depicted by the resources.
- Note the kind of bio-mass that is available in the village.
- Any other that the GP-DP Team may identify.
- In cross-checking the Resource Map the Cadastral Map (like the one shown in Fig. 3.9) may come handy.

Inference from a Resource Map

After a Resource Map is analysed, the next step is to draw inferences. As in case of a Social Map it is not possible to indicate what could be

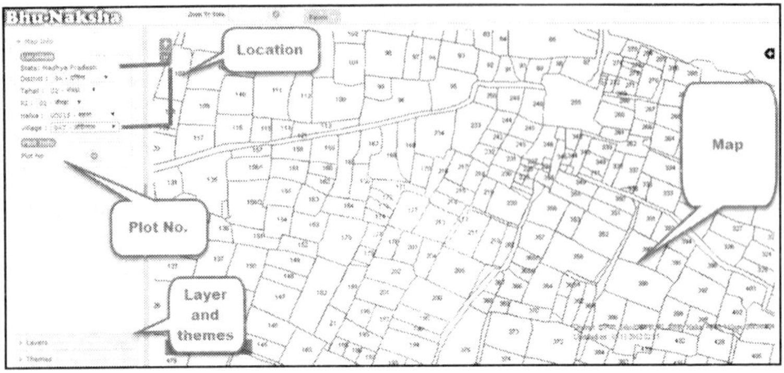

Fig. 3.9: Inference from a Resource Map.

the inferences drawn from a Resource Map but some examples may be helpful.

- For example if the Resource Map reveals that *HHs which are the female-headed households manage their resources and households with PwDs, old age, homeless manages their resources well, then conservation measures initiated by the Government have worked.*
- *Households of manual scavengers, transgenders, victims of trafficking etc. have access to land and water and forests, without let or hindrance then development of natural resource base would not be a problem.*

These are some examples only of how inferences can be drawn.

Material Needed as per need

- *Drawing on soft ground*: Coloured powders, sticks and other local material.
- *Drawing on cemented/hard floor*: Coloured chalks, and other local material.
- *Drawing on Chart Paper*: Large Sized Chart Paper, Pencils, Permanent Markers, Sketch Pens, *Bindis*, and other material as appropriate.
- The Cadastral Map.
- The Topo Sheets.

Analysis of Power or Institutions: Venn Digaram

Meaning of Venn Diagrams

In Gram Panchayat Planning it may be important to anayse the various institution in terms of their importance, efficiency, accessibility and other charateristics of the insitutions within the Gram Panchayt. These local level institutions are not only centres of power, but may play very important roles in implementinmg the Gram Panchayat Plan. Most important these intitutions themselves may need upgradation and improvement for the well-being of the community. Venn Diagram for institutional analysis is a convenient tool in this regard. Often, the diagram is left open, with local people defining which organizations they feel are important to their lives in general terms. Within the framework of institutional analysis, Venn diagrams can also be used to explore a variety of linkages. However, Venn diagrams can also be used to analyze the influence of organization in relation to more specific issues.

Venn diagrams were introduced in 1880 by John Venn in mathematics about the different ways to represent propositions by diagrams. It was borrowed into development economics to:

- Show the relationships between two stakeholders, especially between communities (say villagers) on the one part and institutions designed to serve them (such as police station, post office, dispensary, Block Development Officers' Office) on the other.
- Perception of communities about institutions.
- Analyze the *comparative* strengthens and weaknesses of a set of institutions in terms of their attributes.

It is always community's views and perceptions of institutions which are discussed. Analysis of different ideas within a community is possible through comparison of a number of Venn Diagrams with a range of groups.

Key Components of Venn Diagrams

- The institutions that are relevant to the area (read Gram Panchayat). The institutions may even be located outside the Gram Panchayat.

- The key attributes (importance, usefulness, helpfulness, utility, efficiency, integrity, honesty, life span etc.) of the institutions.
- The *de facto* powers they have in the Gram Panchayat area.
- The *de facto* roles the institutions play in the Gram Panchayat area.
- The perceptions that the community have of the institutions (in terms of their attributes).
- Demonstrate the *comparative* strengthens and weaknesses of a set of institutions in terms of their attributes.

Use of Venn Diagrams

- The roles and significance of various institutions/individuals/places to people in a locality.
- The roles and significance of various institutions/individuals/places to a specific organization/individuals/places.
- Levels of communication between organization/individuals/places.
- The role of development bodies and their interventions in the Gram Panchayats.
- Improving missing links between existing organizations/individuals/places.
- Potential for working through existing organizations,—which ones and with which links.
- Potential roles for new organizations/individuals/places.
- Assessing the possible future roles of the institutions in Gram Panchayat plan implementation, monitoring and evaluation.

Some Key Questions for Venn Diagrams

- How many institutions are there which are relevant to the Community?
- For how long are these institutions in operations?
- Do the institutions have the mandate to work in the area?
- How many of the institutions are formal institutions and how many are informal?
- Are there traditional institutions like *Pani Panchayts, Khap Panchayats*?
- How many institutions are there which are relevant for Gram Panchayat Planning/M&E?

- How are the institutions perceived by the community against various attributes?
- What are the underlying reasons for judging the institutions they are judged so by the community. For example, if the community perceives the Anganwadi as important, find out why and since when?
- Are the institutions relevant (important, useful, helpful, have utility, efficient, have integrity and work honestly) for the marginalized groups the SCs/STs/OBCs/PwD/Manual Scavengers/minorities etc.
- Are there traditional and non-traditional institutions which especially cater to the marginalized groups like the SCs/STs/ OBCs/PwD/Manual Scavengers/Minorities etc.
- Are there intra-institutional tensions?
- Do the traditional institutions impede the working of the non-traditional ones and *vice versa*?

Steps in Venn Diagramming

- First, explain the meaning of institutions to the community.
- Facilitate listing of all institutions and facilities in the area.
- Ask the community to choose two features (importance, utility, efficiency, accessibility, helpfulness and impact) of the institutions and facilities in the area under consideration.
- Suppose the community chooses importance and accessibility as the two attributes of the institutions to be studied.
- Now, first facilitate ranking of the communities according to their *importance* using any of the scoring and ranking methods.
- Then facilitate ranking of the communities according to their *accessibility* using any of the scoring and ranking methods.
- Now, discuss with the community and explain to them that there are two ways of showing the two attributes chosen by them: circles and distances.
- Suppose they choose circles to represent the importance of the institutions/facilities.
- Explain to them that they can show the relative importance of the institutions/facilities by varying the size of the circles. The more important an institution is, the bigger the circle. It is possible that two or more institutions/facilities can be of

similar importance and so the circles representing them will be of almost the same size.

- Each institution is assigned a circle according to their importance. The more important the institution, greater the circle assigned to it. As stated above, two or more institutions which are equally important may be assigned the same size circle.
- The communities make circles or *chapattis* out of paper to represent the various institutions.
- There will be as many circles as there are institutions.
- Now, indicate a point on a large sheet of paper or on the ground. *This point represents the community or village.*
- Explain to the community that now they have to indicate the accessibility of the institutions which they have ranked in order of their importance.
- Explain to the community that accessibility of an institution is shown by the distance of the institution from the community. Thus, the institution which is least accessible to the community, irrespective of its importance, will be furthest away from the point representing the community. Similarly, the institution which is most accessible to the community, irrespective of its importance, will be nearest to the point representing the community. An institution is so close that it may overlap the community.
- Now, the community arranges the paper circles or "*chapattis*", representing the institutions on the paper or the ground according to the accessibility of the institution named in the paper circle, following the principle mentioned in the foregoing sub-paragraph.
- Two or more institutions can be of equal importance. In that case all of institutions of equal importance will be shown at the same distance from the point representing the community.
- Once these steps are completed, the Venn Diagram is ready with three componenets:
  - (a) A point or sign representing the community.
  - (b) "*Chappatis*" or paper circles of various shapes representing the different institutions of different importance.
  - (c) The *Chappatis* or paper circles placed around the point at varying distances showing their relative accessibility: further a circle is from the centre less accessible it is.

- Now, request the community to review the diagram and indicate if they would like to make any change. If not stick the paper circle on the paper.
- If the Diagram was constructed on the ground, replicate it on a large sheet of paper.

Analysis of a Venn Diagram

- What are the roles played by outside institutions?
- Are the community members happy with roles played by outside institutions?
- Why so?
- What are the roles played by village institutions?
- Are the community members happy with roles played by village institutions?
- Why so?
- What are the roles played by informal groupings?
- What are the roles played by traditional institutions?
- Are the community members happy with the informal and traditional institutions?
- The reason why the community members happy (or unhappy) with the informal and traditional institutions?
- What is the condition of the institutions which serve the marginalized groups? Are they sensitive to specific issues relating to these groups (like access to health care for PwDs)?
- What are the relationships between individuals (at family and community level)?
- What are the local facilities, local infrastructure and self-help systems in the community?
- What arc thc institutional and individual support systems?
- What are the credit or health support systems?
- What are the institutions involved in management of natural resources management, agriculture, irrigation, fishing?
- Are they working (or non-working) well and the reasons therefor?
- What are the institutions working livestock diseases and their linkages?
- What are the income generating institutions for women? Are they good and why?

- What are the links between GO, NGO, religious, individual and community groups?
- What are the institutional aspects of conflict/dispute resolution?
- Aspects of policy, interventions and grant systems.
- What are the possible new interventions and new structures or changes to old structures required?
- What are the community's perceptions of project and implementing institutions?
- What are the importance of problems and their relationships to each other with regard to project and implementing institutions?
- Any other issue that the Gram Panchayat Planning Team may deem necessary.

Inference from a Venn Diagram

Like in any other participatory tool, the inferences will be specific to the situation and they differ from place to place. As an indicative list one can infer if the traditional institutions and the non-traditional ones co-function efficiently. One can have inferences about the need and efficiency of the traditional institutions including their role in entrenching traditional values which are not in the best interest of the community. Inferences can be drawn about efficiency of the institutions that deal with social sectors (like health, education sanitation and drinking water) and is (efficiency's) relationship with the quality of these services provided.

Material Needed as per Need

- *Drawing on soft ground*: Coloured powders, sticks and other local material.
- *Drawing on cemented/hard floor*: Coloured chalks, and other local material.
- *Drawing on Chart Paper*: Large Sized Chart Paper, Pencils, Permanent Markers, Sketch Pens, *Bindis*, and other material as appropriate.
- Several pairs of scissors.
- Glue or gum for pasting.

Step-6. Problem Identification

The discussion of the situation analysis above will bring out a range of problems faced by the villagers in the GP: like problems of livelihoods in lean months, poor primary health care or non-existent primary education; problems faced by women in terms of privacy due to open defecation, access to food and health care and so on.

Problems can be of five kinds relating to—

(i) Problems relating to infrastructure (such *kucca* roads, mud housing, lack of water for agriculture, school is held under the trees in the absence of school building etc.). *Source:* Resource Map, Social Map and Thematic Maps.

(ii) Problems to tackle Seasonality (Seasonal Variations) like need for seasonal unemployment, poor conservation of common property resources (which provide food, fruits, fodder and shelter in stress periods), crumbling of traditional water harvesting structures. *Source:* Resource Map.

(iii) Problems relating to Institutions (absence of adequate number of school teachers, health centres, absence of anganwadi centre etc.) *Source*: Social Map and Thematic Maps.

(iv) Problems relating to Social Issues (such as gender discrimination, casteism, untouchability etc.). *Source:* Social Map and Thematic Maps.

(v) Problems relating to preferences (such as seeking traditional medicines *vis-à-vis* allopathic medicines, sending children to school *vis-à-vis* work; creating employment opprtunities in the village *vis-à-vis* migration etc.). *Source:* Social Map and Thematic Maps.

Corresponding to the five kinds of problems there should be five tables of problems. An hypothetical example is given below where the problems are also ranked using free scoring method:

Kinds of Needs

Needs can be of five kinds relating to the five kinds of problems idetified (as shown in Step-6 above):

(i) Needs relating to Infrastructure (such improved roads, better housing, irrigation facilities etc.). *Source:* Resource Map, Social Map and Thematic Maps.

(ii) Needs to tackle Seasonality (Seasonal Variations) like need for seasonal employment, long-run conservation of common property resources, restoration of traditional water harvesting structures. *Source:* Resource Map.

(iii) Needs relating to Institutions (better school buildings, health centres, anganwadi centre etc.). *Source*: Social Map and Thematic Maps.

(iv) Needs relating to Social Issues (such as end gender discrimination, casteism etc.). *Source:* Social Map and Thematic Maps.

(v) Preferences (such as seeking traditional medicines *vis-à-vis* allopathic medicines, sending children to school *vis-à-vis* work; creating employment opprtunities in the village *vis-à-vis* migration etc.). *Source:* Social Map and Thematic Maps.

Prepare following five Tables one for each kind of needs. All the tables should have a heading, date and place/village to which it relates.

A Caveat: The GP-DP Team may adopt any other grouping/ classification of the needs. The only consideration is that all the needs are preseneted in a consolidated manner.

Problems relating to Infrastructure

Serial Number	*Problems*	*No. of Seeds*	*Score*	*Rank*
1.	Poor condition of *Kucca* roads	****************	15	2
2.	Leaking Primary School building	***********	10	5
3.	Absence of health centre	*************	12	3
4.	Non-availability of toilets at homes	************	11	4
5.	Broken drainage	********	8	7
6.	Lack of irrigation	******************	17	1
7.	No veterinary doctor in Village	**********	9	6

Problems relating to Seasonality

Serial Number	*Problems*	*No. of Seeds*	*Score*	*Rank*
1.	Uneven rainfall during cultivation season	******************	18	1
2.	Flash floods	************	10	5
3.	No. employment after Kartik	*************	12	3
4.	Stomach diseases in Asadh, Sawan, Bhado.	************	11	4
5.	High domestic expenditure in Poush, Magh	***********	10	5
6.	Lack of food in summer months	******************	17	2
7.	Pest attack in Rabi crop	**********	9	6

Problems relating to Institutions

Serial Number	*Problems*	*No. of Seeds*	*Score*	*Rank*
1.	Teachers are irregular	******************	18	1
2.	Anganwadi food is poor	************	12	3
3.	Police Station is far away	**********	10	5
4.	Panchayat unhelpful	***********	11	4
5.	No. Bus connection	**********	10	5
6.	No. toilet for girls in school	*************	13	2
7.	Extension workers not available	*********	9	6
8.	Health Centre lacks medicine	******	6	7

Problems relating to Social Issues

Serial Number	*Problems*	*No. of Seeds*	*Score*	*Rank*
1.	Gender discrimination	*************	14	3
2.	Girl children not sent to school	****************	16	2
3.	ST colony is segregated	******************	18	1
4.	SCs have no access to village pond	**********	10	6
5.	Dowry is common	***********	11	5
6.	Scavengers have separate tea cups in Tea Stall	*************	13	4
7.	High rates of suicides amongst women	**********	10	6

Problems relating to Preferences

Serial Number	*Problems*	*No. of Seeds*	*Score*	*Rank*
1.	Migration is preferred	*************	14	3
2.	Prefer women to stay in doors	***********	9	6
3.	Faith Healers are active	****************	16	2
4.	Prefer children to work	******************	18	1
5.	Preference for male child	**********	10	5
6.	Agriculture not given priority as vocation	***********	11	4

A Caveat: The GP-DP Team may adopt any other grouping/ classification of the problems. The only consideration is that all the problems are preseneted in a consolidated manner.

Step-7: Needs Identification

The situation analysis will pave the way for the identification of commmunty's problems from which the community's needs are derived and the community's potential understood. Needs identification is a step following the situation analysis and problem identification.

It needs to be clearly reiterated and underscored that the discussion of the situation analysis above will bring out a range of problems faced by the villages in the GP: like problems of livelihoods in lean months, poor primary health care or non-existent primary education; problems faced by women in terms of privacy due to open defecation, access to food and health care and so on. These problems also reflect the needs of the community. If there is, for instance, the problem of privacy faced by women due to open defecation, the need is to have toilets in the households. If there are problems of livelihoods in lean months, then there is a need to have employment opportunities during lean seasons like MNREGA.

It is open for the GP-DP Team to use either method. Problems and needs are two sides of the same coin. In the following discussion, the Manual has taken the needs route.

Step-8: Needs Prioritization

Generally, the number of needs that emerge from participatory sessions could be very large. Unfortunately, resources are limited though the list of needs requiring attention is very long. Hence, the need to prioritize them, that need attention. The needs identified in Step-6, thus, need to be placed in an ordered sequence in terms of their importance. Needs prioritization is fairly straight-forward through *Scoring-Ranking.*

Scoring of the problems can be done in four ways: ***Cardinal*** Scoring, ***Free*** Scoring, ***Fixed*** scoring and ***Voting***.

In *Cardinal scoring* the items/issues are given a score out of a range of scores like between 1 to 100, or 1 to 10 etc. The most important problem can have a maximum of 100 marks and the least important problem can get the lowest mark of 1. The intervening problems can be assigned marks between 100 and 1, in descending order of their importance.

Agriculture Constraints	*Ranking*	*Solutions*
Lack of availability of fertiliser		Fertilise department in the panchayat
Lack of Knowledge in modern agriculture		Gram sevak should visit regularly
Lack of water of irrigation		• Deep boring well • Dug wells in the fields • Lift irrigation ponds • Motor for well
Lack of agriculture equipments (tractor, sprayer etc.)	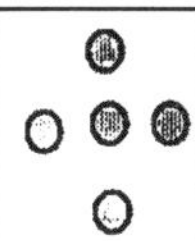	• Demonstration of equipment • Tools to be made • Supply of equipment!
Lack of availability of pesticides	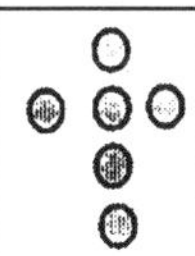	Pesticide department in panchayat (Ghapuli)
Lack of credit facilities		Easy term loan may be provided

Fig. 3.10: Fixed Scoring and Ranking.

In *fixed scoring* the scores are fixed between 1 and the number of items/issues to be scored. For example if there are 12 problems to be scored, then in fixed scoring the range of score will be from 1 to 12 (12 being the score for the most important problem and 1 being the score for the least important problem). For example if there are 8 problems to be scored then the range of score will be from 1 to 8 (8 being the score for the most important problem and 1 being the score for the least important problem). Similarly for other sets of problems. See an example of fixed Scoring below where the Score was fixed between 1 and 6 as the items were six.

In *free scoring*, the items are scored with non-specific quantity of things or elements. Suppose we have to rank five problems. Suppose further that we are using seeds (of any kind) to demonstrate the preferred livelihood option. Under ordinal scoring a certain quantity of seeds is placed against the most important problem. Then a lesser quantity of seeds is placed against the next most important problem. An even lesser quantity of seeds will be placed against the third most important problem and so on. Below is an example of free scoring, with the small circle in the boxes representing the pebbles used in the exercise.

Activities \ Involved Individuals	Female	Male	Boy	Girl	Timing
Cleaning of cowshed	o o o o o o o o o o	—	—	o o o	1 Hour
Grazing	—	o o o o o o o o	o o o o o o	—	6 a.m. to 6 p.m.
Giving feed	o o o o	o o o o o	o o	o o	15 minutes
Milking	o o o o	o o o o o o	—	—	30 minutes
Taking animal to dispensary	—	o o o o o o o o	—	—	1 Day

Fig. 3.11: Free Scoring.

Under the *voting method*, each of the stakeholders or participant in the process is asked to vote his or her preference by using some sign, like placing a seed or pasting a sticker on the item/issue she/he is voting for.

Steps in scoring and ranking are shown below.

Prioritizing the Needs relating to Space (such as lack of roads, lack of housing, irrigation facilities etc.) using Cardinal Scoring:

- Suppose we are trying to ascertain the priority of the community in respect of the eight needs faced by the community: (i) poor roads, (ii) poor school, (iii) "absence of health centre", (iv) non-availability of toilets, (v) broken drainage, (vi) lack of irrigation, (vii) poor housing, and (viii) no veterinary doctor.
- And suppose that we are using the **Cardinal Scoring** method.
- The community is facilitated to first list the needs faced by it.
- The name of each need faced by the community is written on separate flash cards.

- Since, in our example the community has eight needs, there will be eight flash cards with the name of one need written on one card.
- Place the cards as one column on the ground or the floor or table if there is a large table to accommodate all the flash cards.
- Now, request the community to identify the most important need.
- Suppose no health centre, is considered the most important need.
- Request the community to assign a score between 1 and 100 against the need it considers as most important: "absence of health centre".
- Suppose the community gives a score of 90 against "absence of health centre".
- Now, request the community to write 90 against the need emerging from "absence of health centre".
- Now, request the community to identify the *second* most important need.
- Suppose it is non-availability of toilets.
- Request the community to assign it a score which is less than 90 to "non-availability of toilets" because they have given 90 to their most important need, *viz.* absence of health centre.
- Suppose non-availability of toilets is given a score of 74. Request the community to write 74 against the need emerging out of "non-availability of toilets".
- Now, request the community to identify the *third* most important non-availability of toilets.
- The poor school is identified as the *third* most important non-availability of toilets.
- Request the community to assign it a score. Since, the *second* most important non-availability of toilets has been assigned a score of 74, the score to the *third* most important non-availability of toilets will be less than 74. Say 60.
- Community is encouraged to write 60 against poor school.
- Repeat the process with the other needs till all of them are scored.

- The need which scores the highest score, in our example 90, is the most important need and the one which receives the lowest score, say 60, is the least important.
- Thus, the need which gets the highest score is ranked "First". The one which gets the next best score is "Second" and so on, till all the need have been scored and ranked.
- It is underscored that more than one need can get the same score if the community considers them as being equally important.
- Record the outcomes on a chart paper and display at a prominent place for everyone to see.

Prioritizing the needs Relating to Space (such as Lack of Roads, Lack of Housing, Irrigation Facilities etc.) using Fixed Scoring Method

- Suppose we are trying to ascertain the priority of the community in respect of the eight needs faced by the community. And now we are using the *fixed scoring* method. Because there are 8 problems (items) to be scored, under this method the range of scores will be between 1 and 8. Thus, a maximum score that a need can get is 8 (the most important need) and the minimum a need can get is 1 (the least important need).
- Suppose we are trying to ascertain the priority of the community in respect of the same eight needs of the community: (i) better *pucca* roads, (ii) improved primary school buildings, (iii) establishing of health centre, (iv) provision of toilets, (v) restoration of village drainage system, (vi) provide irrigation, (vii) improve housing, and (viii) provide veterinary doctor.
- The community is facilitated to first list the needs faced by it.
- The name of each need faced by the community is written on a flash card.
- Since, in our example the community has eight need, there will be eight flash cards with the name of one need written on one card.
- Place the cards as one column on the ground or the floor or table if there is a large table to accommodate all the flash cards.

- Now, request the community to identify the most important need.
- Suppose "establishing health centre", is considered the most important need.
- Request the community to assign thc score between 1 and 8 (8 being the highest score for the most important problem) against the need it considers as most important.
- Suppose the community gives a score of 8 against "establishing health centre".
- Request the community to write 8 against the need of "establishing health centre".
- Now, request the community to identify the *second* most important need.
- Suppose it is "provision of toilets".
- Request the community to assign it a score which is less than 8 to "provision of toilets" because they have given 8 to their most important need, *viz*. establishing health centre.
- Suppose it is given a score of 7. Request the community to write 7 against the need for "provision of toilets".
- Now, request the community to identify the *third* most important need.
- "improved primary school buildings" is identified as the *third* most important need.
- Request the community to assign it a score. Since, the *second* most important need has been assigned a score of 7, the score to the *third* most important need will be less than 7. Say 5.
- Community is encouraged to write 5 against improved school buildings.
- Repeat the process with the other needs till all of them are scored.
- The need which scores the highest score, in our example 8, is the most important need and the one which receives the lowest score, say 1, is the least important.
- Thus, the need which gets the highest score is ranked "First". The one which gets the next best score is "Second" and so on, till all the need that gets a score of 1 is arrived at which is the least important need.
- It is underscored that more than one need can get the same score if the community considers them as being equally important.

- Record the outcomes on a chart paper and display at a prominent place for everyone to see.

Prioritizing the Needs relating to Space (such as Roads, Housing, Irrigation Facilities etc.) using Free Scoring Method

Needs can also be prioritized using *free scoring* method. The steps in this case are similar to the ones described in p. 76, but instead of using numerical figures for scoring, the GP-DP Team use quantities of local commodities like seeds, pebbles etc. to score. The most important need gets the maximum number of seeds, the next most important need is assigned a lesser number/quantity of seeds etc. Successively lesser number/lower quantity of seeds/ pebbles is assigned to the needs in descending order of their importance. The least important need is assigned the least number of seeds etc.

Prioritizing the Needs Relating to Space (such as better Roads, better Housing, Irrigation Facilities etc.) using Voting Method

Suppose GP-DP Team is trying to ascertain the priority of the community in respect of the same eight needs used by the community. And suppose neither of the three methods discussed above has worked. Then the *voting method* may be adopted as a last resort; last resort because voting has the potential of dividing the community.

- The community is facilitated to first list the needs it faces.
- The name of each need is written on one flash card separately.
- If the community is prioritizing 8 needs, there will be 8 flash cards with the name of one need written on one card.
- Place the cards with the name of one need written on them as one column on the ground or the floor or table if there is a large table to accommodate all the flash cards.
- Now, give *each* community member one seed or pebble or one *post-it* sticker or any comparable thing. The seed or pebble or *post-it* sticker will be used for voting.
- Now, request each of the community members to place the seed or pebble or sticker on the need she/he considers as her/his first priority.

- After everyone has cast his/her vote, ask for a volunteer from the community.
- Request the volunteer to count the number of votes (in terms of seed or pebble or stickers) that each need has received and write the number on a separate card and place it alongside the name of the problem.
- The need which gets the highest number of votes is the most important one and the one which receives the lowest number of votes, say 0, is the least preferred.
- Thus, the one need which gets the highest number of votes is ranked "First". The one which gets the next best number of votes is "Second" and so on, till all the needs have been ranked.
- Record the outcomes on a chart paper and display at a prominent place for everyone to see.

A Few Caveats: Finding out the priority of the GP is a crucial step. The prioritized needs, as revealed in this step, become the *objectives* of the plan. For instance, if the need identified is to stop the depletion of common property resources (CPRs), then the objective of the plan will be to "halt degradation" of the CPRs. If the need identified is better delivery of Health Services, then the objective of the plan will be to "improve the quality of Health Services", and so on.

Prioritization of needs has to be done for each of the areas identified above. That is, there will be at least five sets of needs each set rcorded on seperate Chart Papers. If the GP-DP Team so desires it can have more sets of problems depending what emerges from the analyses.

All the methods for scoring and ranking need not be used for needs prioritization. But more than one method is advisable for "triangulation" or cross-checking.

Step-9*:* Needs Matrix

Once Step-8 is completed the GP-DP Team will have charts similar to one displayed below:

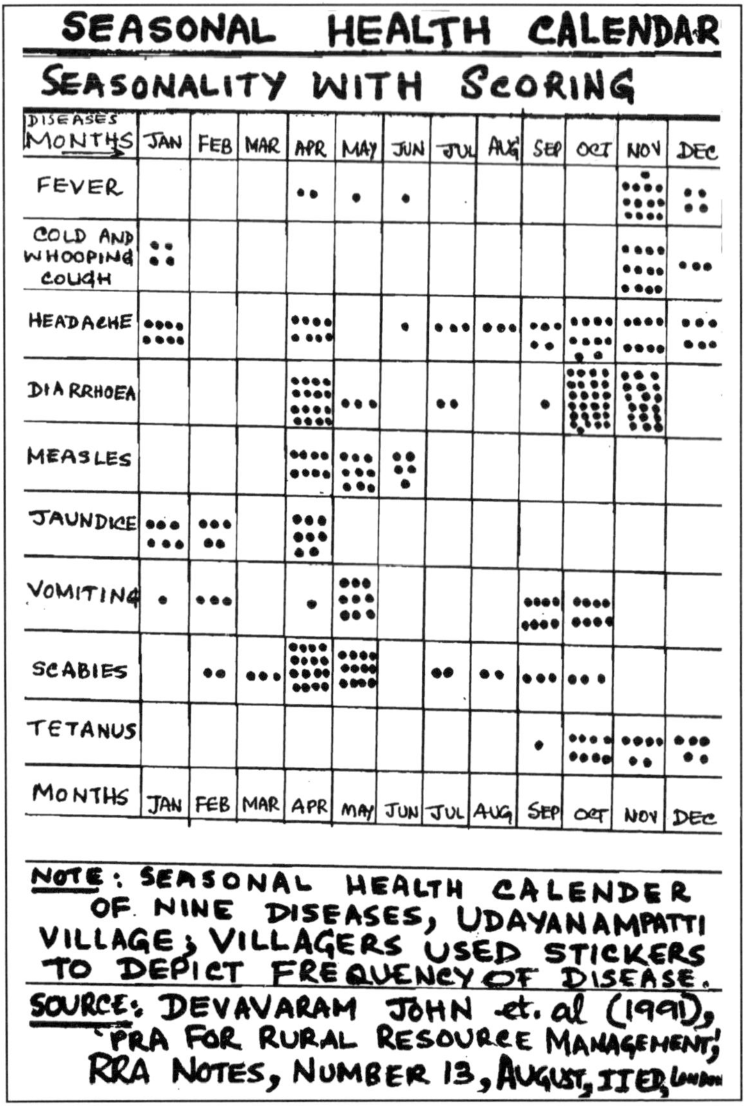

Fig. 3.12: Free Scoring.

Chart 3.1: Needs relating to Infrastructure

Serial Number	*Needs*	*No. of Seeds*	*Score*	*Rank*
1.	Improvement of *Kucca* roads	***************	15	2
2.	Primary School building	***********	10	5
3.	Establishing health centre	************	12	3
4.	Provision of toilets at homes	***********	11	4
5.	Restoration of village drainage	********	8	7
6.	Irrigation facilities	*****************	17	1
7.	Posting veterinary doctor in Village	*********	9	6

Chart 3.2: Needs relating to Seasonality

Serial Number	*Needs*	*No. of Seeds*	*Score*	*Rank*
1.	Irrigation during cultivation season	*****************	18	1
2.	DRR against Flash floods	***********	10	5
3.	Employment after Kartik during lean season	************	12	3
4.	Preventive medicine for stomach diseases in Asadh, Sawan, Bhado	***********	11	4
5.	Provision of credit during high domestic expenditure months of Poush and Magh	**********	10	5
6.	Additional foodgrains in PDS during summer months	*****************	17	2
7.	Supply pestisicides to attack in Rabi crop	*********	9	6

Chart 3.3: Needs relating to Institutions/Organizations

Serial Number	*Needs*	*No. of Seeds*	*Score*	*Rank*
1.	Improve Teacher Attendance	*****************	18	1
2.	Anganwadi food is improved	************	12	3
3.	Police Station is set-up	**********	10	6
4.	Panchayat be made to be more helpful	***********	11	4
5.	Bus connection be provided to nearby market	**********	10	5
6.	Construct toilet for girls in school	*************	13	2
7.	Attendance of Extension workers be checked	*********	9	7
8.	Provide Medicines in Health Centres	******	6	8

Chart 3.4: Needs relating to Social Issues

S. No.	*Needs*	*No. of Seeds*	*Score*	*Rank*
1.	Campaign against gender discrimination	*************	14	3
2.	Make attendance of Girl children to school mandatory	****************	16	2
3.	End ST colony segregation	******************	18	1
4.	Village pond be open to all	**********	10	6
5.	Campaign against Dowry invloving the Police	***********	11	5
6.	Penalty for Tea Stalls that have separate tea cups for SCs in Tea Stall	*************	13	4
7.	Prompt investigation into suicides amongst women	**********	10	6

Chart 3.5: Needs relating to Preferences

S. No.	*Needs*	*No. of Seeds*	*Score*	*Rank*
1.	Migration	*************	14	3
2.	Prefer women to seek more outdoor work	***********	9	6
3.	Removing Faith Healers	****************	16	2
4.	Prefer children to Schools	******************	18	1
5.	Preference for male child be ended	**********	10	5
6.	Agriculture to be given priority as vocation	***********	11	4

Once the prirotized "need charts" are available, the GP-DP Team may consolidate all the Charts. The consolidated charts will generate the *Needs Matrix* for the GP. An example is shown below:

NEEDS MATRIX

	Need-1	*Need-2*	*Need-3*	*Need-4*	*Need-5*	*Need-6*	*Need n-1*	*Need-n*
Sectors								
Needs relating to Infrastructure								
Needs relating to Seasonality								
Needs relating to Institutions								
Needs relating to Social Issues								
Needs relating to Preferences							....	

A Caveat: The GP-DP Team may adopt any other grouping/ classification of the needs. The only consideration is that all the needs are preseneted in a consolidated manner.

Step-10: The Aggregation Needs

The steps mentioned in Section IV (p. 28) above are all applicable to a village. If the village is very large, say has more than 100 households, then these steps have to be applied to different localities or *Tolas/ Mohallas* of the villages. In a Gram Panchayat there will be several villages and each village will generate one or more of the Situation Analyses and Problem Matrix and the corresponsing Needs Matrix. Thus, there will be several Situation Analyses and Problem and Need Matrices.

Because the GPDP Team will be developing a Gram Panchayat Development Plan, it would be necessary to have a picture of the GP as a whole and not of the individual villages, localities or Mohallas. GP-DP Team will need to aggregate the information collected from different villages and localities/*Mohallas*/*Tolas*. GP-DP Team may follow the following process, in technical term called the Delphi Method:

- First collect all the *common* needs emerging from the villages which have been ranked first.

- Then collate all the needs emerging from the villages which have been ranked first but are not common.
- Second collect all the *common* needs emerging from the villages which have been ranked second.
- Then again collate all the needs emerging from the villages which have been ranked second but are not common.

The GP-DP Team will have to follow this iterative process until all the needs have been categorised into two groups: common need and uncommon need. All the common needs ranked will constitute the *Common Lists* of Needs of the GP and all the uncommon ranked needs will be the *Exception List* of Needs of the GP which are *village(s) specific*. Where the Exception List appears, those needs may be specific to villages and would be second priority set of needs for the GP-DP. Thus, at the end of the exercise the GP-DP Team will have:

1. One set of needs common for all villages.
2. One set of needs which are specific to villages.

Step-11: Finding Solutions

Once the lists of needs are arrived at, solutions to those needs have to be located. There can be two sources of solutions.

One, the community will come up with its solutions, which may be based on indigenous knowledge (tacit knowledge), indigenous technology, traditional wisdom and practices. In terms of *Johari's Window,* this is based on Box-2 (They Know-We Do Not Know) of *Johar's Window.* (p. 23).

Secondly, the GP-DP Team may have to supply the community with knowledge which they have such as technical knowledge, knowledge about Government Scheme, details of bank credit, insurances of different kinds etc. [as in Box-3 of *Johari's Window* (We Know-They Do Not Know, p. 23)] and help the Community make an informed choice, generate alternative solutions and take a final decision. This will enable the Community to make an informed choice. There are several ways to arrive at Solutions. *Semi-Structured Interview, Card Sorting Method* and *Problem Activity Matrix* are some of the methods, which have been used with good results.

Spatial Planning

The final step in the tactical planning phase is the spatial planning—Each of the activities has to be located in the space. For instance, if a series of water harvesting structures is to be constructed, the exact locations of the structures have to be decided. Similarly, for other activities there is a need to find the exact location where they will be grounded. Generally, there will be three kinds of activities. Activities giving individual benefit to households (such as support for housing to a widow-headed households) for giving individual benefits, a "well-being grouping map" may be used and each household marked. Then locate/mark especially the households which will receive the benefits. For activities or benefits accruing community owned assets (say a pond), a natural resource map may be used and the location of the new pond marked. If activities which are in the nature of public good, are to be provided, use may be made of a infrastructure map (for locating, for example, a school or a Public Health Centre) and mark the location of the new school or Primary Health Centre on the infrastructure map. Activities accruing benefits to Community owned assets and activities which are in the nature of public goods, the best course is to use mapping of various kinds.

Fig. 3.13: Spatial Planning.

Source: *Planning Training Manual, District Level*, Agricultural Projects Services Centre, Kathmandu, Nepal, Undated.

Annexure-I

Particulars	Details
Number of primary schools	
Number of children below the age of 15	
Number of children below the age of 15 going to school	
Number of children below the age of 15 dropped out of school	
Female literacy	
Number of anganwadis	
Number of Kasturba Gandhi Bal Vidyalayas	
Ratio of teacher: student in the primary school	
Number of PHCs/Sub-Centres	
Number of institutional deliveries recorded	
Ratio of patient: doctor	
Number of libraries	
Number of children identified as malnourished in GP	
Number of children identified as underweight	
Number of women identified as anaemic	
Number of children identified as anaemic	
Infant Mortality Rate (IMR)	
Maternal Mortality Rate (MMR)	
Number of Bharat Nirman Volunteers	
Number of crimes reported	
Number of police stations	
Ratio of constable: citizens	
Number of FIRs registered	
Number of households with toilets	
Number of households with no access to toilets	
Number of common sanitation complexes	
Does GP Bhawan have toilets	
Does hospital have a toilet	
Number of trees in the GP	
Number of BPL families	
Number of SC Households	
Number of ST households	
Number of landless households	
Number of IAY beneficiaries	
Number of FRA beneficiaries	

DETAILS OF ACTIVITIES

Personal Development

Activity: Hygienic Behaviour and Practices

Aim	• Improving personal hygiene for all consisting of ▪ Daily cleaning of teeth ▪ Use of Sanitary Towel ▪ Daily Bath ▪ Washing hands after toilet and before eating ▪ Wearing clean clothes ▪ Personal menstrual hygiene of adolescent girls and women
Strategy	▪ House-to-house campaign through health volunteers and Swachhata Mitras ▪ Education through anganwadi centres, schools, SHGs, and organization of camps. ▪ Wall Writings; Information Boards at relevant locations ▪ Street Plays, Film Shows etc. ▪ Community Radio, if established, can be a very useful medium.
Schemes	▪ NHM ▪ ICDS ▪ Swachh Bharat Mission
Outputs	▪ Formation of health brigade from the youth volunteers ▪ House visits by health brigade ▪ Encouraging early adopters and follow up with defaulters
Outcomes	▪ Reduced incidence of diarrhoea and other infectious diseases ▪ Reduction of other personal illness ▪ Improved sense of well-being

Activity: Inculcating Habits of Regular Physical Exercise

Aim	▪ Mandatory physical exercise everyday as per the requirements of the gender and age groups, individually or in groups
Strategy	▪ Providing variety of options: Gym, yoga, walking/jogging, sports for everyone to choose from ▪ Health volunteers to guide and follow up personally

Schemes	▪ MPLADS ▪ Nehru Yuvak Kendra Sangathan ▪ MGNREGS ▪ State Government Sports Schemes
Outputs	▪ Setting up playgrounds and parks ▪ Identification and provision of opportunities for physical exercise for all ▪ Engaging with every person in the village and facilitate daily exercise regimen
Outcomes	▪ Prevention of illness ▪ Increased well-being

Activity: Reducing risk Behaviour—Alcoholism, Smoking, Substance Abuse etc.

Aim	▪ Reducing risk behaviours like alcoholism, smoking, substance abuse (drugs/tobacco/*gutka* etc.) among all age groups of population
Strategy	▪ Identification of people addicted ▪ Working on behavioural changes—SHGs and health volunteers ▪ Campaign through Schools, Youth Clubs, SHGs, as well as places of worship ▪ Reducing availability of risk substances in the village
Schemes	▪ NHM ▪ MPLADS (for hardware, as applicable) ▪ Schemes of Health and Family Welfare
Outputs	▪ Identification of risk behaviours and practitioners ▪ Social sanction against risk behaviours ▪ Attacking the source of substances ▪ Working on de-addiction and behavioural change
Outcomes	▪ Increased well-being ▪ Improved health outcomes ▪ Improved peace and harmony at homes and in society ▪ Reduction in violence against women

Human Development

Activity: Health and Nutrition

Aim	▪ Universal access to basic health facilities consisting of health card, medical examination. ▪ Complete immunization. ▪ Balanced nutrition irrespective of economic status, gender and age group. ▪ Balancing the sex-ratio.
Strategy	▪ Identify and fill gaps in health infrastructure and materials. ▪ Identify and fill up vacancies of trained health and para-health professionals. ▪ Identify training needs and capacitate health and para-health professionals, and handhold through follow up. ▪ Organise immunization and de-worming drives through habitation specific camps. ▪ Issuance of health card to each and every person. ▪ Create a calendar of health education interventions through street theatre, puppetry and other social communication methods throughout the year. ▪ Train volunteer groups for behaviour and social change on issues like anaemia, hygiene and health. ▪ Monitor and significantly improve the quality of the noon meal programme in schools and the nutrition component in Anganwadi.
Schemes	▪ The National Health Mission (NHM) ▪ ICDS for nutrition along with SABLA and Saksham schemes.
Outputs	▪ Significant reduction in MMR, IMR, NMR over three years. ▪ Significant increase in immunization of infants and children up to five years of age and institutional delivery of infants over three years. ▪ Significant reduction in the incidence of anaemia and Grade III and IV malnutrition in infants, complete arrest of Grade I and II malnutrition reduction in the incidence of anaemia in adolescents, pregnant women, and lactating mothers.
Outcomes	▪ 100 per cent immunization ▪ 100 per cent institutional delivery. ▪ Significant reduction in malnutrition, especially among children and adolescent girls, pregnant women and lactating mothers. ▪ Significant change in the quality of the health delivery and monitoring system of NHM. ▪ Increased capacity of the health and para-health professionals, who could act as resource persons for the next year. ▪ Significant change in behaviour and attitudes relating to health and hygiene.

Activity: Education for All

Aim	▪ Universal access to education facilities up to Class X. ▪ Conversion of schools into 'smart schools' for providing quality education. ▪ Adult literacy ▪ E-literacy ▪ Village libraries including e-libraries.
Strategy	▪ Identify and fill gaps in education infrastructure and materials. ▪ Identify and fill up vacancies of trained education professionals. ▪ Identify training needs and capacitate education professionals. ▪ Convert the GP schools into 'smart schools'. Smart schools will have IT enabled classrooms, e-libraries, web-based teaching and will make all students e-literate. ▪ This will be done through filling the infrastructure gaps. ▪ Organise adult literacy campaigns to ensure functional literacy through youth volunteers. ▪ Use of cultural forms, *viz.* street theatre, puppetry and other social communication methods throughout the year. ▪ Create local toys and education resource centres and materials using local knowledge and materials. ▪ Start a local newspaper which is conceptualized and run by local youth. ▪ Organise Skype sessions with identified eminent persons from the fields of arts, literature and social reform. ▪ Organise exhibitions on local histories and talks by experts. ▪ Construct and/or equip a fully functional library including e-resources, with a trained librarian. ▪ Conduct training for every person interested in e-learning. ▪ Organise youth groups to ensure every child, particularly girl child is in school, working children be motivated for transition schools and special facilities provided for children with special needs.
Schemes	▪ Sarva Shiksha Abhiyan (SSA) ▪ Rashtriya Madhyamik Shiksha Abhiyan (RMSA), ▪ National Literacy Mission (NLM) ▪ National Child Labour Project (NCLP) ▪ MPLADS
Outputs	▪ Significant increase in the enrolment, attendance, completion and transition at every class level, at least till class X. ▪ Significant decrease in the dropout rates from the first year onwards and a significant increase in retention for all classes. ▪ Improved Minimum Levels of Learning (MLLs) in primary classes ▪ All infrastructure and capacity-building gaps identified and filled. ▪ All vacancies filled up.

	▪ Adults going through functional literacy campaign assessed for numeracy and literacy. ▪ At least one person from every family able to use the computer and the internet.
Outcomes	▪ Developing a reading habit that changes the world-view-awareness about the location of the self and the community in the interconnected world. ▪ Self-reliance and mutual respect. ▪ Ability to articulate choices and decision-making including amicable conflict resolution. ▪ Awareness about rights and responsibilities that bring accountability. ▪ Capability to use technology appropriately and adapt in the present world.

Social Development

Activity: Social Development

Aim	To create a vibrant and harmonious village society through: ▪ Activities for promotion of voluntarism like Bharat Nirman Volunteers. ▪ Capacity building of the people to fully participate and contribute to local development. ▪ Activities for honouring village elders, local role models especially women, freedom fighters and martyrs. ▪ Activities for violence and crime free villages such as. ▪ Citizen Committees. ▪ Sensitization, especially of youth. ▪ Village sports and folk arts festivals. ▪ Having a village song to instill a sense of pride among the people ▪ Celebrating 'Village Day'.
Strategy	▪ Organise citizen education. ▪ Involve youth groups in health camps and adult literacy drives. Create discussion groups through the libraries. ▪ Reclaim local histories and identify/select the village day. ▪ Celebrate the village day through exhibitions and honouring the village elders, and local role models, especially women, freedom fighters and martyrs. ▪ Reclaim local repositories of songs. ▪ Start competitions where different groups create a new song that reflects the spirit of the village, and select the village song for different festivals and occasions.

	■ Start local folk music and arts festivals that reflect the diversity of India. ■ Organise citizen-*mohalla* committees for peaceful and crime free village life. ■ Organise Gender Sensitization programmes and peace education training programmes. ■ Organise village discussions on local production and productivity and employment.
Schemes	■ Bharat Nirman Volunteers. ■ Youth Club schemes. ■ MPLADS. ■ IEC components of appropriate scheme.
Outputs	■ Organization and sustaining of the youth volunteer groups for community development through yearly activities schedule. ■ Constitution of citizen committees. ■ Significant reduction in disputes and crimes, especially crimes against women.
Outcomes	■ United and harmonious village. ■ Crime-free society. ■ Increase in awareness, knowledge and opportunities for self-expression.

Activity: Clean Villages

Aim	Universal access to sanitation consisting of: ■ Household toilets for all. ■ Toilets in all public institutions. ■ Solid and liquid waste management. ■ Toilet linked biogas plants.
Strategy	■ Identify all houses without Individual Household Latrines (IHHL) and facilitate construction of toilets in each household. ■ Identify lack of toilets in all public institutions in the GP and facilitate construction. ■ IEC initiatives to create demand for and promote use of toilets – both individual and institutional. ■ Construct covered drains along with liquid waste treatment pits. ■ Garbage collection, segregation and disposal systems. ■ Initiate behaviour change campaigns on hygiene and sanitation through involvement of youth groups and social communication methods like street theatre and puppetry for open defecation free villages.

	■ Identify appropriate solid and liquid waste management technologies for the particular GP context and roll out in a phased manner.
Schemes	■ MGNREGA.
	■ Swachh Bharat Abhiyaan.
	■ MPLADS.
Outputs	■ Fulfil the norms of Nirmal Gram.
	■ Complete Saturation of IHHL and public infrastructure of toilets in the GP.
	■ Efficient solid and liquid waste management systems.
Outcomes	■ Open Defecation Free village.
	■ Clean streets and public places.

Economic Development

Promoting diversified agricultural livelihoods, including livestock and horticulture, through—

Aim	■ Sustainable Agriculture and Organic Farming.
Strategy	■ Transfer of technology for organic farming to the farmers' groups, especially women.
	■ Preparation of Soil Health Cards.
	■ Setting up Local Seed Banks.
	■ Crop intensification such as SRI (System of Rice Intensification)
	■ Micro-irrigation and Drip Irrigation.
	■ Solar pumping systems.
	■ Agro-service centres.
Schemes	■ Schemes of the Ministry of Agriculture
	■ MKSP under NRLM
	■ MGNREGS
Outputs	■ Soil Health Cards prepared
	■ Seed Banks established
	■ SRI Practiced
	■ Micro-Irrigation Infrastructure established and Agro Service Centres set-up.
Outcomes	■ Reduced use of chemical fertilizer.
	■ Reduced use of chemical pesticides.
	■ Enhanced production of organic manure and use of organic pesticides.
	■ Availability of farm machinery at reasonable hire charges.

Rural Industrialization

Aim	■ Livestock development including Gobar Bank, Cattle Hostel Post-harvest technology applications. ■ Food Processing and Dairy Processing. ■ Other Micro-Enterprises.
Strategy	■ Enhancing livestock based livelihoods through better management practices and well-planned linkages. ■ Conducting cattle health campaigns and fairs. ■ Establishment of Gobar Banks for organic manure. ■ Cattle Hostels with linkage to biogas production, as a model of providing modern integrated common facilities for better care and improving productivity of all cattle in the village. ■ Construction and provision of storage facilities, especially common storage facilities to reduce post-harvest losses. ■ Grading and sorting of produce at the village level. ■ Decentralized small scale food processing activities. ■ Small scale dairy processing coupled with marketing of such produce. ■ Revive rural industries ranging from traditional artisanal occupations such as weaving, and pottery to modern cottage and small scale industries. ■ Activities related to village tourism, including eco-tourism.
Schemes	■ Schemes of Ministry of Agriculture, especially Department of Dairy and Animal Husbandry. Support from NDDB and NABARD. ■ MGNREGS. ■ Schemes of Department of Food Processing and Department of Dairy and Animal Husbandry. ■ Schemes of Ministry of MSME and Ministry of Textiles.
Outputs	■ Construction of worksheds. ■ Establishment of market linkages (especially cooperatives). ■ Establishment and functioning of animal healthcare facilities. ■ Post-harvest storage and grading facilities created. ■ Processing units/cooperative facilities set-up. ■ Rural enterprise units established.
Outcomes	■ Enhanced livestock based incomes. ■ Better price realisation for agricultural and allied produce. ■ Significant/Substantial proportion of agricultural and dairy produce is processed in the village before being marketed outside. ■ Enhanced employment and incomes.

Skill Development for all Eligible Youth

Aim
- Development of skill of the rural community to enhance their livelihoods.
- Identifying skill demand and skill gap.
- Identifying suitable training and certification agencies.
- Skill building for self-employment and placement in the formal sector.
- Introducing vocational education in schools.
- Identifying employers and placement opportunities.
- Identifying self-employment opportunities and setting up support services.
- Continuous skill upgradation for sustained employment.
- Skilling the MGNREGS workers.
- MIS for tracking the progress of trained youth.

Schemes
- National Rural Livelihoods Mission.
- Aajeevika Skills.
- RSETI.
- Schemes of Ministry of MSME.

Outputs
- Trained skilled youth.

Outcomes
- Significant increase in skill levels.
- Gainful employment and enhanced livelihoods.

Organizing Women SHGs and Financial Inclusion

Aim
- Formation of Women's SHGs is the master strategy that provides multiple outcomes ranging from women's empowerment to livelihood enhancement to financial inclusion. The model village should be able to bring together women from all social groups and economic situations into SHGs and connect them to banks as individuals as well as groups.

Strategy
- Universal inclusion through participatory identification of the poor (PIP).
- Organisation of SHGs of women and their federations at the GP and cluster levels.
- Bank linkages.
- Ensure that all women SHG members have individual PMJDY bank accounts.

Schemes
- National Rural Livelihoods Mission.

	■ Pradhan Mantri Jan Dhan Yojana.
	■ Constitution and functioning of SHGs.
	■ Opening of individual bank accounts.
	■ Establishment of bank linkage.
	■ Establishment of household and collective enterprise.
Outcomes	■ Increased incomes through enhanced livelihoods.
	■ Inculcation of saving habit.

Employment under MGNREGA

Aim	■ Implementation of MGNREGA as per the provisions of the Act.
Strategy	■ Effective demand capture through Rozgar Diwas.
	■ Better, participatory planning.
	■ Provision of works as per demand.
	■ Timely payment of wages.
	■ Identification and creation of quality productive assets.
Schemes	■ Mahatma Gandhi National Rural Employment Guarantee Scheme.
Outputs	■ Provision of employment as per demand.
	■ Creation of quality productive assets.
Outcomes	■ Enhanced incomes and poverty reduction.

Environmental Development

Activity: Roadside plantations, Tree plantation in homesteads, schools and public institutions; and Social Forestry

Aim	■ Increase coverage of trees in rural areas.
Strategy	■ Planting trees–those having economic, environmental, social and cultural value – in homesteads and public places, especially road sides, canal bunds, commons, and farm bunds.
	■ Develop green walkways in and around the village.
	■ Assigning usufruct rights over tree in public land to the poorest of the poor households.
	■ Development of local nurseries.
	■ Simplification of systems for payment of maintenance expenditure.
Schemes	■ MGNREGS.
	■ National Horticulture Mission.
	■ Schemes of the Ministry of Environment, Forests and Climate Change (like CAMPA).

Outputs
- Plantations and nurseries of multiple species.
- Development of a village nursery can provide employment to the aged and the differently abled.

Outcomes
- Income and employment from the trees.
- Prevention of soil erosion.
- Increased green cover.
- Mitigating effects of climate change.

Activity: Watershed management especially revival of traditional water bodies

Aim
- Developing the village along the principles of Watershed Management to enhance livelihoods, through improving irrigation, improving drainage, and checking erosion.

Strategy
- Scientific and participatory assessment of the health of the watershed and developing treatment measures.

Schemes
- IWMP and MGNREGS.

Outputs
- Water harvesting and soil conservation structures created, revived, rehabilitated.

Outcomes
- Enhanced irrigation facilities.
- Improved drainage.
- Increased groundwater levels.

Activity: Reducing local pollution of air, water and land

Aim
- Reduce as well as mitigate the impacts of air, water and land pollution.

Strategy
- Quick and participatory assessment of different kinds of pollution affecting the village.
- Making the village open defecation free.
- Soil testing and preparation of soil health cards.
- Composting linked to biogas and preparation of farmyard manure.
- Social ban on use of polythene bags and other harmful pollutants.
- Unnat Chullah for cooking.

Schemes
- Schemes of MNRE as well as MGNREGS.
- Schemes of Ministry of Agriculture.

Outputs
- Social and physical infrastructure for reducing waste and pollution.

Outcomes
- Reduced pollution and profitable use of waste.
- Improved health outcomes.
- Aesthetically appealing surroundings.

Rainwater harvesting—rooftop as well as others

Aim	▪ Popularization of rainwater harvesting as a traditional practice in rural India.
Strategy	▪ Rooftop rainwater harvesting integrated to toilet units in individual houses as well in public buildings.
	▪ Structures such as Eris, *Kunds*, *Tankas* and *Tanklis* in desert and other low rainfall areas.
Schemes	▪ NRDWP (National Rural Drinking Water Programme).
	▪ MGNREGS.
Outputs	▪ IWMP structures created and rehabilitated.
Outcomes	▪ Enhanced availability of water for drinking and other purposes.

Basic Amenities

Activity: Pucca houses for all houseless poor/poor living in *kuccha* houses

Aim	▪ *Pucca* houses for all houseless poor/poor living in *kuccha* house.
Strategy	▪ Identification of all families living in temporary structures and prioritising them based on vulnerability—due priority to the elderly and single member households.
	▪ Taking up housing on a saturation mode, as far as possible in viable clusters.
Schemes	▪ Indira Aawas Yojana.
Outputs	▪ Durable, permanent houses for all.
Outcomes	▪ Improved well-being and dignity of living.

Activity: Drinking water, preferably treated piped water with household taps

Aim	▪ Drinking water, preferably treated piped water with household taps.
Strategy	▪ Survey to identify existing and potential sources of drinking water.
	▪ Assess current and future habitation-specific needs.
	▪ Purify, rehabilitate and sustain the existing sources.
	▪ Preparation of village water security plan.
Schemes	▪ National Rural Drinking Water Programme.
Outputs	▪ Piped water connection for all households.
Outcomes	▪ Improvement in health, reduction in water-borne diseases such as diarrhoea.

Activity: Internal all weather roads with covered drains and all-weather road connectivity to the main network

Aim	▪ Internal all-weather roads with covered drains and all-weather road to the main network.
Strategy	▪ Existing *kuccha* roads in and out of the village may be listed and made *pucca*.
Schemes	▪ Pradhan Mantri Gram Sadak Yojana. ▪ MGNREGA. ▪ Backward Region Grants Fund.
Outputs	▪ Completed construction of all-weather roads that meets the target number of kilometres as identified during the needs assessment exercise.
Outcomes	▪ Improved connectivity to and from the village which will enhance economic activity and access to public services as well as markets.

Activity: Electricity connection to all households including from alternative sources of energy, especially solar

Aim	▪ Electricity connection to all households and street lights including from alternative sources of energy, especially solar.
Strategy	▪ Identify best suited source of renewable energy given topography (e.g. wind, solar, micro hydro etc.). ▪ Baseline survey of households without access to electricity. ▪ Electricity connections provided including from new and renewable energy sources. ▪ Priority given to vulnerable households and public buildings.
Schemes	▪ Rajiv Gandhi Grameen Vidyutikaran Yojana, ▪ MNRE Schemes.
Outputs	▪ 100 per cent electrification of households in the village. ▪ Street lights. ▪ Increase in connectivity through telecom and internet.
Outcomes	▪ Enhancement of economic activity and increase in incomes of households in the village.

Activity: Pucca infrastructure for public institutions—Anganwadis, schools, health institutions, Gram Panchayat Office and Libraries

Aim	▪ *Pucca* infrastructure for public institutions—Anganwadis, schools, health institutions, Gram Panchayat office and libraries.

- All public buildings, especially schools, will be built using environment friendly local technologies using local materials and will have extensive tree coverage.

Strategy

- Through participatory planning methods, the order of priority of the need for public infrastructure to be determined.
- Repair and renovation of existing infrastructure to be given first priority to the extent doable.
- Identification of location for construction of different physical buildings.
- Technical support and supervision provided to prepare estimates, procure tenders and monitor quality of construction.
- Ensuring fully functional facilities in these buildings including barrier free access in accordance with scheme guidelines.

Schemes

- MGNREGA,
- Backward Regions Grant Fund,
- RGPSA.
- Sarva Shiksha Abhiyan,
- ICDS.

Outputs

- Repair/renovation of existing public infrastructure.
- Construction of high quality anganwadis, schools, health institutions, Gram Panchayat office and library where absent and fully functional public services in the village.

Outcomes

- Improvement in quality of services through the public institutions, particularly relating to health and nutrition.
- More accessible Gram Panchayats.
- Developing reading habit and improving learning levels.

Activity: Civic Infrastructure including Community Halls, Buildings for SHG Federations, Playgrounds, PDS Outlets, and Burial Grounds/Crematoria

Aim

- Civic infrastructure including community halls, buildings for SHG federations, playgrounds and PDS outlets, and burial grounds/ crematoria.

Strategy

- Identification of location for construction of different types of civic infrastructures through participatory planning processes.
- Technical support and supervision provided to prepare estimates, procure tenders and monitor quality of construction.

Schemes

- MGNREGA.
- Backward Regions Grant Fund.
- Sarva Shiksha Abhiyan.

	■ MPLADS.
	■ Rajiv Gandhi Khel Abhiyan.
Outputs	■ Construction of high quality community assets.
Outcomes	■ Strengthened SHGs, increase in physical and recreational activities amongst youth, better organisation of community events and festivals, better functioning PDS outlets.

Activity: Village Markets

Aim	■ Develop well-functioning and efficient village markets.
Strategy	■ Consultations with producer groups to identify location, size and nature of village market to be constructed.
	■ Technical support and supervision to prepare estimates, procure tenders and monitor quality of construction.
Schemes	■ National Rural Livelihoods Mission,
	■ MGNREGS.
Outputs	■ Village markets constructed at strategic locations.
Outcomes	■ Improved marketing and sale of agricultural produce and increase in incomes of households.

Activity: Micro-Mini Banks/Post Offices/ATMs and Provision of UIDAI Card

Aim	■ Ensuring linkage of the all rural areas with an efficient banking network.
Strategy	■ Survey existing coverage of bank and post offices in the local area.
	■ Identify banking partners for extending micro ATM services to unserved areas.
	■ Opening of accounts.
	■ Conduct enrolment camps and door to door distribution of UIDAI cards.
Schemes	■ PM Jan Dhan Yojana and other schemes of the Department of Financial Services.
	■ BRGF.
	■ Finance Commission Grants.
Outputs	■ 100 Per cent financial inclusion of all.
	■ 100 Per cent Aadhaar enrolment.
Outcomes	■ Increase in savings, reduced impact of income shocks, and increase in standard of living.

Activity: Broadband, Telecom Connectivity and Common Service Centres

Aim	▪ Broadband, telecom connectivity and Common Service Centres.
Strategy	▪ Common Service Centres may be built as part of Gram Panchayat office.
	▪ E-literacy of citizens may be facilitated through modules and regular classes.
Schemes	▪ CSC Scheme of DEITY,
	▪ National Optical Fibre Network (NOFN)
	▪ Schemes of Telecom Department.
Outputs	▪ 100 Per cent access to internet and mobile connectivity.
Outcomes	▪ Bridging the digital divide.
	▪ Digital literacy, greater access to information and knowledge, increased opportunities for innovation.

Social Security

Activity: Pensions for All Eligible Families—Old Age, Disability and Widow

Aim	▪ Coverage of social security schemes for all eligible persons on principles of Saturation.
Strategy	▪ Door-to-door identification exercise to register all eligible persons under NSAP and the state social pension schemes.
	▪ Time-bound sanction of pension.
	▪ Opening of bank/PO account
	▪ Timely payment of pension through micro ATMs.
Schemes	▪ IGNOAPS, IGNWPS, IGNDPS.
	▪ Other state social pension schemes.
Outputs	▪ All eligible pension beneficiaries receive timely payment into their accounts.
Outcomes	▪ Reduced vulnerability of the elderly, widows and persons with disability to health and income shocks, and enhanced dignity of life.

Activity: Insurance Schemes

Aim	▪ Universal coverage of insurance schemes.
Strategy	▪ Door-to-door identification exercise to register all eligible persons under PMJDY, RSBY and AABY.

	■ Time bound sanction of insurance.
	■ Systems for preparation of claims using SHG network.
Schemes	■ Aam Aadmi Bima Yojana,
	■ RSBY/State health insurance schemes.
	■ PMJDY.
Outputs	■ Saturated coverage of all households eligible for AABY and RSBY under the programme coverage.
	■ Coverage of all eligible households under PMJDY.
Outcomes	■ Reduced risk of health and income shocks and enhanced social security.

Activity: PDS-Universal Access to All Eligible Households

Aim	■ Universal coverage of PDS.
Strategy	■ Door-to-door identification of beneficiaries and distribution of ration cards to all in accordance with the provisions of the NFSA.
	■ Timely distribution of full entitlement of grain to families according to the provisions of the NFSA.
	■ Social audit of the PDS institutions.
Schemes	■ National Food Security Act.
	■ State PDS schemes.
Outputs	■ Implementation of all provisions of NFSA.
Outcomes	■ Enhanced food security and improved nutritional outcomes.

Good Governance

Strengthening Gram Panchayats

Aim	■ Strengthening local democracy and improving capacity of Gram Panchayats to perform their functions particularly in relation to public service delivery.
Strategy	■ Providing basic infrastructure for Gram Panchayats like Panchayat Bhavan, computers etc.
	■ Capacity-building of elected functionaries and officials.
	■ Activating Standing Committees of Panchayats.
	■ Creating Functional Committees and vitalizing participatory for a like Watershed Committees, Village Health and Sanitation Committees, PTAs etc.

Schemes	▪ BRGF. ▪ RGPSA. ▪ MGNREGS.
Outputs	▪ Good infrastructure for Gram Panchayats. ▪ Functioning committees. ▪ Trained functionaries.
Outcomes	▪ Deeper local democracy.

Activity: Social Audit

Aim	▪ Half-yearly Social Audit of all components done by the Gram Sabha.
Strategy	▪ Rope in Social Audit Unit (SAU) of the State to facilitate the Gram Sabha of the GP in conducting a social audit. ▪ Information collected above to be shared with the members of the community, SHG members, Village Resource Persons, District Resource Persons of the SAU 15 days prior to the Social Audit being conducted. ▪ Conducting a 100 Per cent house-to-house verification to verify the records with individual testimonies. ▪ Recording of individual testimonies and grievances in writing during the verification. ▪ Conduct of a Social Audit Gram Sabha where findings of the social audits are read out in front of the Gram Sabha which shall be attended by functionaries from the implementing agencies, independent observers etc. where decisions will be taken on each of the findings read out.
Schemes	▪ All schemes.
Outputs	▪ All schemes being implemented in the selected GP having gone through a social audit conducted by the Gram Sabha.
Outcomes	▪ Complete transparency of expenditure of public funds to the community.

Proactive Disclosure

Aim	▪ Proactive disclosure of all information pertaining to the implementation of the programme in the public domain.
Strategy	▪ Identify the following categories of information pertaining to all programmes/interventions that are being made in the selected gram Panchayat through the SAGY.

	▪ Job chart of functionaries responsible for carrying out duties with their designations and contact details. ▪ Prerequisites to be identified as a beneficiary under the programme/Intervention. ▪ Norms of delivery of benefit including service standards. ▪ List of beneficiaries of the programme/intervention in the GP. ▪ Amount of benefit/amount allocated to each beneficiary. ▪ Order of prioritization of the beneficiaries. ▪ Item-wise approved budget and expenditure for the scheme in the GP. ▪ Statement of records held by the Department concerned at the Block and District Level. ▪ Name and contact details of Project Implementing Agency (PIA). ▪ Collate this information for the GP and ensure its disclosure through wall paintings, notice boards and public places in the GP.
Schemes	▪ Right to Information Act, 2005.
Outputs	▪ Compliance of the GP with all provisions of Section 4 of the Right to Information Act, 2005.
Outcomes	▪ Complete transparency of expenditure of public funds to the community.

Activity: Timely Grievance Redressal

Aim	▪ Ensure redressal of all grievances faced by citizens within a well defined time period.
Strategy	▪ All inhabitants of the selected village will be able to submit their complaints in writing to the Panchayat and be entitled to a dated receipt. ▪ Gram Panchayat to remain open everyday to receive complaints from members of the community. ▪ Gram Panchayat to submit the grievances received to concerned departments for redressal. ▪ Concerned departments to ensure that the complainant receives a written response to the grievance submitted by him/her stating the decision taken and outcome of the grievance submitted within 21 days. ▪ Panchayats may also put in place regular public hearings where grievances will be heard and redressed in the public domain.
Schemes	▪ All schemes.

Outputs	▪ Timely redressal of grievances lodged by citizens.
Outcomes	▪ Putting in place of a uniform and standard grievance redress mechanism for all development schemes rolling out in the GP.

Activity: Time Bound Service Delivery in Line with Department's Citizens Charter

Aim	▪ Time bound service delivery in line with Citizens Charter E-Governance to improve quality of service delivery.
Strategy	▪ Develop a Citizens Charter of the scheme which shall mandatorily include key services, job charts and service standards.
	▪ Communicate and disseminate the contents of the charter to all community members.
	▪ Ensure regular and punctual attendance of government and panchayat staff.
	▪ Facilitate citizens in filing grievances where services are not provided to citizens within the prescribed time-frame and ensure its redressal.
	▪ Provision of computers to the Gram Panchayat.
	▪ Introduction of E-Governance applications like PRIA Soft, PLANPLUS, NREGA Soft, Awaas Soft and GIS based applications for local planning and mobile based applications for monitoring programmes and grievance redressal.
	▪ Capacity-building for E-Governance.
Schemes	▪ RGPSA.
	▪ MGNREGA.
	▪ MPLADS.
	▪ BRGF.
Outputs	▪ Ensure timely provision of key services to citizens.
	▪ Proper monitoring of important schemes.
Outcomes	▪ Ensure accountable and timely service delivery to citizens Improved local governance.

Activity: Holding of Gram Sabha, Mahila Sabha and Bal Sabha

Aim	▪ Participatory decision-making through regular (at least once a quarter), inclusive and transparent gram sabhas, mahila sabhas and bal sabhas.

Strategy	▪ Create awareness amongst people about importance of participatory platforms for people to make decisions. ▪ Conduct special women gram sabhas (Mahila Sabhas) to deliberate on issues relating to women and child development and priority issues such as sanitation. ▪ Conduct special children's gram sabha (Bal Sabha) to discuss issues of their education, recreation and safety. ▪ Encourage elected representatives, MPs, MLAs to attend the Gram Sabhas. ▪ Encourage SHG Women to participate and organise women to attend Gram Sabhas.
Schemes	▪ Panchayati Raj Act of the State.
Outputs	▪ All decisions taken by the GP pertaining to utilization of resources and monitoring to be based on the needs and aspirations of all sections of the community.
Outcomes	▪ Flourishing democratic engagement at the grassroots.

Manual of Micro-Level Planning for G.P.

Particulars	*Details*
Number of Households headed by single women.	
Number of Households headed by physically handicapped persons.	
Number of SHGs.	
Number of active SHGs.	
Number of federations.	
Number of SHG leaders.	
Number of persons having a bank account.	
Distance from the Bank Branch.	
Distance from the Post Office.	
Presence of ATM in the village.	
Area of cultivable land.	
Area of irrigated land.	
Area of unirrigated land.	
Area of common land.	
Area of fallow land.	
Category-wise livestock in the GP.	
Details of production in the Gram Panchayat.	
1. Agriculture.	
2. Animal Husbandry.	
3. Village Industries.	
Number of functional water bodies.	

Area within 2 km of the reach of functional water bodies.

Number of active Job Card holders under MGNREGA.

Number of active Job Card holders who have completed 100 days of work.

Number of food storage facilities.

Number of dairy processing units.

Number of Households who do not have pucca houses.

Number of households who do not have household taps for treated potable water.

Number of roads within the GP.

Number of roads within the GP which are not all weather.

Number of Households which do not have electricity connection.

Number of anganwadis in the GP.

Number of Fair Price Shops/PDS outlets in the GP.

Number of CSC in the GP.

Number of eligible Households for pension (old age, widow, disability).

Number of eligible Households who are not receiving pension.

Number of Households eligible for Ration Card.

Number of eligible HHs who have a ration card.

Number of households covered under RSBY.

Number of HHs covered under AABY.

Number of shops selling alcohol.

NOTES

1. *(i)* Analysis of Space through *Social Mapping, Resource Mapping etc.; (ii)* Analysis of Time through *Historical Transect, Time Line, Oral History, etc.; (iii)* Analysis of Relationships through *Venn Diagramming, Relational Matrices, Mapping and SSI; (iv)* Analysis of Institutions through *Venn Diagramming Scoring-Ranking and Matrix-Ranking, Matrix Scoring; and (v)* Analysis of Preferences through *Scoring-Ranking and Matrix-Ranking, Matrix Scoring, Pair-wise Ranking etc.*
2. The process of scoring and ranking are discussed in, p. 76 given below.

4

How to Apply PLA in Gram Panchayat Planning?

Preparation Stage

I. Introduction

Before Fieldwork

There are some steps which need to be taken by the PLA Facilitation Team in order to gather and analyse reliable and precise information. These steps before fieldwork are as follows:

Use of Secondary Information

A study of secondary data of the area/households for whom PLA exercise is being undertaken is very important. It provides the background information and basic assumptions of fact that the rural people provide. A careful review and assessment of the secondary data are necessary from secondary sources before fieldwork. It may be helpful in developing topics, sub-topics or checklists to be used in acquiring information. The team must know why they are in a village? They must know what kind of village they are going to? What kind of people to expect?

Selection of Interdisciplinary Team (See Chapter 1.4., p. 6)

Developing Sub-topics

Generally, a brainstorming session is organized for developing topics or sub-topics around which PLA exercises are to be facilitated. Ideally, number of experienced people, not necessarily team members are invited in the session to generate specific issues on a particular area. The raised issues in the session are listed in flip chart or board, depending on the availability. The issues are repeatedly discussed in the session relating to the practical situation and are finalized as guidelines for collecting required information. For example, if we are seeking information on wood fuel production the following could be the sub-topics.

See Annexure 1 for Check List of Sub-topics

The team members should also discuss how to carry out fieldwork, especially tools to be applied for collecting the required information. Generally, the choice of tools depends on topics and expected output. The team should consider the situation and select the tools which fit better for collecting reliable and precise information. Therefore, it is the team that decides which tools and techniques fit better for a particular area.

It is preferable to go for a short field visit to identify key informants, to observe the initial site and to try out the tools. This preparation may be assigned to a single team member, probably someone who is familiar with the locality. Based on the short field visit, the pre-designed tools may have to be changed or modified.

During Fieldwork

The fieldwork is people-oriented. It seeks information on indigenous knowledge, local customs and practices. Therefore, the team should begin analyzing and evaluating data at the very start of the work and continue on throughout the fieldwork.

Rapport Building

Rapport building is an important task for the team for collecting reliable information. It is usually done to develop communications and to establish working relationships with the local people. Generally, rapport building is initiated immediately as the team enters a village. This may help the team to bring closer to the village people. The team could follow the following steps suggested by Pokharel *et al.* (1997) for carrying out PLA:

- Start talking to the people in their local language or at least saying "*local Hello*" whenever you meet them, such as on the trail, agricultural fields, tea shops, homes etc.
- Learn a local trait by doing it (Learning by doing) like ploughing the field, "driving" a bullock cart, harvesting crops and the like.
- Be culturally sensitive: treat and respect people as per their local custom.
- Ask the knowledgeable people about a subject or area in a village.
- Try to meet with local leaders and officials before starting work in the field.
- Clearly explain reasons for coming to the area.
- Show genuine interest in the local issues.
- Choose time and venue that are convenient for the local people.

Maintaining Protocols

Maintaining protocols in the team is the basic rule in PRA methods. Grandstaff *et al.* (1995) defines protocols as a set of rules governing how people act in a given situation, a code of conduct. They further elaborated that PRA protocols are rules of interpersonal behaviour by which a PRA team agrees to operate. The following are the protocols suggested by Messerschmidt (1991) for conducting PRA in the rural communities:

- A facilitator (from the team) controls the interview process by singling start, filling gaps etc.;
- Each team member pursues a sub-topic, following one's own line of questioning and reasoning;
- The order of interviewing sequence (who starts, who follows, who finishes) predetermined, members take notes during each other's turn;
- Unanticipated questions that arise out of turn are held for later;
- Unwanted persons (e.g. drunks, trouble makers etc.) are politely diverted by a team member; and
- After each day's sessions, the members debrief as a group, discuss findings to verify and also incomplete information are noted down for recollection.

Data Collection by Applying Tools and Techniques

Start collecting information by applying appropriate tools and techniques once the rapport is developed in a village. Also, apply probing and iterating techniques for collecting more indepth and reliable information. Some techniques for collecting information are:

Semi-Structured Interviewing (SSI)

Semi-structured interviewing is the principal method used in RRA. It is conducted using the sub-topics to guide the specific questions thought up by the researchers during the interview. SSI is conducted with key informants, who have good knowledge about the history of the village and its resources, and others using pre-selected sub-topics as guidelines. In this method, actual questions are created during the interview. Questions should be precise and easy to understand. Leading questions should not be used while conducting interviews.

Iteration

Iteration is one of the techniques for collecting information in PRA methods. In this technique, the same question is repeatedly asked in different situation for confirming the given information. A very high pay off from flexibility of the methodology through iteration occurs in *PRA—Participatory Rural Appraisal* is the ability to reform questions and formulate new questions, especially within the interview itself (Grandstaff and Grandstaff, 1989).

Probing

The main function of a probe is to encourage the respondent to answer more fully and accurately. Furthermore, it also helps to structure the respondent's answer and make sure that all topics of interest are covered. Always start questions with the 'six helpers': ***who, what, why, when, where, whom*** and ***how*** for helping to establish the basic situation.

Direct Observation

This is also used as a technique especially in the social sciences since a long time. In this technique, related indicators are used in the field to verify the collected information or to generate questions. For example, if the dung is used for cooking purposes, it means that there is a scarcity of firewood in the area. Similarly, there are a wide range of participatory tools available which can be used according to the situation or needs. The most common PRA tools and techniques are (See chapter 2.1):

Sharing

Sharing sessions and discussions are important during the fieldwork. The team members review their field notes after their fieldwork since, delay causes significant loss of memory and may seriously affect the results.

After Fieldwork

A discussion should be carried out by the team about the collected information and going back for more should be arranged if it is necessary. Each team member is assigned tasks and results are held by group members' consensus. The findings are also presented in workshops or seminars for the comments. The comments/suggestions are taken care of and are incorporated in the final reports.

II. PLA Tools and Methods: Used in Community-Based Gram Panchayat Planning

Direct observation—Observations are related to questions: What? When? Where? Who? Why? How?

Do it yourself—Villagers are encouraged to teach the researcher how to do various activities. The researcher will learn how much skill and strength are required to do day-to-day rural activities, gaining an insider's perspective on a situation. Roles are reversed: villagers are the "experts" and attitudes are challenged.

Participatory mapping and modelling—Using local materials, villagers draw or model current or historical conditions. The researcher then interviews the villager by "interviewing the map". This technique can be used to show watersheds, forests, farms, home gardens, residential areas, soils, water sources, wealth rankings, household assets, land-use patterns, changes in farming practices, constraints, trends, health and welfare conditions, and the distribution of various resources.

Transect walks and guided field walks—The researcher and key informants conduct a walking tour through areas of interest to observe, to listen, to identify different zones or conditions, and to ask questions to identify problems and possible solutions. With this method, the outsider can quickly learn about topography, soils, land-use, forests, watersheds, and community assets.

Seasonal calendars—Variables such as rainfall, labour, income, expenditures, debt, animal fodder or pests, and harvesting periods can be drawn (or created with stones, seeds, and sticks) to show month-to-month variations and seasonal constraints and to highlight opportunities for action. An 18-month calendar can better illustrate variations than a 12-month calendar.

Daily-activity profiles—Researchers can explore and compare the daily-activity patterns of men, women, youth, and elders by charting the amount of time taken to complete tasks.

Semi-structured interviewing—A semi-structured interviewing and listening technique uses some predetermined questions and topics but allows new topics to be pursued as the interview develops. The interviews are informal and conversational but carefully controlled.

Types, sequencing, and chain interviews—Individual, pair, and group interviews are combined in a sequence to take advantage of key informants and specialist groups.

Permanent-group interviews—Established groups, farmers' groups, or people using the same water source can be interviewed together. This technique can help identify collective problems or solutions.

Time lines—Major historical community events and changes are dated and listed. Understanding the cycles of change can help communities focus on future actions and information requirements.

Local histories—Local histories are similar to time lines but give a more detailed account of how things have changed or are changing. For example, histories can be developed for crops, population changes, community health trends and epidemics, education changes, road developments, and trees and forests.

Local researchers and village analysts—With some training, local people can conduct the research process (for example, collect, analyse, use, and present data; conduct transects; interview with other villagers; draw maps; make observations).

Venn diagrams—To show the relationship between things, overlapping circles are used to represent people, villages, or institutions; lines are added to reflect inputs and outputs.

Participatory diagramming—People are encouraged to display their knowledge on pie and bar charts and flow diagrams.

Wealth and well-being rankings—People are asked to sort cards (or slips of paper) representing individuals or households from rich to poor or from sick to healthy. This technique can be used for cross-checking information and for initiating discussions on a specific topic (for example, poverty). The technique can also be used to produce a benchmark against which future development interventions can be measured or evaluated.

Direct-matrix pair-wise ranking and scoring—Direct-matrix pair-wise ranking and scoring is a tool used to discover local attitudes on various topics. People rank and compare individual items, using their own categories and criteria, by raising hands or placing representative objects on a board. For example, six different shrubs can be ranked from best to worst for their fuel, fodder, and erosion-control attributes. Other resources can be ranked in terms of taste or marketability. Wealth ranking can be used to identify wealth criteria and establish the relative position of households.

Matrices—Matrices can be used to gather information and to facilitate or focus analyses and discussions. For example, a problem opportunity matrix could have columns with the following labels: soil type, land-use, cropping patterns, and available resources; and rows with the following labels: problems, constraints, local solutions, and initiatives already tried.

Traditional management systems and local-resource collections—Local people collect samples (for example, of soils, plants). This can be an efficient way to learn about the local biodiversity, management systems, and taxonomies.

Portraits, profiles, case studies, and stories—Household histories or stories of how a certain conflict was resolved are recorded. This can provide short but insightful descriptions of characteristic problems and how they are dealt with.

Key probes—A question addressing a key issue is asked of different informants, and the answers are compared. The question might be something like "If my goat enters your field and eats your crops, what do you and I do?"

Folklore, songs, poetry, and dance—Local folklore, songs, dance, and poetry are analyzed to provide insight into values, history, practices, and beliefs.

Futures possible—People are asked how they would like things to be in 1 year and to predict what will happen if nothing is done or if something is done. People's desires, wishes, and expectations are revealed.

Diagrams exhibition—Diagrams, maps, charts, and photos of the research activity are displayed in a public place to share information, facilitate discussions, and provide an additional cross-checking device. The exhibition can inspire other villagers to take part in research activities.

Shared presentations and analysis—Participants are encouraged to present their findings to other villagers and to outsiders, providing another opportunity for cross-checking, feedback, comment, and criticism.

Night halts—The researchers live in the village during the research process. This facilitates all interactions between the outsiders and the villagers, invites change in the outsiders' attitudes, and allows for early-morning and evening discussions, when villagers tend to have more leisure time.

Short questionnaires—Short and issue-specific questionnaires can be useful if conducted late in the research process.

Field report writing—Key findings are recorded before "leaving" the village. (This assumes that the community has consented to having the research data leave the village.) Brief summaries are made of each diagram, model, and map, as well as of the process involved in creating them.

Survey of villagers' attitudes towards PRA—To improve the PRA process and techniques and maintain realistic expectations, the researcher asks the villagers what they expected and what they learned from the PRA research process.

Intriguing practices and beliefs—Indigenous practices and beliefs are noted, even if they are based on myth or superstition. Even practices that are unusual or do not fit in with conventional scientific thinking are worth exploring because they are meaningful to local people.

Individual Tools

III. Daily Schedules

Definition

Daily Schedule is a pictorial depiction of a person's or of a household's activities during the waking hours of a day. It does not include personal chores.

Key Components

- Analysis of time on a daily basis.
- One should add seasonal, gender, age group, education, well-being and locational comparisons.
- Analysis of space has to be added if "DAILY SCHEDULES" are extended to cover mobility also.

Use of Daily Schedules

Daily schedules are used to identify daily working patterns and other activities. It is possible to discuss both types of work and distribution of workloads throughout the day. For comparative analysis between different individuals, daily schedules of different people may be compared and contrasted. The main uses of daily schedules are:

- To document different types of activities, *per se.*
- To document the timing of activities.
- To document time spent in different activities.
- To document time available for rest and leisure.
- To note periods where more than one activity are carried out concurrently.
- To discover difference or otherwise of workload of women and men separately.
- To locate differences in workloads of urban and rural women and men.
- To analyse "outside home" and "inside home" workloads.
- For discussing new activities and their implications for time use.
- For discovering suitable times for meetings and training sessions.
- For comparison of differences between schedules.

Daily schedules have also been used to illustrate mobility and periods spent away from the home.

Applications

There are numerous examples, where comparisons have been carried out not only of the variation in individual's workloads over time, but also between men and women, or women from different background. The seasonal variation is most notable in relation to agricultural activities. Within one gender, differences are notable between the young and old, the rural and urban, professional and domestic etc.

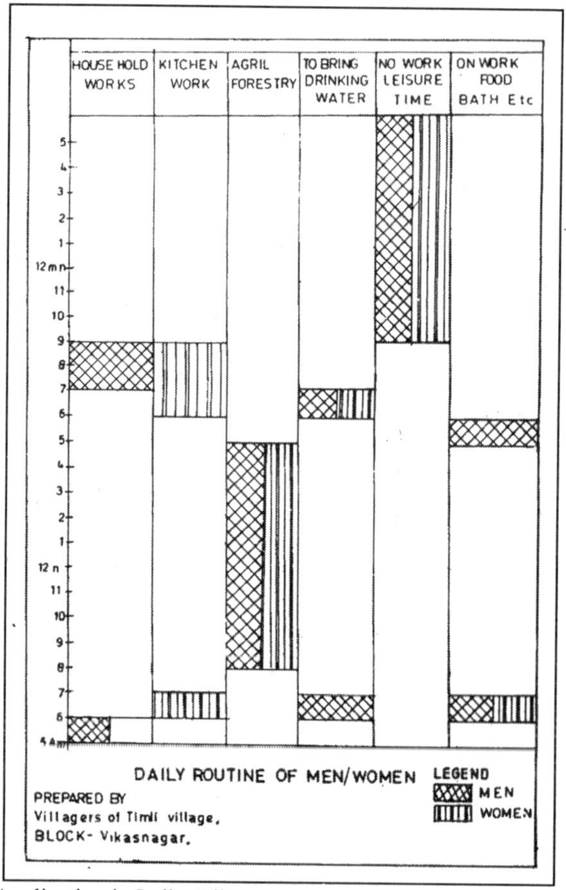

Fig. 4.1: Application in India: Vikasnagar.

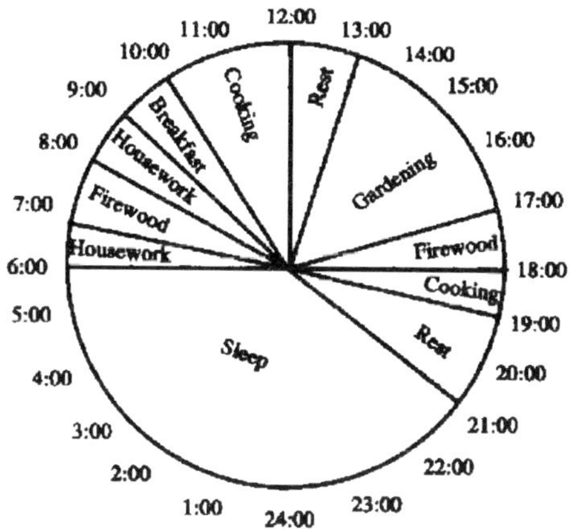

Fig. 4.2: Daily Routine Work Time.

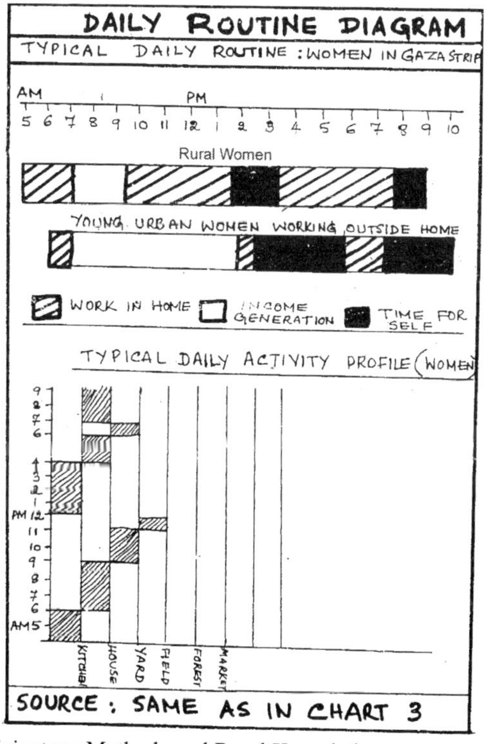

Fig. 4.3: Participatory Methods and Rural Knowledge.

significant differences in perception can be found through an examination of women's ideas on men's time allocation, compared with men's, and men's ideas on women's time allocation, compared with women's. These illustrate the importance of involving all sections of the population, especially those with whom it is intended to work in the longer term.

Steps in the Preparation of Daily Schedule

- Choose a place for the exercise which should be a public place and accessible to all.
- As far as possible ensure that people sit in a circle.
- Explain to the participants the purpose of the exercise: we wish to learn from them how they typically spend their 24 hours in a day.
- You can facilitate the process either on the floor or on a large sheet of paper. Two or more chart papers may be joined together to have a large sheet of paper.
- Remember Daily Schedules are always done separately for women and men, girls and boys because their schedules are different.
- Request the participants to catalogue all that they do in a 24-hour period. Every activity is noted down in another Chart Paper. The noting should be in large letters so that they can be seen from a distance.
- Hang the chart paper somewhere such that it is visible to everyone of the participants.
- Facilitate the process where the participants draw a straight line to the left on the floor or the large sheet of paper. Alternatively they may also draw a large circle at the centre.
- Ask the participants to divide the line or the circumference of the circle into 24 parts, by marking each of the 24 divisions with small lines. Each part representing one hour, starting from 1 AM to 12 PM or 1.00 hour to 24 hours.
- Request the participants to label each division starting from 1 AM to 12 PM or from 1.00 hour to 24 hours.
- Request the participants now to match the list of their activities with the hours when they are performed.
- Ask the participants to review the output. If the participants want to change anything, encourage them to do the same.

- The daily schedule is ready.
- Display it in a prominent place.
- Interview the daily schedule with open ended questions as mentioned earlier. Record the findings.

Strengths and Weaknesses

Simple strong and relatively versatile, but with the dangers of becoming routinised as it is easy to use. The potential of using relative measures and avoiding dependency, literacy and time awareness is strong. Potential is best with small groups sizes, conducting a number of schedules for comparison.

2. TRANSECT WALK

Definition

A transect walk is a systematic walk along a defined path (transect) across the community area together with the local people to explore the vegetation, habitation, infrastructure, water and sanitation conditions, crops, undulation of the topography etc. by observing, asking, listening and producing a transect diagram. It is best to walk a route, which will cover the greatest diversity in terms of vegetation, habitation, infrastructure, water and sanitation conditions, crops etc. The transect walk is conducted jointly with the villagers or community members. The information collected during the walk is used to present the findings visually in the form of a diagram.

Either the different participants can be asked to form different team members for separate transect walks, showing the areas of most importance to them or each group can have responsibility for a different topics while they all walk together, or everybody has the joint responsibility for all the issues under consideration. For example, one group may focus on soils, land-use and cultivation, a second on trees, vegetation and water resources, and a third, on infrastructure, housing and services. Alternatively, all the participants can walk together and have joint responsibility for all aspects under review.

Key Components

- The nature of the terrain.

- The nature and variety of soil conditions.
- The nature of the vegetation.
- One should add seasonal, gender, age group, education, well-being and locational comparisons.

Use of Transects

- To understand the different types of soil conditions, vegetations etc. obtaining in the village.
- To understand the nature of the terrain in the village like gradients, slopes and undulating nature of land surface in the village.
- To document the timing of activities.
- To document time spent in different activities.
- To document time available for rest and leisure.
- To note periods where more than one activity are carried out concurrently.
- To discover difference or otherwise of workload of women and men separately.
- To locate differences in workloads of urban and rural women and men.
- To analyse "outside home" and "inside home" workloads.
- For discussing new activities and their implications for time use.
- For discovering suitable times for meetings and training sessions.
- For comparison of differences between schedules.

Daily schedules have also been used to illustrate mobility and periods spent away from the home.

Applications

Strengths and Weaknesses

Suggested Way to Conduct a Transect Walk

- Organize 2 or 3 groups with a mix of participants such as women and men, young and old.
- Explain to the participants the purpose of the exercise.

- Using existing Village Maps, if any and/or on the advice of the community members, choose a more-or-less straight line through the area, say from East to West or from North to South.
- The line chosen should take in as many of the different physical zones, types of vegetation, land-use areas and sections of the community as possible. It is often a good idea to start from the highest point in the area and walk straight (as far as practicable) to the other end.
- Start walking from one end towards the other end along the designated line, East to West or North to South.
- A Transect walk is always carried out on foot.
- While undertaking the transect walk, listen, ask questions about each zone, soil conditions, vegetations, livelihoods, problems, solutions etc. in the village. Everything heard is written down as the transect proceeds.
- During the transect walk, make time for brief and informal interviews (always with open ended questions) with women and men met along the way.
- During these interviews, discuss the critical issues faced by the community and ask whether there are other issues as well.
- During the walk attempt to find out if it is possible to locate soil zones, ecological zones or vegetation zones or cropping zones.
- If it is possible to divide the path into such zones, try and locate the problems peculiar to each zone.
- Seek their views on opportunities and solutions to problems, if any. One of the advantages of doing a transect walk is that often people may be found more willing to discuss sensitive issues such as land ownership patterns when they are in a group than individually.
- Allow sufficient time for the transect walk.
- It may take several hours depending on what discussions are held amongst the Facilitators' Team and the community and the distance to be covered.
- After completing the transect walk the groups share the information from their walks to construct the transect diagram(s) together. Or there could be separate thematic Transect Diagrams. Alternatively there could be one single

diagram if all the participants had joint responsibility. See diagram on Transect attached.

- Once the Transect Diagram is completed, interview the Transect (Diagram) through open ended questions.
- Record the information gathered during the process of interviewing the Transect. This is a must.

  ***Note*:** A transect walk is not a mapping exercise and does not involve going round the village on roads and alleys.

TRANSECT

VILLAGE OF SIDRA KORDOFAN, SUDAN

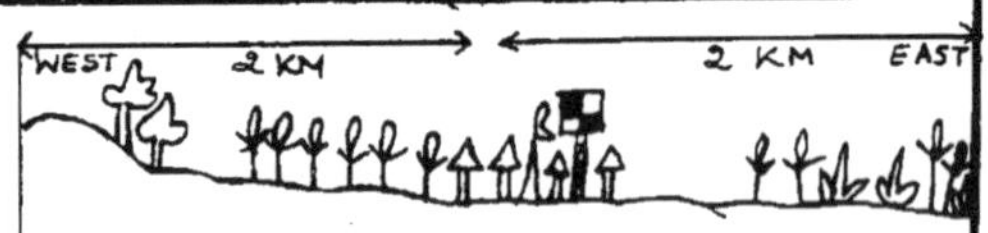

SOIL	rocky	gravel	gravel	sand	clay
LANDUSE	forest	farmland village	village	farmland grazing	farmland
CROPS AND VEGETATION	trees, bamboo	grass, shrubs, millet, sesame		sesame, beans, hibiscus	sorghum, groundnuts
PROBLEMS	erosion	drought, pests		drought, pests, low soil fertility	drought
OPPORTUNITIES	fuelwood, timber, bamboo	pasture, rainfed farming	market, transport, water, credit, health-care, school	pasture, rainfed farming	flood-recession farming

SOURCE: THEIS JOACHIM AND GRADY HEATHER M., (1991), PARTICIPATORY RAPID APPRAISAL FOR COMMUNITY DEVELOPMENT, A TRAINING MANUAL BASED ON EXPERIENCES IN THE MIDDLE EAST AND NORTH AFRICA, I.I.E.D. AND SAVE THE CHILDREN FEDERATION, LONDON.

Fig. 4.4: Transect Village of Sidra Kordofan, Sudan.

3. HISTORICAL TRANSECTS

Definition

A Historical Transect is a pictorial depiction of the changes in several variables over a long period of time in a community, such as changes in forest cover, changes in availability of water, changes in grazing land and micro-environments and the like. It can also be used to show social variables like changes in density of population, cattle wealth, status and number of houses and education.

Key Components

- Temporal analysis on a historical basis.
- Spatial analysis of stable and changing resources.

Use of Historical Transects?

Historical transects illustrate changes, particularly in land-use, natural resources, common property etc. over time, although Historical transects have been used to indicate other aspects of historical information which have a spatial dimension, like the state of housing, the state of infrastructure and so on. Most commonly, a period of several decades is covered. A less well documented tool than many other tools and they have been used mainly to:

- Generate a trend in land-use, changes in environment natural resources use etc.
- Identify changes that have occurred over time and place.
- Identify the reason why changes have taken place.
- Examine the implications and causes of these changes.

The use of transects means that a number of different aspects can be considered over time in a clear visual manner.

Application

Most historical transects have focused on land-use as changes over time are easily displayed in transect form. Agriculture and forest area/type are indicated as well as changes in numbers of stock, housing, infrastructure etc. transects can deal with each of these issues in more or less detail. For example, some go into greater detail of soils and erosion others into forest management and tree species/production. Fisheries and changes in fishing methods have been examined as have changes in public participation in meetings. Many of the examples so far are rural based, but there are cases where urban historical transects have provided useful information on infrastructure and urban changes.

Strengths and Weaknesses

Strengths

Good as a summary of visible changes. Adaptations to include of systems, utility and even rights make the discussion stronger and more informative. The timings of transects can be related to significant external events if necessary. It is not clear whether actual walked transects have been used as a starting point for development historical transects, but there would seem to be potential for this to take place.

Weakness

Some worrying methods of "production" emerged in one case. There appeared to be no discussion of the different aspects of the Transect. The key informants were told exactly what to fill in where. There are cases where "transects" are drawn from Semi-structured Interviews (SSIs) and written information by the "facilitators" alone. There is confusion of nomenclature; some graphs have been labelled as transects.

How to Facilitate a Historical Transect?

- Decide on a place to facilitate the Historical Transect, preferably a public place accessible to all.
- Explain to the participants the purpose of the exercise: to learn how different aspects of their community have changed over the years!
- List the issues or items or aspects of community life (like water resources, conditions of housing, state of health care, literacy etc.) on which you see a historical perspective.

- Facilitate the process by which the community members write down the issues to be investigated (forest cover, availability of water, population, number of animals, availability of grazing land and so on) on flash cards. One item or issue is to be written on one flash card.
- Request the community members to place the flash cards as *one column*.
- Now, request the community members to recall major events in their lives, staring from the earliest to the latest.
- Relate the events to years (approximately), if accurate year is not understood by the community. Associate the event to the calendar years/dates as far as possible.
- The community members to write down the dates on another set of flash cards, with only one year written on one flash card.
- Now, help the community members to place the cards with years as one row in such a manner that the items/issues appear as the first column and the dates/years appear as the first row of a Matrix.
- Take the oldest date/year. Say 1980. The community members to indicate the state of the first issue or item in that year, below the item/issue, on the first row. Suppose the first item is Forest. The state of forest by symbols of trees.
- Then take the second date and request the community members to indicate if there has been a change in the item/ issue between the first date and the year under discussion. Indicate the change. In our example, forest, say the forest cover has improved or deteriorated. Then indicate the change by a larger number or smaller number of symbols depicting trees, depending on whether the forest cover has improved or deteriorated.
- Repeat the same process for all the years for the first item, "forest cover" in our example.
- Repeat the same process for all the years for the second item, say "availability of water" in our example.
- Now, facilitate a process by which the status of all the items/ issues is shown for all the years.
- Interview the Historical Transect that is so prepared.

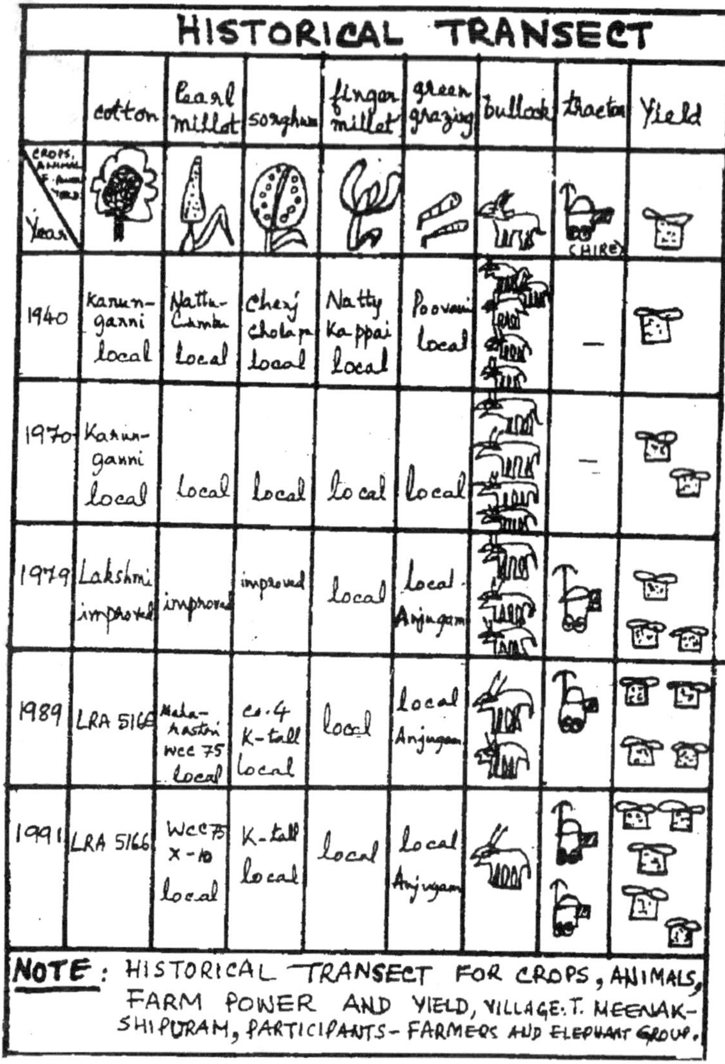

Fig. 4.5: Historical Transect.

Source: Theis Joachim and Grady Heather M.: *Participatory Rapid Appraisal for Community Development, A Training Manual Based on Experiences in the Middle East and North Africa,* IIED & SCF, London.

4. LIVELIHOOD ANALYSIS

Definition

Livelihood analysis is a visual depiction of the forms of livelihoods, their availability and their outcomes as also problems and opportunities associated with each livelihood over a period of time, usually one year, in a community.

Key Components

- Livelihood analysis on an individual, household or community scale.
- Temporal analysis of changes in livelihoods.

Use of Livelihood Analysis

Livelihood analysis aims to examine the details of individuals or groups livelihoods, in terms of seasonality, income, assets, expenditure, consumption etc. which can provide a picture of livelihood of an individual, household or community (as the case may be). Livelihood Analysis can also give a breakdown on a monthly or annual basis of the livelihoods of an individual, household or community (as the case may be).

In Livelihood Analysis a variety of methods are used to discuss a broad range of livelihood related issues. For example, a Map of the Village can be used to depict the livelihood of each household and then get a picture of the range of livelihoods pursued by different households. A Seasonality Diagram of Employment Availability can give the seasonal character of livelihoods. A Bar Chart of wages *vis-à-vis* Livelihoods give the picture of the viability of livelihood. and so on.

Two main categories of analysis can be considered in a Livelihood Analysis.

First, occupational and employment issues are raised, generally at community level, which provide a profile of the area. Ownership of livestock and agricultural production, for example, can also be discussed at the community level.

Second, individual livelihoods are examined, which tend to focus on income, expenditure etc., as well as food consumption and its distribution within the household. Seasonal changes and changes over time can also be discussed. A livelihood analysis forms an

MONTH	AVAILABILITY AND NATURE OF LIVELIHOOD	FOR WHOM?	INCOME AND SAVINGS	FOOD CONSUMPTION
BAISAKH, JYAISTHA, ASHAR (APRIL TO JULY)	HARD LABOUR, DIGGING AND SOIL PREPARATION WORK•	MEN	NO SAVINGS, WAGE USED TO BUY RICE	ABLE TO EAT TWO MEALS - BARE MINIMUM
SRABON (JULY TO AUGUST)	GREATER AVAILABILITY OF FARMING WORK•	MEN AND WOMEN	INCOME INCREASE, ABLE TO SAVE	ABLE TO EAT BETTER
BHADRA, ASWIN (AUGUST TO OCTOBER)	NO FARMING WORK, CATCH FISH AND SELL	MEN AND WOMEN	LITTLE INCOME FROM FISH, DEPLETE SAVINGS	NO EVENING MEAL, CONSUME LITTLE FISH, CANNOT EAT SNAILS
KARTICK (OCTOBER TO NOVEMBER)	NO FARMING WORK, CATCH FISH AND SELL	MEN AND WOMEN	LITTLE INCOME FROM FISH, DEPLETE SAVINGS	— DO —
AGHRAYAN (NOVEMBER TO DECEMBER)	FARMING WORK• - HARVESTING IN OTHER FIELDS	MEN AND WOMEN	WAGE - Rs 20/- PER DAY AND BREAKFAST, ABLE TO SAVE	ABLE TO EAT AND ALSO STORE GRAINS FOR FUTURE
POUSH (DECEMBER TO JANUARY)	FARMING WORK• - HUSKING AND THRESHING	MEN	ABLE TO SAVE, BUY CLOTHES	ABLE TO EAT AND ALSO STORE GRAINS FOR FUTURE
MAGH (JANUARY TO FEBRUARY)	NO FARMING WORK CATCH FISH AND SELL	MEN AND WOMEN	DEPLETE SAVINGS, INCOME FALLS	EAT A PART OF STORED GRAINS AND OTHERS
PHALGUN (FEBRUARY TO MARCH)	NO FARMING WORK, SELL FIREWOOD	MEN AND WOMEN	DEPLETE SAVINGS, INCOME FALLS FURTHER	— DO —
CHAITRA (MARCH TO APRIL)	NO WORK, SELL FIREWOOD	MEN AND WOMEN	HARD LIFE, NO SAVINGS	FOOD IN SHORT SUPPLY FORCED TO SKIP A MEAL

NOTE: • FARMING WORK AVAILABLE WITH BETTER-OFF FARMERS

ANALYSTS: SOME COMMUNITY MEMBERS OF VILLAGE KRISHNA RAKSHIT CHAK — FACILITATOR - NEELA MUKHERJEE

Fig. 4.6: Seasonal Livelihood Calendar and Coping Strategies.

important opening for discussing specific details of employment, income etc.

Strengths and Weaknesses

Livelihood analysis is not a specific tool *per se*, but rather an adaptation of a number of other tools to the analysis of a specific subject. The strengths and weaknesses of each exercise depends on the individual tools used and the ability of the facilitator to facilitate that exercise, as well as choice of tool for each situation. Indeed, this is one of the strengths, that such a wide range of tools can be used to look at similar issues, allowing for selection depending on the circumstances.

A wide range of subject matter is also included under "livelihood analysis" which is in part dependent on the structure of economy in the area, and in part in the agenda set both by facilitators and participants. This may seem at first sight confusing but again allows for exploration of wide range of issues.

The strength of many forms of livelihood analysis lies in allowing people a non-threatening way of expressing income and related issues. It also enables strong comparative analysis between individuals, between men and women, and between different forms of livelihoods. In some cases this may work better with groups, where people may be more comfortable in discussing these issues in a group setting, rather than one to one with a stranger. In order to cases, working with individuals may be easier. "Best judgement" is required.

5. LINKAGE DIAGRAMS—NETWORKS AND FLOWS

Definition

Linkage Diagrams—Networks and Flow Diagrams study the relationships between different groups and individuals or issues. They illustrate relationship among elements within a system. Flow diagrams additionally discover and identify resources or activity flows and illustrate causal flows, impacts and linkages.

Key Components

- Systematic analysis of a wide range of issues.

- Examination of impacts, cause-effects, relationships, flows of resources.

Use of Linkage Diagrams

1. Network diagrams can act as a basis for discussing the relationships between different group's individuals or issues: illustrate relationship between elements within a system.
2. Flow diagrams discover and analysis impact, resources or activity flows: illustrate causal flows, impacts and linkages.
3. Current situations, constraints problems and opportunities can be discussed, as can the effects of specific problems or interventions. These types of diagram can:
   - Highlight gaps in understanding or indicate "missing" potential connections.
   - Identify points at which "negative" or vicious circles can be broken and identify significant issues.
   - Indicate the impact of development interventions, plan and evaluate.

It is possible to obtain a high level of detail from these diagrams, depending on circumstances. Both broader issues and very detailed specific ones can be studied. It is also possible to undertake comparative analysis, i.e. of resource flows from richer/poorer households.

Applications

There have been numerous applications of such diagrams within PRA, as any subject involving relationships, linkages, causes or outcomes can be portrayed. The following list is indicative, and includes the analysis of systems, problems, coping mechanisms, institutional interactions and decision-making strategies:

- Household systems, farm systems.
- Resource flows, incomes and expenditures.
- Household energy flows.
- Agriculture, and other production systems, marketing systems, or product flows, nutrient flows.
- Credit systems or credit flows.

- Household/community level enterprise systems.
- Forest users/forest management systems.
- Forest product flows.
- Causal diagram for deforestation.
- Impact of drought.
- Indigenous knowledge systems.
- Health, diseases, child death cause/effect flows.
- Effect of husbands/fathers drinking.
- Effects of male/female child births.
- Impact of project interventions.
- Problem/solution analysis.

Strengths and Weaknesses

Networks and flows can represent a complexity which is often difficult to articulate. A wealth of information can be presented, and potentially detailed analysis carried out. The connections between external and internal factors also be represented. Many such diagrams appear to occur spontaneously from other discussions, and require little forward planning, unlike some other exercises which may be planned in advance.

However, if there is not an easy lead in from discussion, the concept of network can be difficult to explain. There is a need for facilitators to be clear about the specific issue/problem under discussion, and be careful to phrase questions clearly and most importantly simply. There are a number of cases where confusion had arisen through lack of understanding.

Confusion can also arise if the diagram becomes too complicated, as boxes become too numerous and interactions too detailed. However, there is the concern that rigorous analysis is limited through attempts to simplify complex reality, limiting its value as a planning tool, particularly if the elements and links are limited by the facilitator. Others feel that discussing interactions in this way enables more meaningful planning and understanding of the potential dynamics of intervention.

Facilitation is very important, for the reasons mentioned above, and because diagramming networks is so complex that care must be taken to examine the issue from a number of angles to ensure there are no significant omissions. One facilitator felt after the event that they had missed out all the negative interactions, partly because of

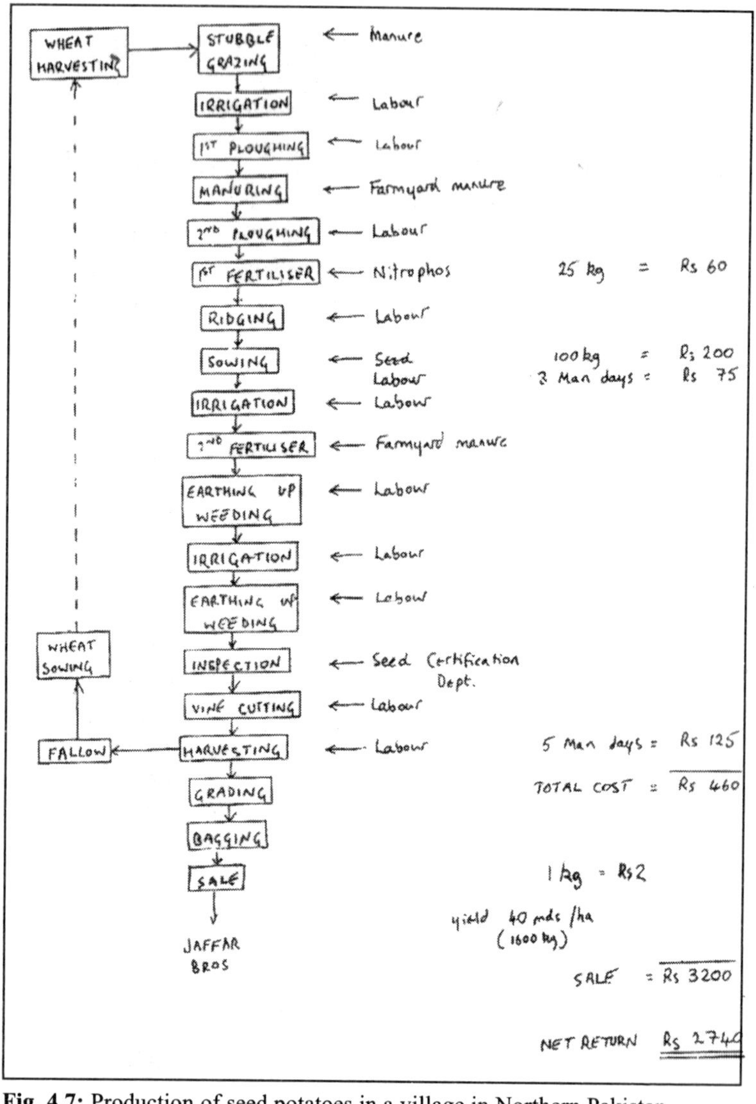

Fig. 4.7: Production of seed potatoes in a village in Northern Pakistan.

the way the opening question had been phrased, and because further questions had only focused on positive interactions.

It may be particularly important to triangulate ideas with a number of different groups as the items raised are highly dependent on the situation. For example when examining causes of poverty it was found that how far down a chain of ideas the people went was in large part dependant on the probing of the facilitator, and that people found it interesting to compare different analysis.

In other cases, flow diagrams were drawn by facilitators on the strength of a number of SSIs, or farm systems drawn later, although on maps that farmers had produced the required linkages. Liner, written "flows" have also been created from interviews. This changes the diagram completely, and means that analysis is that of the outsiders, not the local people. One outsider felt that decision or problem trees could only be produced after interviews and were not a participatory technique – "difficult to produce and of little value". This introduces the dangers of retrospective memory of the situation, and the temptation to use one's own rationalization for interpreting issues. Diagrams drawn in this way should be clearly labelled as such to avoid confusion with participatory techniques and local analysis.

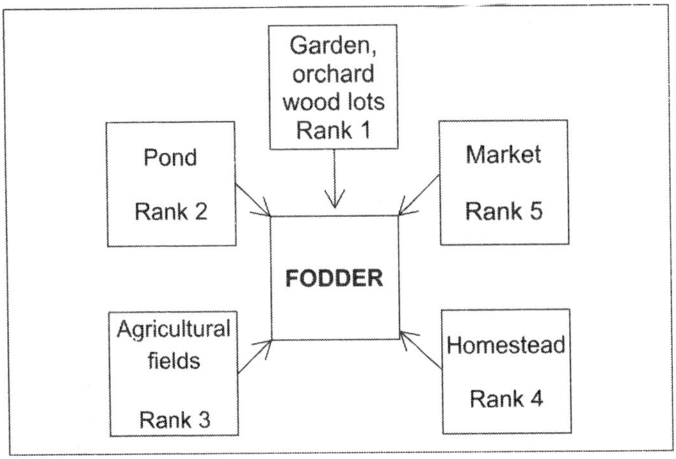

Note: Sources of fodder identified and ranked in village Panchma by a group of local villagers.

Facilitator: Jamal.

Source: Neela Mukherjee, *Participatory Learning and Action*, Concept Publishing Co., New Delhi, 2003.

Fig. 4.8: Source Diagram.

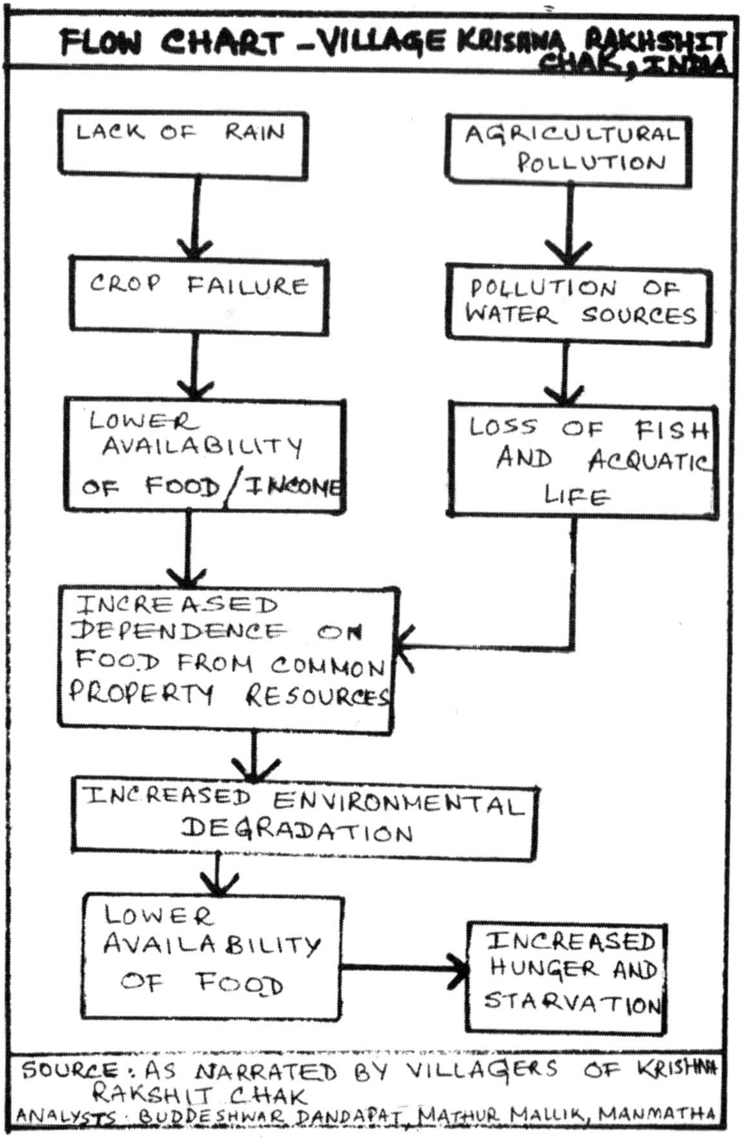

Fig. 4.9: Flow Chart—Village Krisana Rakshit Chak, India.

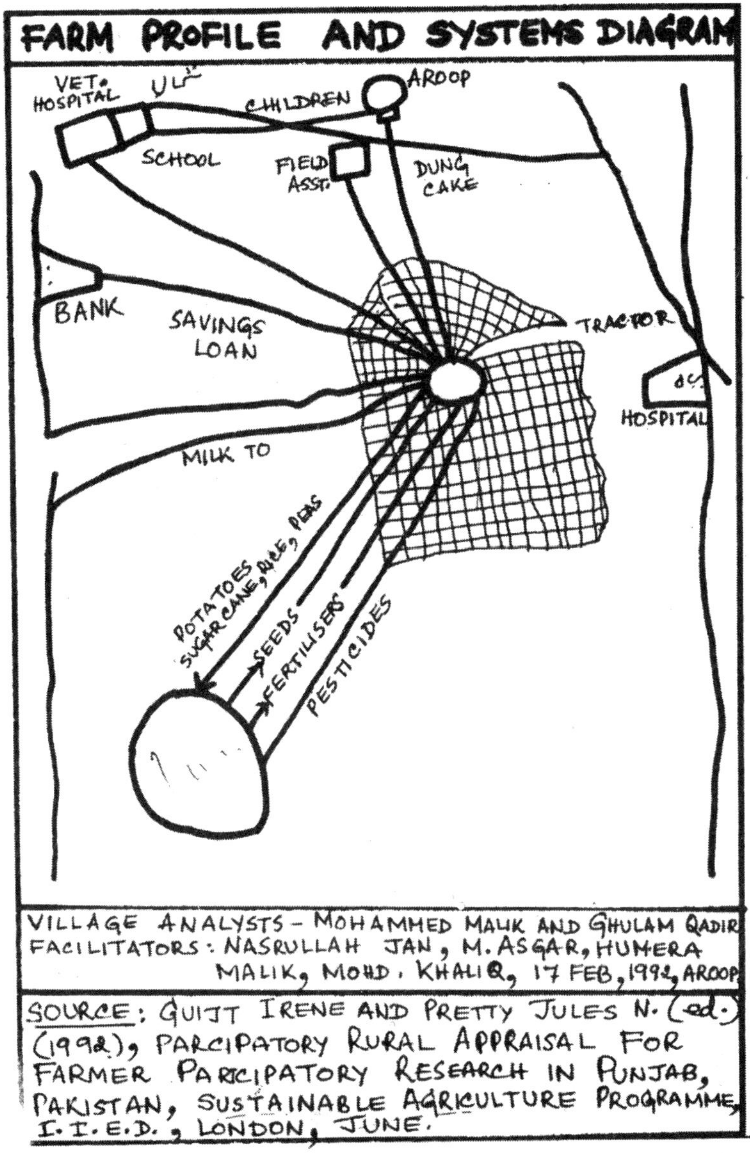

Fig. 4.10: Farm Profile and System Diagram.

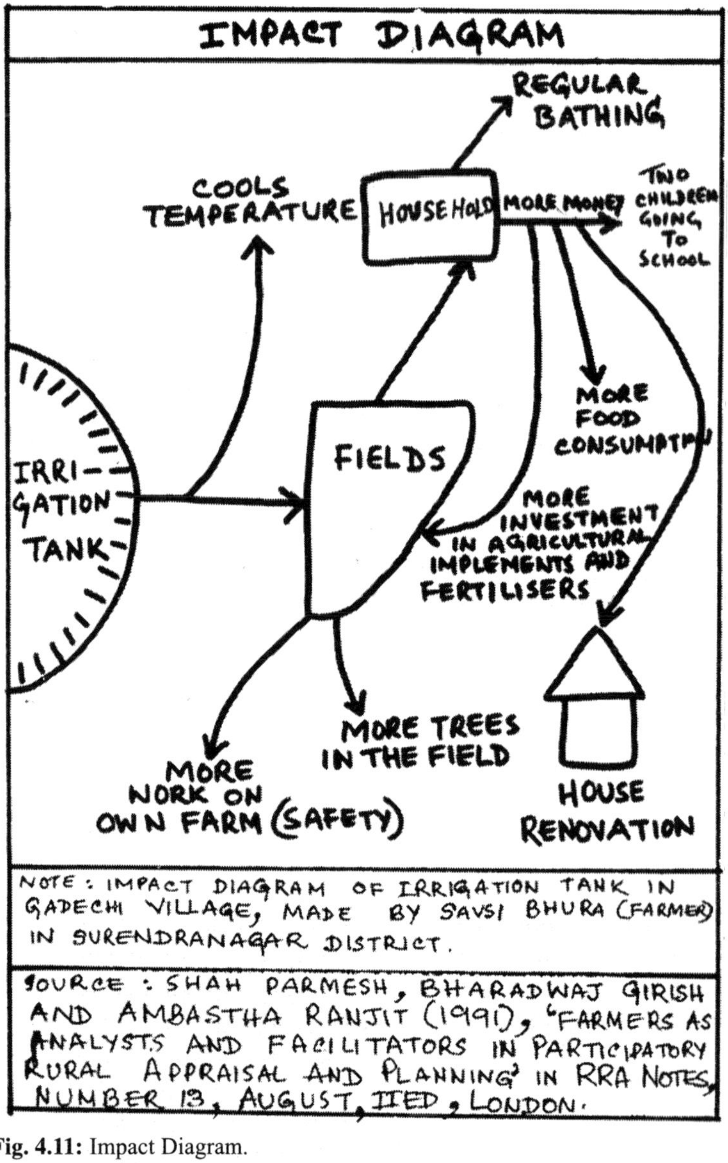

Fig. 4.11: Impact Diagram.

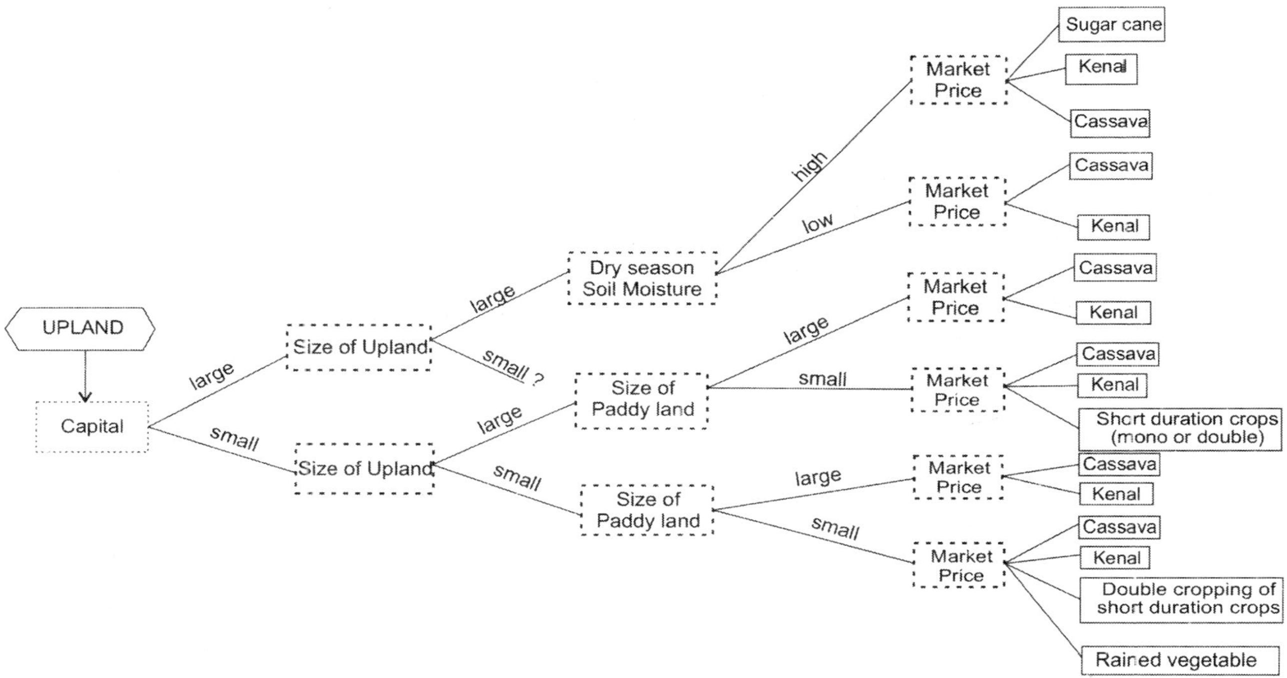

Fig. 4.12: Decision tree showing key determinants that influence farmer decisions on crop selection in uplands of Northeast Thailand (Limpinuntana, 1987)

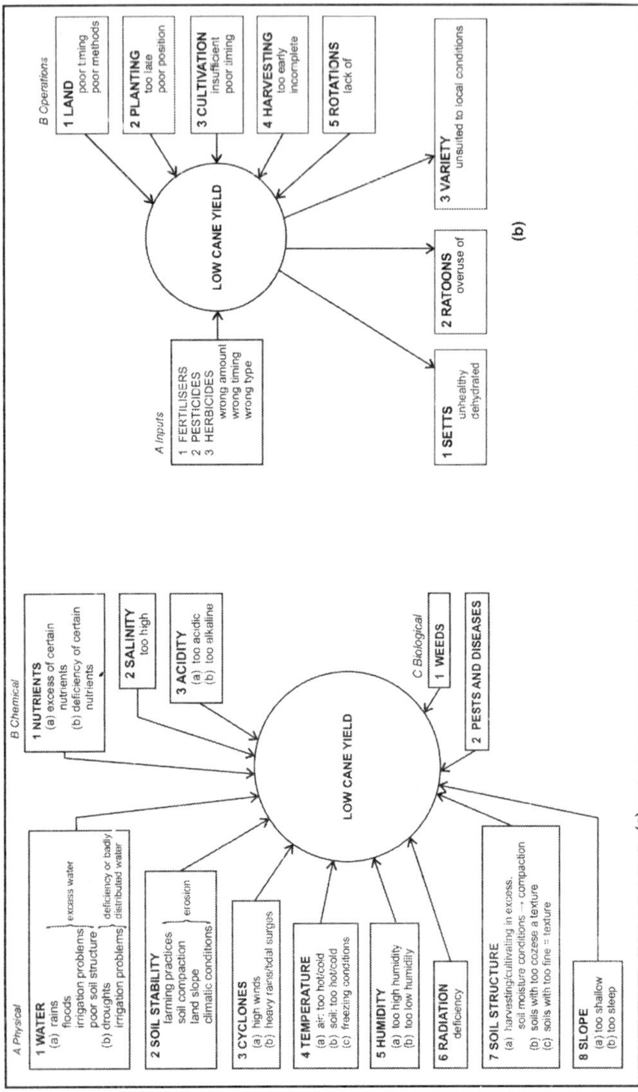

Fig. 4.13: Preliminary diagrammatic hypothesis on possible causal factors of Fiji's low sugarcane yields (J.A. McCracken *et al.*: An Introduction to Rapid Rural Appraisal for Agricultural Development, IIED, London, 1988.): (a) Environmental Conditions and (b) Farming Practices.

6. TIME LINES

Key Components

- Temporal analysis on a historical basis.
- Analysis of key events on a group or individual basis.

Use of Time Lines

Time Lines identify historical sequences of events, generally over a period of years or decades. They discuss both significant events and identify major changes:

- Identification of sequences of significant events/changes over time and identifying coping strategies.
- Provide reference points for trend/change analysis and monitoring the impact of these identified changes.
- Understanding past interventions.

Time lines can examine both general issues and specific activities, and consider phases or periods of activity/inactivity as well as individuals events. They promote discussion of events, consequences and associated issues in a historical context.

Steps in Facilitating Time Lines

- Time Lines can be done on paper or on the ground/floor.
- Choose a paper or place which is visible to all participants. The place should be big enough for all the participants to sit properly.
- As far as possible make the participants sit in a circle.
- Request the community to recall the significant events in their lives (life of the community).
- Now, request them to put a date (in some cases approximate) against each significant event.
- Let the community draw a straight line across the paper or on the ground.
- Let the community mark the dates along a straight line drawn on the paper or on the ground.

- Facilitate the process so that the events are recorded against the event. This generates the time line.
- Request the community to think again and reflect if they have left out any significant event. If they recall additional events then, they should mark it on the line.
- Now, request the community to mark on the Time Line why they consider the significant events important.
- Make sure the community mentions the place, date and names of participants in preparing the Time Line.
- Now, interview the Time Line using the seven helpers and through open ended questions.

Applications

Specific subject studied using time lines are diverse. The most common are village histories, where significant events in the development of the village are considered. This may include: leadership or local activist changes and administrative/political events; changes in the natural resources – forests, land and agriculture; the development of infrastructure such as roads, clinics, schools etc.; emergencies/crisis periods; and the introduction of firsts – TVs, bikes, cars etc. personal histories have also been examined this way, and may include influencing external factors and constraints. Project histories, such as for health or irrigation, can be looked at from the community's perspective, as can employment histories, or industrial changes. Climatic variation, the timing of droughts, the introduction of different varieties and cropping systems, yields and harvest, stock numbers and fishing activities have all been examined using time lines.

Strengths and Weaknesses

Weaknesses

Significant dangers relate to the dominance of the written word and pens/paper, and therefore, those on one side of the paper have a clear view. Firstly, there is a greater tendency for only one pen to be used, with potential for hijacking of the process by one individual, in group work. Secondly, there is the tendency for the process to become facilitator driven, especially where literacy levels are low. There appears to be a temptation for facilitators to construct the time line themselves, either in view of the informants or in isolation from the "result" of individual interviews. More visual time lines have potential to overcome these issues. It is recognized that there may need to be a trade off of exact dates, particularly over events that happened far in the past. In addition, some facilitators feel that older key informants may have a tendency to "romanticize" the past.

Strengths

Time lines can be combined with illustrations, and be related to other aspects of historical change to provide a greater depth of analysis. They can relate individual, cultural, environmental, agricultural, economic, political and social events. Other "methods" such as time trends, transects and historical matrices have emerged from time lines. The methods are simple, and one dimensional. Facilitation to discuss all available relevant information is important, particularly where the line is not focused on a specific topic but discusses general issues.

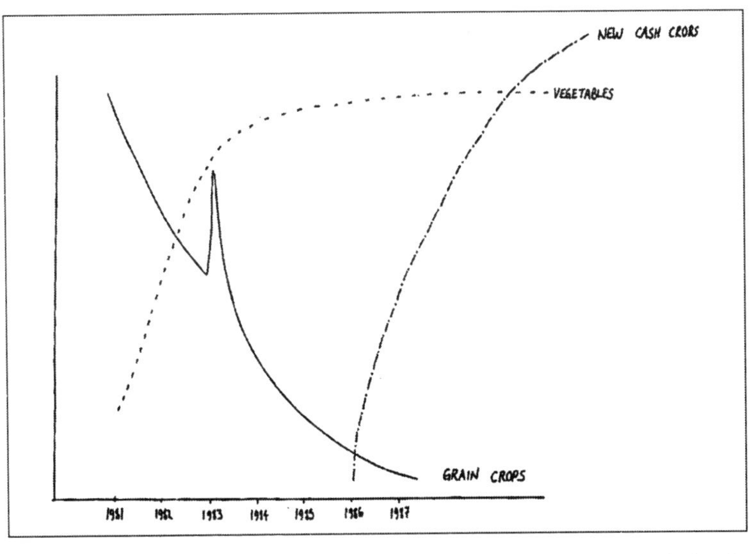

Fig. 4.14: Cropping trends in the irrigated land of a Peasant Association in Wollo, Ethiopia (Ethiopian Red Cross Society, 1988).

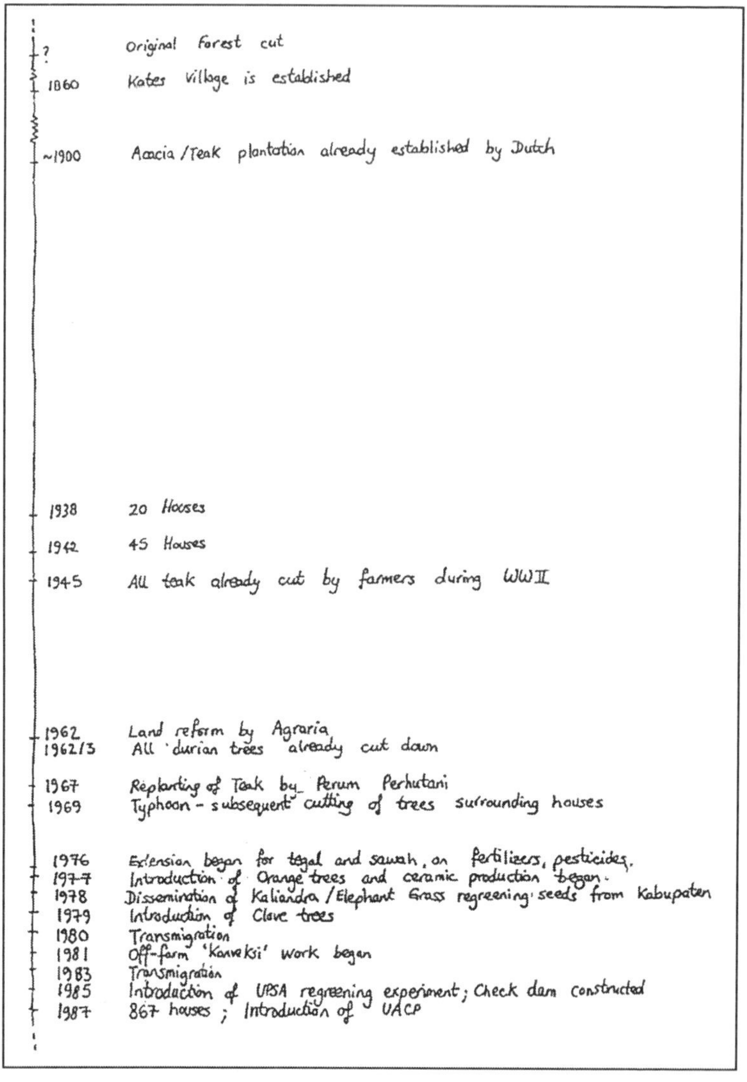

Fig. 4.15: Historical Profile of a village in East Java.

TIME LINE

APPROXI-MATE YEAR	WAGE RATE PER DAY	KIND OF FOOD	TREES
1920	Re 0·06	CHAPPATI, GOOD QUALITY RICE	
1940–45	Re 0·15	CHAPPATI, GOOD QUALITY RICE, MEAT OCCASIONALLY	
1980	Rs 1·20	INFERIOR RICE, PULSES, POTATOES	
1985	Rs 10·00	INFERIOR RICE, DILUTED PULSES, POTATOES	
1990	Rs 15·00	RATION RICE, POTATOES, DILUTED* PULSES (*PREPARED WITH MORE WATER, LESS PULSES)	

ANALYST – SRI ACHAIAH, VILLAGE MADHAPUR, HYDERABAD, (ANDHRA PRADESH), INDIA.

Fig. 4.16: Time Line.

YEAR	SOCIAL PROFILE	WAGE RATE	PRICES AND FOOD	ROLE OF FOREST AND COPING STRATEGIES
1942 (YEAR OF BENGAL FAMINE)	14 TO 15 HOUSEHOLDS, NO LAND OWNERSHIP; POSSIBLE TO WORK AS SHARE-CROPPERS-50:50; COST OF CULTIVATION WHOLLY BORNE BY SHARE-CROPPERS	AS AGRICULTURAL LABOUR WAGE WAS 2 ANNAS PER DAY OR EQUIVALENT RICE	RICE 4 P/SEER BRINJAL 1P/SEER PULSES 2P/SEER NON-VEGETARIAN ITEM AFTER EVERY 2 DAYS	FOREST AND CPRs PROVIDE FRUITS, EDIBLE POTATOES, 'KUNDRI', ROOTS, LEAVES ETC., DEPENDENCE ON FOREST "PRODUCE" DURING OFF-SEASON- 'MAGH' TO 'ASHAR' (JANUARY TO JUNE)
1965 (YEAR OF WAR WITH PAKISTAN AND BOMBING OF KALAKUNDA)	70-75 HOUSEHOLDS; NO LAND OWNERSHIP; SHARE CROPPING CONTINUED	AGRICULTURAL WAGE- Rs. 2.50 OR RS. 3.50 OR 2 SEERS OF RICE	RICE 14 ANNA/ 15 ANNA/SEER	FORESTS & CPRs PROVIDE FOOD AND NON-FOOD ITEMS DURING SEASONS AND FOOD SECURITY DURING OFF-SEASONS SOME ITEMS FROM FOREST AND CPRs BARTERED FOR OTHER ITEMS
1975-76 (EMERGENCY DECLARED)	80 HOUSEHOLDS; 'BARGA' RECORDING JUST STARTED; 50:50 SHARE-CROPPING CONTINUED; COW DUNG CONTINUED AS MANURE; ONLY 10 TO 12 HOUSEHOLDS HAD COWS	AGRICULTURAL WAGE- Rs. 5.00 TO Rs. 6.00	RICE - Rs. 2.50 PER KG, COOKING OIL RS. 2.25/LITRE	SINCE 1967-68, THEY WERE DISALLOWED MANY OF THEIR EARLIER BENEFITS FROM FOREST, BECAME POOR BY 1967-68, FOREST ALSO STARTED DEGRADING; THEY CAUGHT FISH AND SOLD THEM FROM 'SRABON' TO 'KARTICK' (JULY TO NOVEMBER)
1980 ONWARDS	MANY HOUSEHOLDS HAVE SOME LIVESTOCK SINCE 1983, MANY BECAME OWNER OF LAND UNDER OPERATION 'BARGA' OF THE STATE GOVERNMENT	AGRICULTURAL WAGE- Rs. 10.00 PER DAY	RICE - Rs. 3.00 PER KG RICE WAS SUBSTITUTED BY FLOUR MADE FROM BOILED GRAMS & TAMARIND POWDER; ALSO SUBSTITUTED BY WILD LEAVES & PUMPKIN	FROM 1980-88, EMPLOYMENT OPPORTUNITIES BY FOREST DEPARTMENT TO DIG PITS, TO PLANT TREES AND CUT GRASS (Rs. 10 AS DAILY WAGE FOR DIGGING 100 PITS) FROM 'MAGH' TO 'BAISAKH' (JANUARY TO MAY) AND 'KARTICK' (OCTOBER TO NOVEMBER)
1990 ON WARDS	NO MORE SHARE-CROPPING; FERTILISERS USED; SOIL FERTILITY ON DECLINE 125 HOUSEHOLDS, SOME HOUSEHOLDS STILL DO NOT HAVE LAND	AGRICULTURAL WAGE RS. 20.00 PER DAY	RICE - RS 5.00 PER KG DURING 1977-83 NO RATION RICE FROM FAIR PRICE SHOPS - AFTER 1983 MOSTLY KEROSENE & SUGAR FROM FAIR PRICE SHOP	FOREST AND CPRs DEGRADED, FISH IS OFTEN DISEASED DUE TO POLLUTION IN WATER BODIES; GRAM PANCHAYAT HAS FUNDS FROM JAWAHAR ROZGAR YOJANA, FOOD INTAKE SEVERELY AFFECTED IN OFF-SEASONS

NOTE - P STANDS FOR PAISE, Rs. FOR RUPEES; CPR - COMMON PROPERTY RESOURCES; 'BARGA' - LAND DISTRIBUTION PROGRAMME OF STATE GOVERNMENT
VILLAGE ANALYSTS - AS NARRATED BY KEDAR PRAMANICK, AGE - OVER 80 YEARS AND MATHUR MALLIK, AGE - AROUND 60 YEARS, KRISHNA RAKSHIT CHAK, WEST BENGAL, FACILITATOR - NEELA MUKHERJEE & MIHIR KUMAR PRAMANICK

Fig. 4.17: Time Line.

7. VENN DIAGRAMS

Key Components

- A two dimensional institutional analysis.
- Comparative analysis of institutions against two different parameters such as importance, utility, efficiency, accessibility, helpfulness and impact.

Use of Venn Diagrams

Venn diagrams are usually used to depict key institutions, organization and individuals, and their relationship with the local community or other group. Key players in decision-making are shown. Institutions and organizations, which affect specific local issues and community (or sections of the community), can be examined. The institutions analysed can be both local ones internal to the community and external ones which have a local influence.

Place of important social significance and interchange can also be included. Both formal and non-formal groups and their levels of co-operation may be discussed, highlighting opportunities and problems.

On the Venn diagram, each institution/individual/place is presented, usually by a circle. The **size** of the circle represents the importance, significance or power of that institution/individual/place. The **distance** from the centre (which may represent the community or the village), or the degree of overlap with the central analysis group, is the level of interaction/accessibility/utility of the relative institutions. The nearness of the institutions/individual/place to the community is not geographical distance. It is the mental distance. Institutions can be broadly defined to include elected bodies, schools, hospitals, Block Office, Collectorate, temple, caste, religion etc. A narrower definition could be also utilized depending on what issues are sought to be examined.

Venn diagrams can form a basis for discussion of:

- The roles and significance of various institutions/individuals/ places to people in a locality.
- The roles and significance of various institutions/individuals/ places to a specific organization/individuals/places.

- Levels of communication between organization/individuals/ places.
- The role of project bodies and their interventions.
- Improving missing links between existing organizations/ individuals/places.
- Potential for working through existing organizations,—which ones and with which links.
- Potential roles for new organizations/individuals/places.

It is always local perceptions which are discussed. Analysis of different ideas within a locality is possible through comparison of a number of diagrams with a range of groups.

Applications

Within the framework of institutional analysis, Venn diagrams have been used to explore a variety of linkages. Often, the diagram is left open, with local people defining which organizations they feel are important to their lives in general terms. However, Venn diagrams can also be used to analyze the influence of organization in relation to more specific issues:

- Examination of the role played by outside agencies.
- Examination of the role played by village agencies.
- Examination of the role played by informal groupings.
- Relationships between individuals (at family and community level).
- Local facilities, local infrastructure and self-help systems.
- Institutional and individual support systems.
- Credit or health support systems.
- Forest management, agriculture, irrigation, and fishing.
- Livestock diseases and their linkages.
- Income generating institutions for women.
- Links between GO, NGO, religious, individual and community groups.
- Institutional aspects of conflict/dispute resolution.
- Aspects of policy, interventions and grant systems.
- Assessment of interventions, new structures, changes to old structures.
- Perceptions of project and implementing agencies.

- Importance of problems and their relationships to each other.
- And others.

Steps Involved in Facilitating a Venn Diagram

- First, explain the meaning of institutions to the community.
- Facilitate listing of all institutions and facilities in the area.
- Ask the community to choose two features (importance, utility, efficiency, accessibility, helpfulness and impact) of the institutions and facilities in the area under consideration.
- Suppose the community chooses importance and accessibility as the two attributes of the institutions to be studied.
- Now, first facilitate ranking of the communities according to their *importance* using any of the scoring and ranking methods.
- Then facilitate ranking of thc communities according to their *accessibility* using any of the scoring and ranking methods.
- Now, discuss with the community and explain to them that there are two ways of showing the two attributes chosen by them: circles and distances.
- Suppose they choose circles to represent the importance of the institutions/facilities.
- Explain to them that they can show the relative importance of the institutions/facilities by varying the size of the circles. The more important an institution is, the bigger the circle. It is possible that two or more institutions/facilities can be of similar importance and so the circles representing them will be of almost the same size.
- Each institution is assigned a circle according to their importance. The more important the institution, greater the circle assigned to it. As stated above, two or more institutions which are equally important may be assigned the same size circle.
- The communities make circles or *chapattis* out of paper to represent the various institutions.
- There will be as many circles as there are institutions.
- Now, indicate a point on a large sheet of paper or on the ground. *This point represents the community or village.*
- Explain to the community that now they have to indicate the accessibility of the institutions which they have ranked in order of their importance.

- Explain to the community that accessibility of an institution is shown by the distance of the institution from the community. Thus, the institution which is least accessible to the community, irrespective of its importance, will be furthest away from the point representing the community. Similarly, the institution which is most accessible to the community, irrespective of its importance, will be nearest to the point representing the community. An institution is so close that it may overlap the community.
- Now, the community arranges the paper circles or "*chapattis*", representing the institutions on the paper or the ground according to the accessibility of the institution named in the paper circle, following the principle mentioned in the foregoing sub-paragraph.
- Two or more institutions can be of equal importance. In that case all of institutions of equal importance will be shown at the same distance from the point representing the community.
- Once these steps are completed, the Venn Diagram is ready with three components
  (a) A point or sign representing the community.
  (b) "*Chapattis*" or paper circles of various shapes representing the different institutions of different importance.
  (c) The "*Chapatttis*" or paper circles placed around the point at varying distances showing their relative accessibility: further a circle is from the centre less accessible it is.
- The contact between all the institutions can also be shown by the distance between the circles on the map depending upon the facilitator.
- Largely distanced circles: no or little contact or co-operation.
- Circles close to each other: only loose contacts exist.
- Touching circles: some co-operation.
- Overlapping circles: close co-operation.
- Now, request the community to review the diagram and indicate if they would like to make any changes. Encourage them to do so. Now, stick the paper circle on the paper.
- Now, interview the Venn Diagram using the seven helpers and through open ended questions.

If the Diagram was constructed on the ground, replicate it on a large sheet of paper.

Strength and Weaknesses

Strengths

Institutional analysis is an important component of PLA, especially for planning, implementation, monitoring and evaluation, whether it be for forestry, livestock, health, poverty, urban etc. understanding local institutions and their relationship with the broader political economy is considered crucial. Venn diagrams offer an opening into this understanding. Most facilitators have found that the discussion which emerges around the diagrams can provide interesting insights. In one case there was a dispute over whether to include the local bar, since several women thought it was evil. One, however, thought it was good, as a source of employment for her husband. In other cases, participants included roads and rivers as important road-linked villages to other forms of infrastructures, and rivers were seen as important focal points. The Venn diagram is, therefore considerably more versatile than is apparent at first sight.

Other facilitators point to the importance of using local leaders, who "know" all the organizations. These leaders are likely to have their *own agendas,* and it may be important to understand these, but then try to get beyond them. There was one case where local leaders placed the local women's group as small size at a great distance, while the chief was placed centrally. Comparative analysis would be interesting!

Facilitators must also be sensitive to the fact that if *their own organization* is one of the groups being studied that their presence does not affect the positioning.

8. SEASONALITY ANALYSIS

Key Components

- Analysis of variations in issues/dimensions affecting the lives of people, like food availability, availability of employment, prevalence of diseases) according to season/month/time.

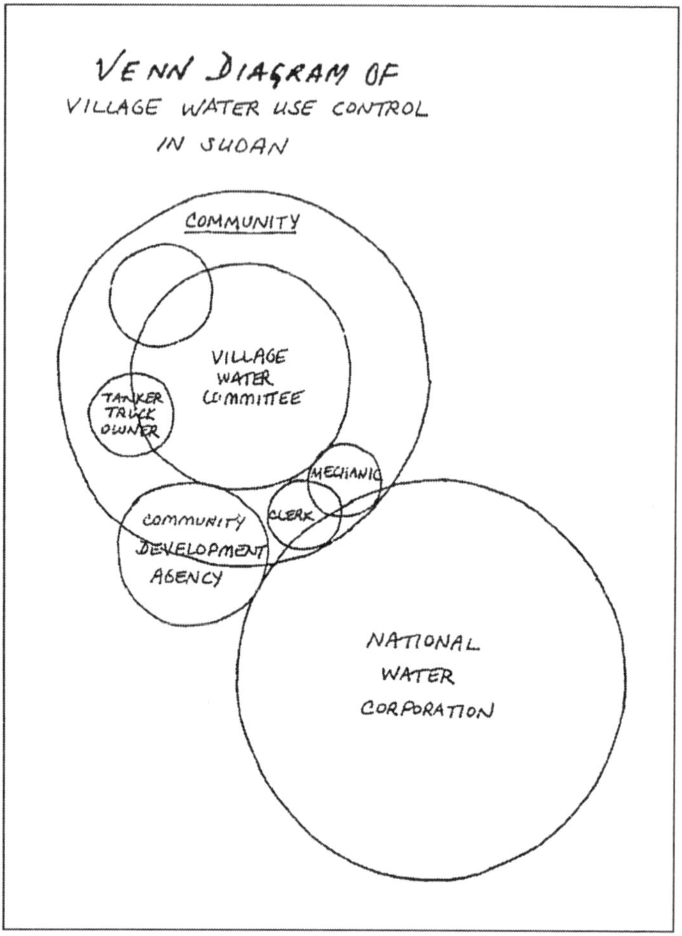

Fig. 4.18: Venn Diagram of Village Water Use Control in Sudan.

- Analysis of variations in livelihood of people/communities according to season/month.
- Analysis of seasonal variation in community's response to processes, institutions, structures, policies etc.

Use of Daily Schedules/Seasonal Calendar

- To document different types of activities, undertaken in different seasons/times/months of the year.

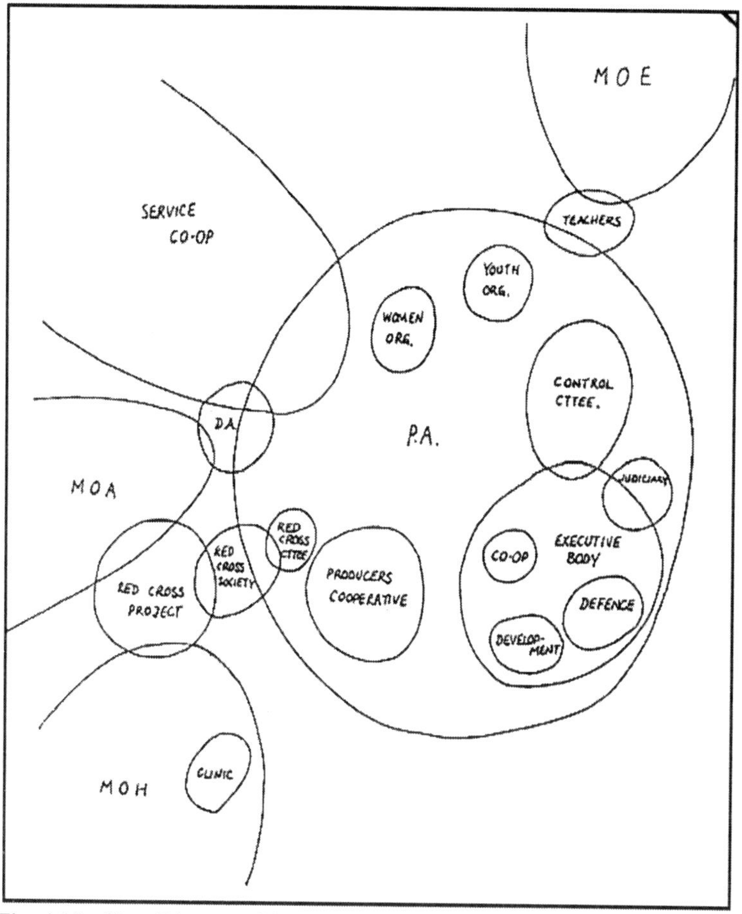

Fig. 4.19: Venn Diagram of decision-makers in a Peasant Association in Wollo, Ethiopia (Ethiopian Red Cross Society, 1988).

- To document time available for rest and leisure in different seasons/times/months of the year.
- To note variations in multiple activities undertaken in different seasons/times/months of the year where more than one activity are carried out concurrently.
- To discover difference or otherwise of work load of women and men separately in different seasons/times/months of the year.
- For discussing which new activities and their implications for time use in different seasons/times/months of the year.

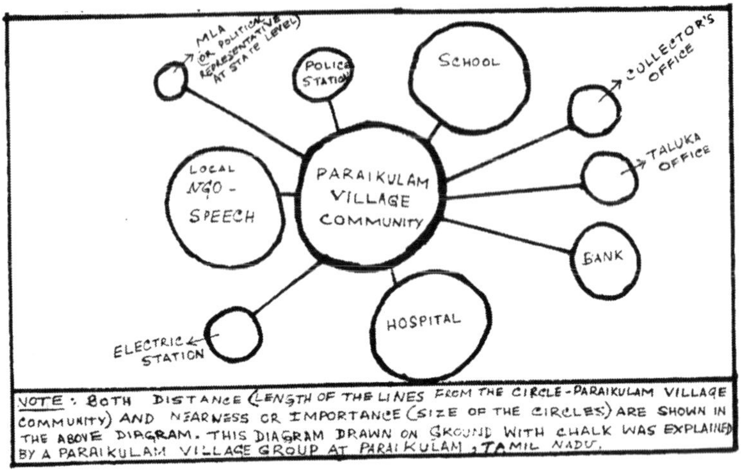

Fig. 4.20: Venn or '*Chappati*' Diagram.

- For discovering suitable times for interventions that can be planned in different seasons/times/months of the year.
- To compare differences in food security, employment opportunities, incidence of disease, income-expenditure pattern etc. in different seasons/times/months of the year.
- To compare differences in food security, employment opportunities, incidence of disease, income-expenditure pattern etc. in different seasons/times/months of the year.
- Seasonality Analysis has also been used to illustrate mobility and periods spent away from the home during different seasons/months/periods of the year.

Steps in Seasonality Analysis

- Suppose we are trying to analyze the seasonality of prevalence of diseases.
- Choose a place to carry out the exercise preferably a public place and sufficiently large to hold the people.
- Explain the purpose of the exercise.
- The exercise can be done on paper or on the floor/ground.
- Request the community to draw a grid or matrix with 12 rows and 12 columns to begin with like the one shown on p. 159.

	1	2	3	4	5	6	7	8	9	10	11	12
1	•	•	•	•	•	•	•	•	•	•	•	•
2	•	•	•	•	•	•	•	•	•	•	•	•
3	•	•	•	•	•	•	•	•	•	•	•	•
4	•	•	•	•	•	•	•	•	•	•	•	•
5	•	•	•	•	•	•	•	•	•	•	•	•
6	•	•	•	•	•	•	•	•	•	•	•	•
7	•	•	•	•	•	•	•	•	•	•	•	•
8	•	•	•	•	•	•	•	•	•	•	•	•
9	•	•	•	•	•	•	•	•	•	•	•	•
10	•	•	•	•	•	•	•	•	•	•	•	•
11	•	•	•	•	•	•	•	•	•	•	•	•
12	•	•	•	•	•	•	•	•	•	•	•	•

Fig. 4.20(a): Community to draw a grid matrix.

- Request the community to write the names of the months as the first column.
- Now, request them to list out the names of the diseases from which they suffer during various months of the year.
- Make them write the names of the diseases as the first row of the matrix.
- Suppose the community says that they suffer from fever, diarrhoea, asthma and scabies and the months are from January to December.

- If the community uses twelve months and the four diseases, there will be a 12 by 4 matrix with names of the 12 months appearing as the first column and the names of the 4 diseases appearing in the first row.
- Let us take the first disease fever.
- Ask the community the names of the months in which they suffer from fever.
- Ask the community in which month they suffer from fever most. Soppose they say May. Using a free scoring method, the community puts 10 against May under fever.
- Now, ask the community another month in which they have fever but less than what they suffer in May. Say the community says it is the month of July. Using the free scoring method the community may write any number less than 10, say 8 against July under fever.
- The community to repeat the process for all the months in which they suffer from fever.
- Now, repeat the process for all the months *vis-à-vis* diarrhoea. And repeat the process similarly for asthma and scabies.
- Once this is done ask the community to review the diagram. If they want to make any change, encourage the same.
- Finalize and copy the diagram on paper if the diagram was drawn on the floor/ground. Make sure nothing is omitted.
- Now, interview the diagram using the seven helpers discussed earlier. Not down what the community discusses.

Applications

It has been widely applied in the study of seasonality dimension of food, hunger, employment, depths of poverty, migration, cyclical labour movement, rainfall, incidence of diseases, school drop-outs, availability of Non-timber forest produce, cropping patterns, farming cycles, incidence of natural calamities etc.

Strengths and Weaknesses

Strengths

The methods help the community and the outsider to see the role of time element in the lives of communities. It is an invaluable aid to

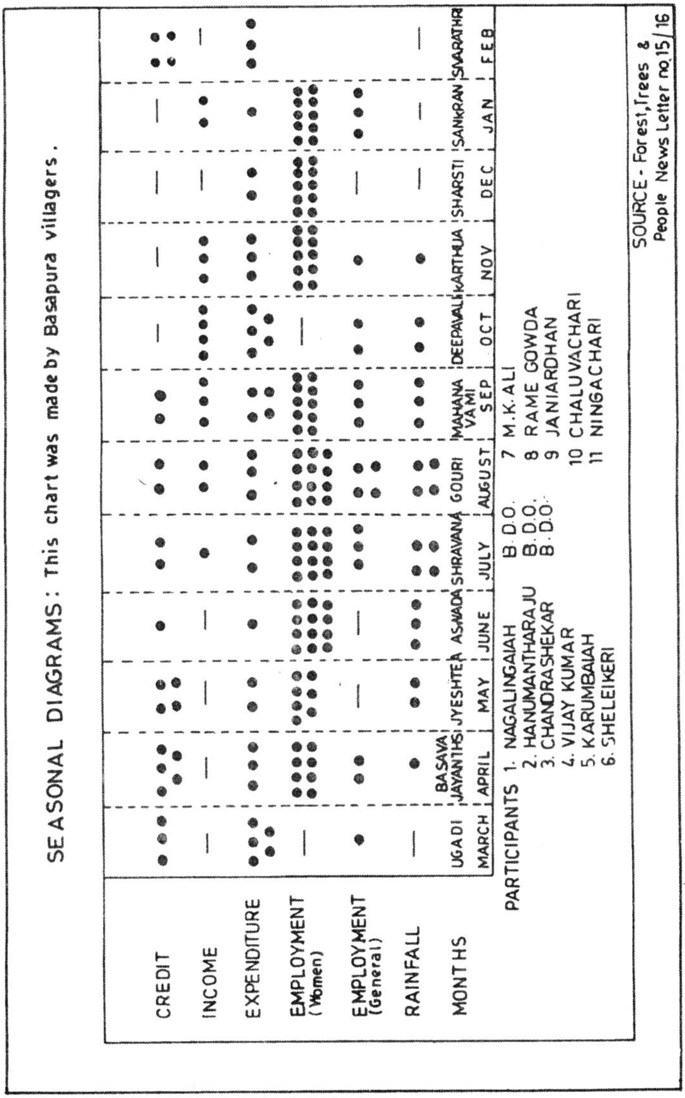

Fig. 4.21: Seasonal Diagrams: This chart was made by Basapura villagers.

development professionals to identity the impact of season on interventions. It helps to identify the lean periods when interventions/ consultations can be targeted/planned. Seasonality analysis helps locate the periods of stress and avoid overloading people with tasks in any season/mc nth which is otherwise stressful for the communities.

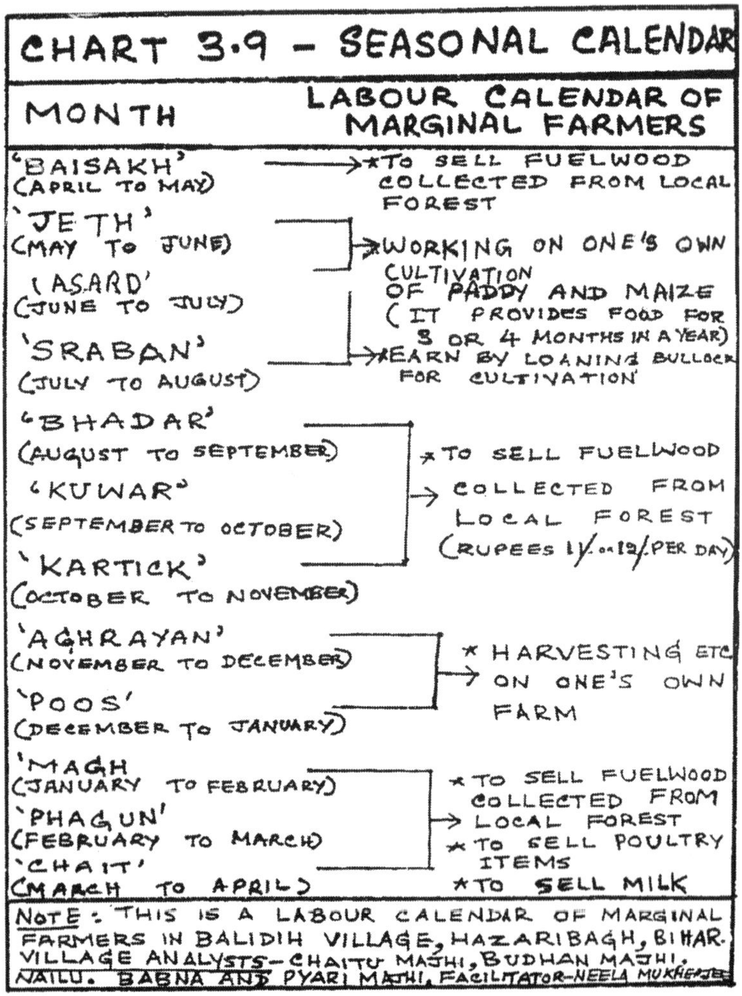

Fig. 4.22: Seasonal Calendar.

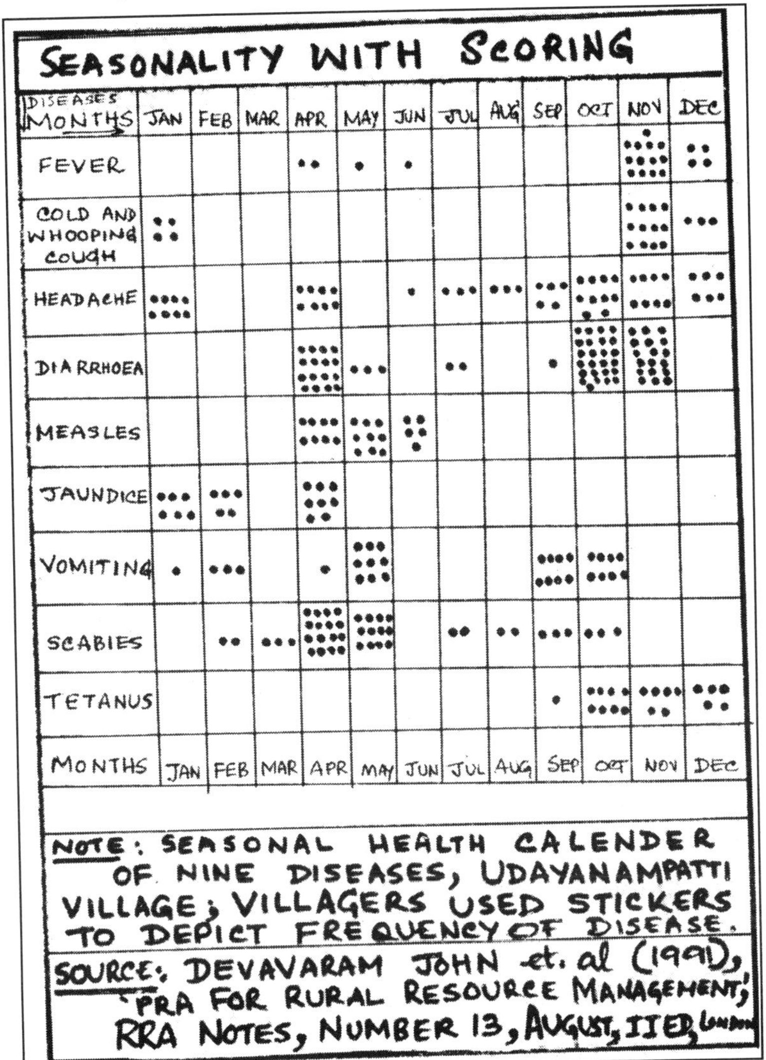

Fig. 4.23: Seasonal Health Calendar Seasonality with Scoring.

SEASONAL FOOD CALENDAR– MALE ADULT / FEMALE ADULT																								
MONTHS	CHAITRA		BAISHAK		JYAISTHA		ASHAR		SRABON		BHADRA		ASWIN		KARTIK		AGRAHYAN		POUSH		MAGH		PHALGUN	
ITEMS	M	F	M	F	M	F	M	F	M	F	M	F	M	F	M	F	M	F	M	F	M	F	M	F
RICE	2	2	6	5	7	6	9	8	9	8	7	6	6	5	5	4	8	7	6	3	6	5	6	5
CHAPPATI	5	4	0	0	0	0	0	0	0	0	0	0	0	0	2	2	0	0	0	0	3	2	3	2
VEGETABLES	1	1	2	2	6	6	10	10	7	7	5	5	4	3	6	4	3	3	3	2	2	2	2	2
PULSES	10	10	5	5	4	4	2	2	3	2	6	6	7	7	7	6	7	6	9	7	8	8	9	9
FISH	1	1	5	2	4	3	2	3	5	2	3	3	8	3	8	2	5	2	4	2	1	2	2	2
EGG	3	2	4	2	3	2	3	2	4	1	4	2	8	3	10	4	9	9	10	9	8	7	7	6
MILK	11	10	5	5	4	4	3	3	3	2	3	3	4	3	2	2	2	2	2	2	2	2	8	8
MANGO	-	-	-	-	4	4	-	-	-	-	-	-	-	-	-	-	-	-	-	-	-	-	-	-
JACKFRUIT	-	-	-	-	9	6	8	5	-	-	-	-	-	-	-	-	-	VILLAGE ANALYSTS - REHANA PARVIN AND FERDUSI BEGUM VILLAGE BANSTAOL, DISTRICT TANGAIL, BANGLADESH						
NOTE: THE FIGURES SHOW THE NO. OF SEEDS USED IN SCORING; M STANDS FOR MALE, F FOR FEMALE																								

Fig. 4.24: Food Discrimination Seasonal Food Calendar–Male Adult/Female Adult.

SEASONAL FOOD CALENDAR – GIRL CHILD/MALE CHILD - ONE YEAR OLD

MONTHS / ITEMS	CHAITRA		BAISAKH		JAISTHA		ASHAR		SRABON		BHADRA		ASWIN		KARTIK		AGRAHAYAN		POUSH		MAGH		PHALGUN	
	M	F	M	F	M	F	M	F	M	F	M	F	M	F	M	F	M	F	M	F	M	F	M	F
RICE	2	1	3	2	5	3	6	4	6	5	7	6	8	7	6	5	7	6	8	7	9	8	6	5
PULSES	7	6	6	5	4	3	6	4	5	4	7	6	7	6	6	5	6	5	6	5	5	4	7	6
VEGE-TABLES	3	2	4	3	3	2	4	4	4	3	6	5	7	6	5	3	4	3	7	6	6	5	5	4
FISH	2	1	2	1	2	1	3	2	3	2	4	3	5	4	4	3	4	3	5	4	6	5	4	3
EGG	6	4	4	3	3	2	3	2	4	3	5	4	6	5	4	3	7	5	8	7	4	3	10	9
MILK	9	7	4	3	5	3	4	3	4	3	5	4	6	5	6	5	6	3	8	7	6	5	7	6
BANANA	7	3	6	4	4	3	3	2	4	3	5	4	7	6	6	5	4	4	6	5	5	4	8	7
ORANGE	4	3	4	2	3	2	2	1	3	2	2	1	4	3	4	3	4	4	5	4				
MANGO							3	2																
JACK-FRUIT							4	3																
PINE-APPLE											2	1	1		3	2	4	3	5	4				
APPLE													2	1	4	3	4	3			5	4		
PAPAYA											4	3											6	5
BISCUIT	3	1	2	1	2	1	3	2	3	2	2	1	5	4	5	4	5	4	6	5	6	3	7	6

NOTE: SAME AS IN CHART 28 ; VILLAGE ANALYSTS – SAME AS IN CHART 28

Note: Same as in Fig. 4.26; Village Analysis—Same as in Fig. 4.26.

Fig. 4.25: Food Discrimination Seasonal Food Calendar–Girl Child/Male Child––One Year Old

SEASONAL FOOD CALENDAR

MONTH \ ITEMS	RICE (NO. OF STONES)	POTATO (NO. OF STONES)	PULSES (NO. OF STONES)	VEGETABLES	FRUITS	FOOD FROM OTHER SOURCES	OTHERS FROM WILD
MAGH (mid-Jan. to mid-Feb.)	15	13	3	CABBAGE			WILD BORUMS WILD RABBITS
PHALGUN (mid-Feb. to mid-March)	9	11	2	SPINACH			'NEEM' LEAVES
CHAITRA (mid-March to mid-April)	4	4	2	PUMPKIN		FISH AND WILD WATER PLANTS	
BAISAKH (mid-April to mid-May)	4	3	1	'PUI' LEAVES (HERBS)	MANGO* JACK-FRUIT*	FISH, SNAILS AND WILD WATER PLANT	
JYAISTHA (mid-May to mid-June)	4	4	2	'LOTA' LEAVES (HERBS)	MANGO* JACK-FRUIT*	FISH AND WILD WATER PLANTS	
ASHAR (mid-June to mid-July)	4	3	3	'JHINGE'			
SRABON (mid-July to mid-August)	4	4	5	PAPAYA			
BHADRA (mid-August to mid-Sept.)	4	3	3	GREEN BANANA		FISH AND SNAILS	
ASWIN (mid-Sept. to mid-Oct.)	4	3	2				
KARTICK (mid-Oct. to mid-Nov.)	2	4	3	RADDISH LEAVES			
AGRHAYAN (mid-Nov. to mid-Dec.)	2	4	5	TOMATO			
POUSH (mid-Dec. to mid-Jan.)	2	9	6	BRINJAL			WILD RABBITS

NOTE: THE NUMBER SPECIFIED UNDER RICE, POTATO AND PULSES REPRESENT THE NO. OF STONES SHOWN BY VILLAGERS. * SHOW FRUITS OF TREES GROWING NEAR-BY.

WOMEN VILLAGE ANALYSTS – NAMITA MALLIK, BINAPANI DANDAPAT, PRATIMA BHAKTA, SUSHILA MALLIK.

DATE: 4.2.1993, VILLAGE KRISHNA RAKSHIT CHAK, MIDNAPORE

Fig. 4.26: Seasonal Food Calendar.

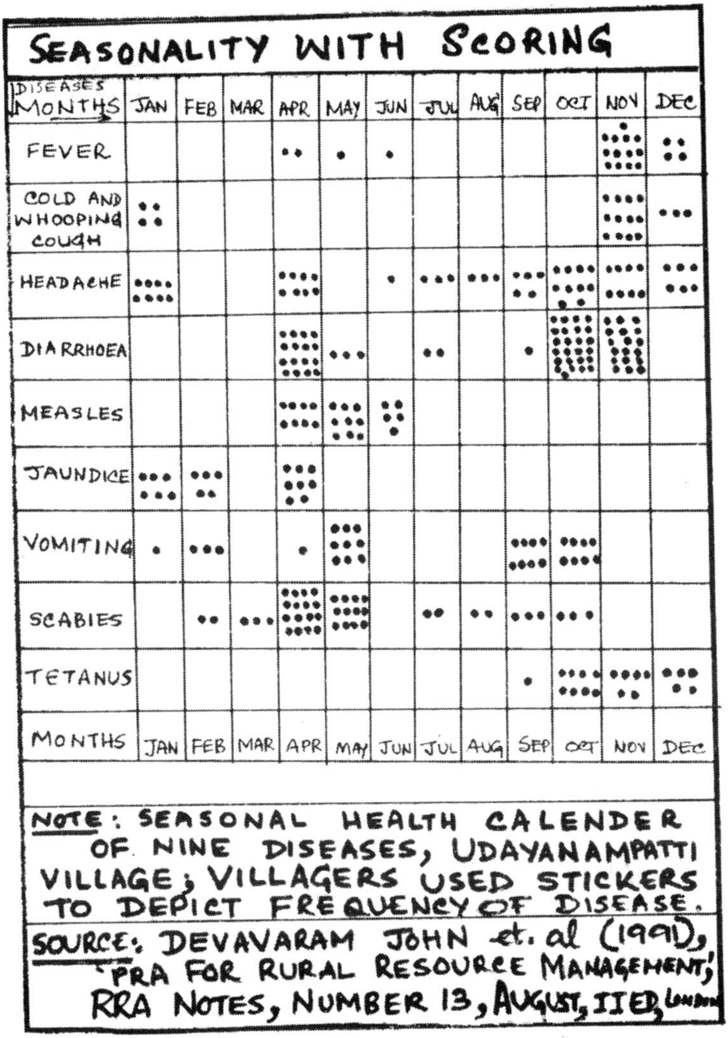

Fig. 4.27: Seasonal Health Calendar Seasonality with Scoring.

9. WELL-BEING ANALYSIS

Definition

Well-being Analysis is a method for investigating well-being differences and inequalities in a community, to discover local indicators and criteria of well-being and wealth. It involves the ranking or grouping of all households in a community according to criteria chosen by the community and thus is also useful for establishing the criteria by which the well-being of households is assessed by the community. The well-being categories may be "well-off", "poor", "very poor" and "poorest of the poor" (PoP) and so on.

Key Components

- Criteria used by people to rank or classify households falling different well-being/ill-being groups.
- Criteria used by people to identify poor households.
- Identification of poor households.
- Ranking and classification of households into different well-being/ill-being groups.

Use of Well-Being Analysis

- To identify households who are very poor/poor, poor and not so poor.
- To rank households in ascending or descending order of well-being/ill-being.
- To classify households into different ill-being/well-being grouping.
- To understand the critical factors that affect the ill-being/well-being levels of households.

Steps in Well-Being Analysis

It is also possible to do a well-being analysis by Wealth Ranking as also by other methods, one of which is described below:

- As stated earlier, fix location (preferably a public place like a Panchayat Bhawan or a School, if it is a holiday) and time for a Well-Ranking Exercise with the community.

- Make a formal invitation to the community members to come for the Well-Ranking Analysis or Wealth Ranking.
- Explain once again to the community members, the purpose of the exercise.
- Request the community members to prepare a list of all the households in the village, may be *mohalla*-wise. Typically a few volunteers will come forward to prepare this list.
- Request the Volunteers to read out the names. If someone's name is missed, include it.
- Now, provide the community members with flash cards.
- Request the community members to write down the name of the households on the card. Ensure that only one name is written per card.
- Now, ask the community to spell out what are the criteria they would use to describe a household as poor. For example landlessness, homelessness, being bonded labour, people with disability etc. could be criteria for identifying who are poor.
- Put up a Chart Paper or Flip Chart on any wall or tree at the place of the exercise. Request the members of the community (may be a volunteer from them) to write down these criteria in block letters in local language on the flip chart as one column.
- Ask the Volunteer to read out the criteria loudly so that everyone can hear. Again seek the community's agreement and make room for them to change should they wish to.
- Help the community to restrict the number of criteria to five or six. In case they evince a very large number of criteria, help them to prioritize them and select five or six. Simple scoring method can be used for the purpose.
- Again put up another Chart Paper or Flip Chart on any wall or tree. Request the members of the community (may be a volunteer from them) to write down these prioritized criteria in block letters in local language on the flip chart as one row.
- Again ask the volunteer to read the prioritized criteria aloud so that all can listen.
- Now, number each criterion and assign each criterion a colour or symbol to represent it. Suppose there are five criteria. For criteria 1, the colour to represent it could be red. For criteria

2, colour to represent it could be yellow. For criteria 3 the colour to represent it could be black. For criteria 4, the colour to represent it could be green. For criteria 5 the colour to represent it could be blue and so on. Instead of colours one can use separate symbols like +, ++, @, *, ** and so on for each criterion.

- Now, request a community member to read out the names of each household **one by one** and request the community members to identify if the household whose name is read out satisfy criterion number 1. If it does, request them to mark the household by red dot. Repeat the process for each household. Then repeat the process for criterion number 2 and request the community to identify those households which have criterion number 2 applicable to it and to mark those households where criterion number 2 applies by yellow dots. Repeat the process for every criterion and every household, until all the households have been considered for all the criteria and appropriate dots placed against them. *Note*—that some households may not have any dots at all if none the stipulated criterion apply to them and some households may have all the dots.
- Now, request the community members to identify those households with the highest number of dots. In the case of our example above households can have a maximum of five dots. Households with five coloured dots, say, will be considered *poorest of the poor*. Then there may be households with four colour dots. Those households which have four coloured dots, say, will be *very very poor.* Those households with three coloured dots, say, will be considered *very poor.* Those households with two coloured dots, say, will be considered *poor.* Those households with one coloured dot, say, will be considered *not so poor*. The rest of the households will be considered as being *not poor*.
- If lesser number of categories of poor are desired, facilitate a process by which the community can club two or more of the different categories into one.
- Invite the community members to review the work they have done and invite them to correct any mistake that might have crept in.

- Now, request the community to keep in separate lots the cards representing households belonging to different categories of poor. Lay them on the floor or on the ground or paste them on the wall. Display the outcome prominently so that everyone can see the output prominently.
- Invite all the members of the community to review the outcome. If they want to make any change, invite them to do so.
- Now, facilitate the process for the community to finalize the list of poor households.
- Interview the well-being analysis using the seven helpers.
- Record the process and outcome of the interview.

10. SCORING AND RANKING

Definition

Scoring and Ranking are facilitated visual methods for ordering and comparing the preference or priorities of a community by the community itself. They can be used for prioritizing needs, problems, solutions, preferences etc.

Key Components

Scoring and Ranking's key components include analysis of preferences, analysis of priorities, analysis of causal relationships and comparison of different elements against a range of criteria.

Use of Scoring and Ranking Exercise

The aims of scoring and ranking are to discover individuals or groups relative prioritization/preferences of components of a single issue. These can be further broken down by criteria which give reasons why the components have been ranked in that particular order. "Ranking and Scoring" can be used to discuss key constraints or opportunities.

Ranking and scoring can be used for understanding preferences. They facilitate initiating discussion of the criteria for selection, and also attempt to develop and understand the basis for making choices and decisions.

It is possible to use these techniques of ranking and scoring as a planning tool, which also stimulates detailed discussion and could be used for basic comparative analysis.

Application of Scoring and Ranking Exercise

Scoring and Ranking have been applied as part of PRA/PLA within almost all contexts. They are one of the most common techniques used.

The following is a selection of issues discussed in Ranking and Scoring:

- Analysis of water use: Preference ranking of different sources of water, and different uses of water.
- Analysis of fuel types, preferences and problems, and comparisons of urban with rural uses.
- Analysis of food preferences, types, staples, fish and vegetables etc.
- Analysis of credit, preference for sources, access, problems, preference for use etc.
- Analysis of income generation. Preference for activity, problems etc.
- Analysis of project preferences, priorities, interventions.
- Analysis of institutions, service provision.
- Analysis of health and education facilities, literacy, food and nutrition, diseases, symptoms.
- Analysis of livestock, preferences, fodder types, species, i.e. for milk, diseases.
- Analysis of soil types, production problems, crop species, varieties, pest damage etc.
- Analysis of forestry: species, preferences, advantages/ disadvantages, utility, varieties, management etc.
- Analysis of gender issues.

Subject matter does not restrict the use of scoring and ranking, and criteria are fully flexible, depending on the context and the participants. Different types of scoring and ranking have also been used at all stages in the project cycle, from appraisal, as planning tools, and for Monitoring and Evaluation.

How to Facilitate Scoring and Ranking Exercise?

Scoring can be normally used of four kinds, ***Free*** Scoring, ***Fixed*** Scoring, ***Ordinal*** Scoring and ***Voting***.

In *free* scoring the items/issues are given a score out of a range of scores like 1 to 10, or 1 to 100.

In *fixed* scoring the scores are fixed between 1 and the number of items/issues to be scored. For example if there are 12 problems to be scored, then in fixed scoring the range of score will be from 1 to 12 (12 being an indicator for the most important problem and 1 showing the least important problem).

In *ordinal* scoring, the items are scored with non-specific quantity of things or elements. Suppose we have to rank 5 livelihood options. Suppose further that we are using seeds (of any kind) to demonstrate the preferred livelihood option. Under ordinal scoring a certain quantity of seeds is placed against the most important livelihood option. Then a lesser quantity of seeds is placed against the next most important livelihood option. An even lesser quantity of seeds will be placed against the third best option and so on.

Under the *voting* method, each of the stakeholders or participant in the process is asked to vote his or her preference by using some sign, like placing a seed or pasting a sticker on the item/issue she/he is voting for.

Free Scoring Method

Suppose we are trying to ascertain the priority of the community in respect of the eight facilities used by the community. And suppose that we are using the free scoring method.

- The community is facilitated to first list the facilities it uses.
- The name of each facility is written on a flash card. If the community is using 8 facilities, there will be eight flash cards with the name of one facility written on one card.
- Place the cards as one column on the ground or the floor or table if there is a large table to accommodate all the flash cards.
- Now, tell the community that it is free to choose a range of score which they will use to score the eight facilities being

prioritized, such as between 1 and 10, or 1 and 50 or 1 and 100 or whatever.

- Suppose the community chose a range between 1 and 10.
- Now, request the community to place a score of 10 against the facility it considers as it first priority or best.
- Then ask the community to identify the next most important facility it uses and give it a score which is less than 10 as it is a little less good than the one which has got a score of 10.
- Suppose the community gives the second best facility a score less than 10, say 9.
- Repeat the process with the other facilities till all the listed facilities are scored.
- It may be possible that two or more facilities may get the same score as they may be equally good.
- The facility which scores the highest score, say 10, is the most preferred and the one which receives the lowest score, say 2, is the least preferred.
- Thus, the one facility which gets the highest score is ranked "First". The one which gets the next best score is "Second" and so on, till all the facilities have been ranked.
- Request the participants to review the scoring and ranking. If they want to change, encourage them to do so but only as a group, not individually.
- Interview the scoring ranking using the seven helpers.
- Record the process and outcome of the interview.

Fixed Scoring Method

- Suppose we are trying to ascertain the priority of the community in respect of the eight facilities used by the community. And suppose that we are using the *fixed scoring* method. Because there are 8 facilities (items) to be scored, under this method the range of scores will be between 1 and 8. Thus, a maximum that a facility can get is 8 and the minimum it can get is 1.
- The community is facilitated to first list the facilities it uses.
- The name of each facility is written on a flash card. If the community is using 8 facilities, there will be eight flash cards with the name of one facility written on one card.

- Place the cards as one column on the ground or the floor or table if there is a large table to accommodate all the flash cards.
- Now, request the community to place a score of 8 against the facility it considers as it first priority.
- Then ask the community to identify the next most important facility it uses and give it a score which is less than 8 as it is a little less good than the one which has got a score of 8.
- The community gives the second best facility a score less than 8 say 7. Repeat the process with the other facilities till all the listed facilities are scored.
- The facility which scores the highest score, say 8, is the most preferred and the one which receives the lowest score, say 1, is the least preferred.
- Thus, the one facility which gets the highest score is ranked "First". The one which gets the next best score is "Second" and so on, till all the facilities have been ranked. The facility which gets the lowest score is ranked as last, noting that the lowest score can be 1.
- The process is similar for Ordinal Scoring.
- Request the participants to review the scoring and ranking. If they want to change, encourage them to do so but only as a group, not individually.
- Interview the scoring ranking using the seven helpers.
- Record the process and outcome of the interview.

Ordinal Scoring Method

- Suppose we are trying to ascertain the priority of the community in respect of the eight facilities used by the community. And suppose that we are using the *ordinal scoring* method.
- The community is facilitated to first list the facilities it uses.
- The name of each facility is written on a flash card. If the community is using 8 facilities, there will be eight flash cards with the name of one facility written on one card.
- Place the cards as one column on the ground or the floor or table if there is a large table to accommodate all the flash cards.

- Now, request the community to place a large quantity of seeds or stones or leaves against the facility it considers as first priority.
- Then ask the community to identify the next most important facility it uses. Request them to place a quantity of seeds or stones or leaves, which is less than the quantity placed against the facility which has been given the highest amount in the previous step.
- The community places a quantity of seeds or stones or leaves against the second best facility an amount less than in the first. Repeat the process with the other facilities till all the listed facilities are scored.
- The facility which has the largest quantity of seeds or stones or leaves etc. placed against it, is the most preferred and the one which receives the least, is the least preferred.
- Thus, the one facility which gets the highest quantity of seeds or stones or leaves is ranked "First". The one which gets the next higher quantity is "Second" and so on, till all the facilities have been ranked, noting that the least quantity being against the least preferred facility.
- The process is similar for free Scoring.
- Request the participants to review the scoring and ranking. If they want to change, encourage them to do so but only as a group, not individually.
- Interview the scoring ranking using the seven helpers and open ended questions.
- Record the process and outcome of the interview.

Voting Method

- Suppose we are trying to ascertain the priority of the community in respect of the eight facilities used by the community. And suppose that we are using the voting method.
- The community is facilitated to first list the facilities it uses.
- The name of each facility is written on a flash card. If the community is using 8 facilities, there will be 8 flash cards with the name of one facility written on one card.
- Place the cards as one column on the ground or the floor or table if there is a large table to accommodate all the flash cards.

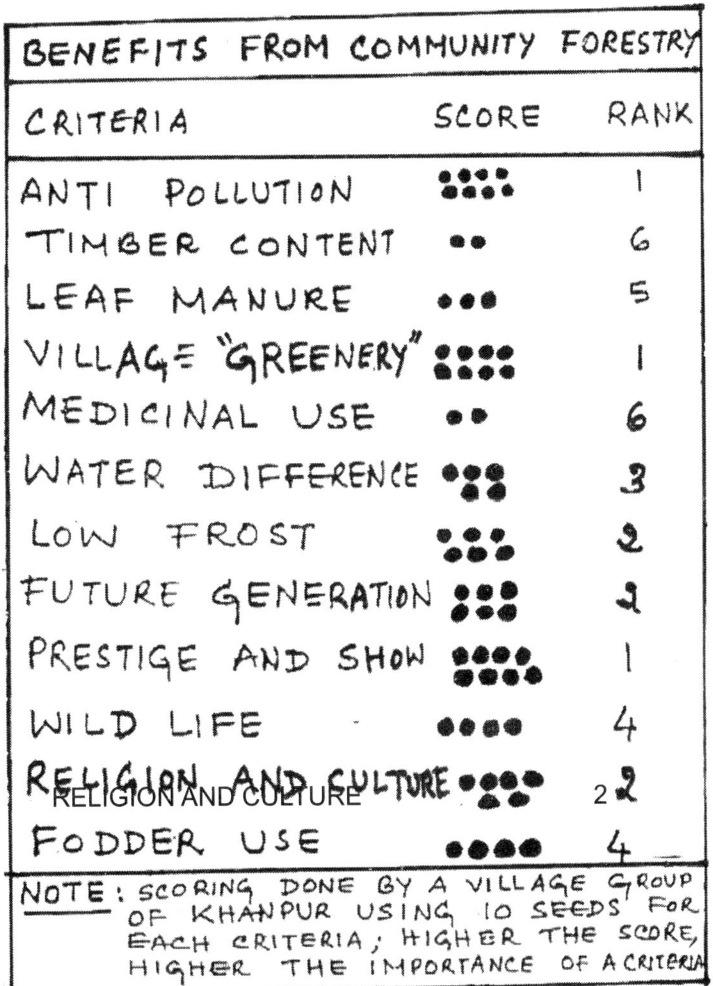

Fig. 4.28: Free Scoring: Group Scoring of Benefits from Community Forestry.
Source: Neela Mukherjee, *Participatory Rural Appraisal* (New Delhi: Concept Publishing Co.) 1997.

- Now, give each community member one post it sticker. The post-it sticker will be used for voting.
- Now, request each of the community members to place the sticker on the facility she/he considers as her first priority.
- After everyone has cast his/her vote, ask for a volunteer from the community.

Ranking of Institutions by Village Group, Karambeli, Penn Taluka, District Raigad

Serial Number	Name of the Institution	Stone Placed	Rank
1	Local NGO	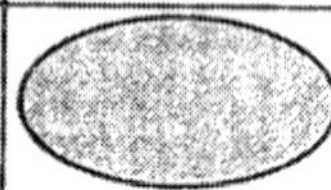	I
2	Zilla Parishad Office	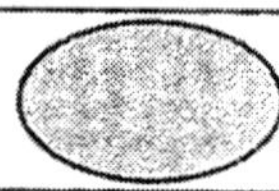	II
3	Panchayat Office	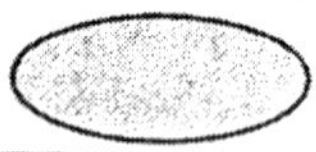	III
4	Gram Panchayat		V
5	Talati Office		IV
6	Tribal Welfare Office (Adibasi Office)		VII
7	Tahsildar's Office (Local Revenue Office)		VI
8	Samaj Kalyan (Social Welfare) Office		X
9	Jangal Samiti (Forest Society)		XI
10	Police Station		VIII
11	Credit Cooperative Society		IX

Notes: Village Analysts: Maruti Pawar, Ram. Pai Ram Pawar, Sonoo Pawar, Rama Wadmore of village Karambelli, on 13-2-2001. Facilitated by Amitava Mukherjee.

Fig. 4.29: Ordinal Scoring.

- Request the volunteer to count the number of votes that each facility has got and write the number on a separate card and place it alongside the name of the facility.
- The facility which gets the highest number of votes is the most preferred and the one which receives the lowest score, say 0, is the least preferred.
- Thus, the one facility which gets the highest number of votes is ranked "First". The one which gets the next best number of votes is "Second" and so on, till all the facilities have been ranked.
- Interview the scoring ranking using the voting method with the help of the "seven helpers".
- Record the process and outcome of the interview.
- *Do not request* the participants to review the scoring and ranking. If they want to change, do not encourage them to do so either as a group, or individually.

11. PAIR-WISE RANKING

Definitaion

Pair-wise Ranking is also a facilitated visual method for ascertaining relative importance, ordering and comparing the preference or priorities of a community, by the community itself, by directly comparing different items/issues amongst themselves *inter se.* It can also be used for prioritizing needs, problems, solutions, preferences etc.

Key Components of Pair-wise Ranking

Pair-wise Ranking's key components include analysis of preferences, analysis of priorities, analysis of causal relationships and comparison of different elements, by directly comparing different items/issues amongst themselves *inter se.*

Use of Pair-wise Ranking

Pair-wise Ranking is a widely used technique in the repertoire of Participatory Learning and Action (PLA, earlier PRA) which compares pairs of elements, such as the preference for specific tree species or prioritization of particular problems and solutions. It leads to analysis of decision-making rationale: as a key to understanding, for example, demand for certain kinds of facilities or social services or natural resource use. It can also highlight the relevance and appropriateness of interventions, through an increased understanding of priorities of the people and other stakeholders. Comparisons of preference and priorities of groups, by gender, age, occupation or history, for example, are possible.

Steps in Facilitating Pair-wise Ranking

- Let us take the example of ranking of facilities in a Village according to their utility.
- Request the community to write down the facilities as one column.
- Now, request the community to write down the same facilities as first row.
- Ensure that the facilities listed as the first row is in the same order as the first column.
- Now, request the community members to draw a matrix (grid) with the names of the facilities appearing both as first column and first row. Now, suppose there are in all five facilities. Request the community members to compare each of the facilities with all other facilities and request them to record which is more important in the squares against them.
- Start by requesting the community to say whether facility number 1 is more important than facility number 2. Suppose they say facility number 1 is more important, then the community members should write 1 in the square under facility 2 and 1. If, on the other hand, facility number 2 is more important than facility number 1, the community members should write 2 the square under facility 2 and 1.
- Then request the community to say whether facility number 1 is more important than facility number 3. If they say 3 is more important that facility number 1, they should record 3 in the square under facility 3 and 1 as in the earlier cases.
- Then request the community to say whether facility number 1 is more important than facility number 4. Ensure they record what they say in the same manner as above.

- Then request the community to say whether facility number 1 is more important than facility number 5. Ensure they record what they say in the same manner as above.
- Repeat the exercise with facility numbers 2, 3, 4 and 5.
- Now count the number of times that facility 1, 2, 3, 4 and 5 appear in the Matrix or Grid.
- List the facilities in order of the number of times they appear. If suppose 2 appears 15 times and 3 appears 10 times, then facility 2 is deemed ranked above 3 in terms of its utility. Similar process may be followed for the other facilities.
- Thus, all the facilities will be ranked from one to five, in our example.
- It may be noted that the some facilities can appear the same number of times and thus have the same rank.
- Interview the scoring and ranking using the seven helpers and open ended questions.
- Record the outcome of the interview in the field itself.

Application

Most of the original applications of Pair-wise ranking were in the fields of agriculture and then forestry. Crop and variety preferences, tree species preferences, agriculture and tree problems have all been explored. Subsequently, problems in delivery of basic services, sources of income, livelihood options, sources of credit, expenditure, diseases, irrigation, children's needs, general problems and potentials etc. have all been the subject of Pair-wise Rankings. Urban applications and use in "northern" settings are increasingly common.

It is possible to examine the importance of different criteria, for example, that were used in a scoring and ranking exercise. By comparing the criteria directly, the relative importance of these different criteria can be discussed, and therefore, the scoring more fully understood.

Strengths and Weaknesses

Strengths

Pair-wise ranking encourages discussion, and the criteria mentioned for selection should be carefully noted. In some cases where participants have expressed a lack of preferences for specific items, claiming to have no detailed knowledge of the subject, pair-wise ranking helps to stimulate discussion and elicits detailed knowledge and understanding. The *process of comparison* is as important as the grid "result" itself.

Weaknesses

Some criteria may be self-evident. For example if you are comparing livestock and the group has limited access to water, then ducks are unlikely to be chosen as livelihood option a water is a problem. Access to basic services which determine preferences may also create problems in reaching group consensus. Choice of food depends just as much on what is available in season as on personal preferences. A discussion which brings out these issues is possibly more rewarding than a ranking exercise itself. Additionally many items are likely to be multi-functional and therefore, simple comparison without criteria may be difficult.

Unless a lively discussion is encouraged both the participants and the facilitators may find pair-wise comparisons tedious. It is also important to limit the number of elements to be ranked to a small

Problems	Lack of Facilities	Pregnancy	School fees	Losing traditional values	Distance from home	Early Marriage
Lack of Facilities		pregnancy	lack of facilities	lack of facilities	lack of facilities	early marriage
Pregnancy			pregnancy	pregnancy	pregnancy	pregnancy
School Fees				school fees	school fees	school fees
Losing Traditional Values					distance from home	early marriage
Distance from home						early marriage
Early Marriage						

Fig. 4.30: Pair-wise ranking.
Source: Rietbergen-Mcracken *et al.* (1998).

number, say 5 or 6, to reduce the risk of boredom. In large part pair-wise ranking is dependent on the quality of facilitation. Facilitators may tend to fill in the grids, either during interviews or after. Lack of visual impact and the discussion around pair-wise ranking also increases the potential for participants to lose interest.

An example of Pair-wise-Ranking of the reasons why girls do not attend school in a village in Gambia.

In the example: (i) Pregnancy appears 5 times. (ii) Lack of facilities appears 3 times, (iii) Early marriage appears 3 times, and (iv) School fees appear 3 times. Thus, the main reason for girls in not attending *schools is pregnancy* (see Fig. 4.31).

12. SOCIAL MAPPING

Definition

A map is a mental picture of a place or community or village. Maps are perhaps amongst the most popular methods in the literature on participation. These are seminal methods, which explore the spatial dimensions of a place or community.

Social Map is a visual depiction of all man-made structures in a village or area. It shows human habitation, the location and nature of housing, infrastructure such as roads, drains, schools, health outlets, drinking-water facilities, water channels and places of worship, settlement patterns including location houses of marginalized groups. A Social Map is prepared by local people and is not drawn to scale. It reflects the perceptions of the social dimensions of people's reality.

Key Components of a Social Map

- Availability of social and economic infrastructure such as roads, bridges, schools, health outlets, places of worship etc., community centre, electricity poles, solar power, hand pumps, wells, shops, ration shops etc. in an area or community.
- Status of social and economic infrastructure (such as gravel roads, broken roads, good roads, culverts or iron bridges etc.), in an area or community.
- Habitation pattern of the people such as houses, kinds of houses (Thatched, *Kucca*, *Pucca*) as well as concentration of particular class or kind of people (like STs, SCs,

Problem	1. Alcoholism	2. Lack of road	3. Lack of community hall	4. Lack of teachers	5. No electricity to Harijan colony	6. Problems of public distribution system	7. Lack of medical facilities	8. Lack of employment	Priority frequency
1. Alcoholism	X	2	3	4	1	1	7	8	2
2. Lack of road	X	X	2	4	2	2	2	2	6
3. Lack of community hall	X	X	X	4	3	3	7	3	4
4. Lack of teachers	X	X	X	X	4	4	4	4	8
5. No electricity to Harijan colony	X	X	X	X	X	6	7	8	0
6. Problem of public distribution system	X	X	X	X	X	X	7	8	1
7. Lack of medical facilities	X	X	X	X	X	X	X	7	5
8. Lack of employment	X	X	X	X	X	X	X	X	3

Participants: Kailash Das, Mohan Das, Poonam, Ram Nayan, Narayan Ram Meghwal, Haridas and Mohan Meghwal
Facilitators: Rameshwar Godara, Indra Kumar Dube and Sankar Sarma

Fig. 4.31: Pair-wise Ranking.

Blacksmiths etc.) in any part of the area or community under discussion.

Use of Social Map

- In developing a Dream Map to visualize the future of a community or village, i.e. developing a perspective for a area or village or community.
- In developing a situation analysis for micro-level planning.
- In ascertaining the location of houses of marginalized people or households.
- In finding out the existence and status of delivery of basic services.
- In finding out common areas like places for bazaars, holding community events, cremation/burial etc.
- Comparing the status of a community or village at two or more points in time in respect of social infrastructure, demographics etc.

Applications of Social Map

Social Map helps in developing a broad understanding of the various facets of social reality, *viz*. social stratification, status of housing, status of electrification, settlement patterns, social infrastructure etc.

A Typical Social Map can neatly depict the lanes, sub-lanes, school, railway track, temple, post-office, well, hand pump, community hall etc. in the village. Using suitable symbols, it can provide household-level details on the educational status of adults and children (even disaggregated by age and by gender), health status of the inhabitants, women headed households, status of houses (*kuccha*, *pucca*, IAY Houses) and social status of the head of the household.

The applications of social maps are, *inter alia*, as follows:

- In carrying out a situation analysis of an area/community/ village.
- Understanding of the physical and social aspects of community or village life.
- Understanding of the demographic and related household dimensions of a community/village.

- Social Map is used as a platform for discussion on different aspects of social life
- Social Map is critical for spatial planning.
- Social Map is used in monitoring and evaluation.

Key Questions

- What are the approximate boundaries of the village with regard to social interaction and social services?
- How many households are found in the village and where are they located?
- Is the number of households growing or shrinking?
- What are the social structures and institutions found in the village?
- What are religious groups found in the village?
- What are ethnic groups found in the village?
- Which are the Female Headed Households and where are they located?
- The diagram above is an example of a typical Social Map. *Source*: S. Kumar: *Methods for Community Participation: A Complete Guide for Practitioners* (New Delhi: Sage) 2000.

Steps in Social Mapping

- Fix the location. Ensure that the locations/venues have enough room to accommodate the expected number of people. See if it is in a central place in the village and accessible to all. Be sure that it is convenient and comfortable for everyone in the community/village. There should be enough shade for the participants. In case you decide to have the map drawn on the ground, make sure the surface fairly smooth for the exercise.
- Avoid the venue for mapping being in a religious place as there may be sensitivities involved.
- Fix a time for the exercise in consultation with the local people.
- Invite them for the mapping exercise.
- Reconsider where you will facilitate the Social Map: On the floor/ground or on Chart Paper. Both have their advantages and limitations.

- If the Map is facilitated on Chart Papers, ensure that more than one chart paper is joined together so that the people are not constrained by space to draw the map.
- Ensure you have the required material for mapping (apart from local material) like *Rangoli* powder, chalks, chart papers, marker pens, flash cards etc. in adequate quantity.
- Once at the venue, clearly explain the purpose of Social Mapping to the people at the start of the process.
- Leave it to the people to use whatever materials they choose.
- "Hand over the Stick" or better still "Hand over the Pen" to the people. Empower them and let the people have total control and initiative.
- Suggest to the people to begin by marking the directions as they deem fit. Deviating from conventional mapping they may indicate the side from which sun rises as the East and mark it as such in the paper/ground.
- Facilitate so that people may start by drawing the prominent features of the area/village such as a Railway Track or the main road, or the Temple or the School Building or an Old Big Tree or whatever. Most of the time people start by drawing the main road or a landmark and then move on to add other details. The houses start appearing later. Generally, the houses are shown mirroring the actual reality: in terms of size, design, kind of the materials used for roofing (like concrete, tiled, thatched etc.).
- Watch who all are actively involved, and who all are being left out. Take proactive steps to involve the left out group in the process.
- Once the mapping is over, ask some people present there to identify their houses in the map.
- Always number the households. It will be essential for finding out their entitlements and deprivation.
- Ask them to depict the household details that are particularly necessary for the planning: like women headed households, households with communicable diseases, households with people who are differently-abled and so on.
- Interview the map with open ended questions. Clarify those aspects which are not clearly shown and request for more information, if necessary. Remember there is no second chance!

Note: if the facilitator has something to add or clarify, he/she must wait for the right moment and not disrupt the process.

- Have the map copied on to chart papers if the map was drawn on the floor or the ground. Ensure accuracy in copying!
- Triangulate the information generated with others in the locality.
- Display the Map at a prominent place where all people have free access so that if any errors have crept in those can be pointed out.
- Facilitate corrections of the errors in the map should any be found.

The outsiders' role is limited to facilitation and they should intervene only when necessary, like when the process is not progressing well or some people are left out.

Advantages and Limitations

Advantages

Social Maps provide a spatial structure for discussion and provides an overview of the community/village, often leading to a common orientation and understanding.

Social Maps generate a wealth of household information. Social mapping helps in problem identification and in planning for development intervention. It is particularly powerful in comprehending the socio-economic stratification of the community/village. A Social Map gives an idea of the community's/village's social resources, and its distribution and control.

Social Map is a versatile tool. It can generate detailed information on a range of issues like demography, education and health status of the villagers; deprivations and entitlements; migration and desertion. Social Map is used extensively for "before and after" or "with and without analysis" in monitoring and evaluation of development projects.

Limitations

Social mapping may be found to be difficult to initiate though once the process starts, it moves on its momentum. Social mapping may be

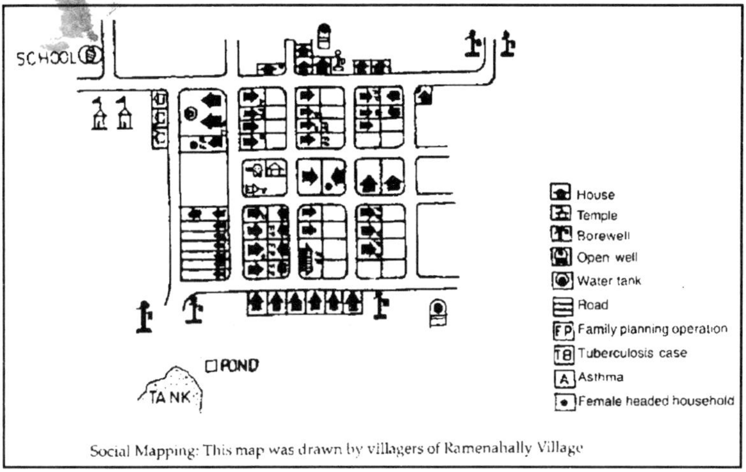

Fig. 4.32: Resource Map.

Source: Forest, Trees and People, *Newsletter*, Number 5/16.

difficult with the illiterate or neo-literate people. Their lack of confidence in themselves and their belief that maps can be drawn by experts only aggravate the situation. Dealing with literate people is not easy either. They are reluctant to do a mapping exercise on the ground for fear of soiling their hands. They feel that when cadastral survey maps and other data are already available, there is no need for exercises like social mapping. Though social mapping enables the poor and marginalized to set forth their realities, they may not come out of their shells and draw a Social Map autonomously. Special efforts on the part of the facilitators are needed. A Social Map is shown on p. 190.

13. RESOURCE MAP

Definition

A Resource Map is a visual depiction of all natural endowments in a village/community. As a corollary to Social Map, one can say Resource map depicts the "nature made structures" (as it were) in a village or area. Thus, a resource map depicts all the natural resources—land, water, forests, flora, fauna, hills, vegetative cover, fields, grazing lands, common property resources etc. A Resource Map thus reflects the natural resources' dimensions of people's reality.

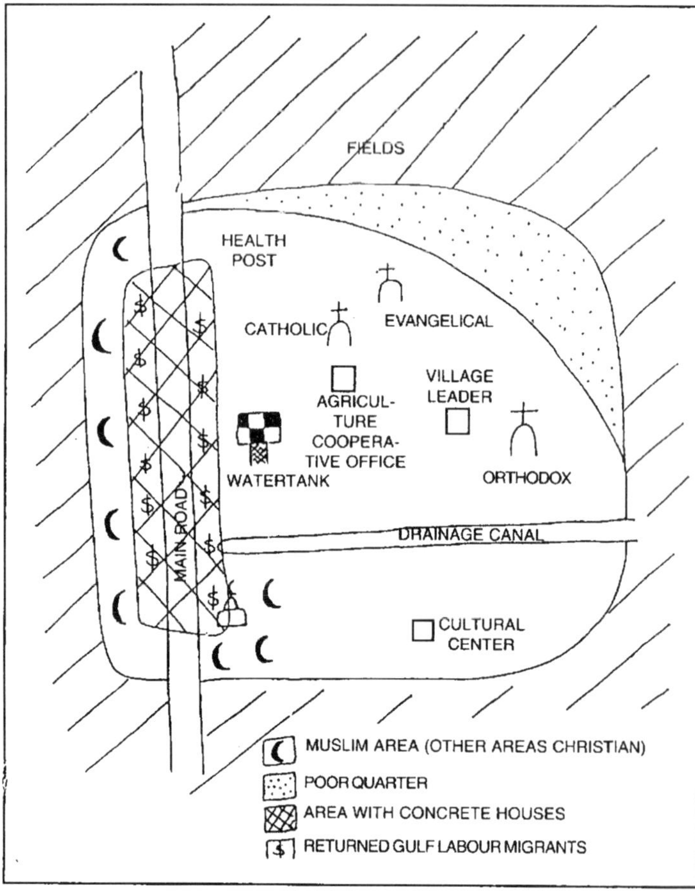

Fig. 4.33: Resource Map.

At times, the distinction between the resource map and social map may get blurred.

A Resource Map using participatory method is, like a Social Map, not drawn to scale, because a Resource Map reflects the people's perceptions (and not precisely measured) of natural resources of the community/village.

Key Components of a Resource Map

Resource Maps depict different aspects of natural resource endowment and management, of a community/area/village including:

- Topography, terrain and slopes of a community's habitation/ village.
- A community's/village's forest, scrub land, vegetation and tree cover and species.
- Soil-type, fertility, erosion and depth of erosion.
- Land and land-use including land-used for agriculture, grazing land, community land etc.
- Command area, tenure, boundaries and ownership of land.
- Availability of water, rivers and their catchment area, other water bodies, sources of irrigation and natural drainage system, watersheds etc...
- Various soil and water conservation measures, denuded areas etc.

Use of Resource Map

A Resource Map is particularly useful because they provide a focused spatial structure for discussion and analysis of the natural resources. A Resource Map helps in creating a common understanding amongst the community about their natural resource base.

A Resource Map well as a baseline for monitoring and evaluation. The process of creating a resource map is full of joy and it instills self-confidence amongst the participants, which later makes the interaction more meaningful. Resource maps have been found particularly useful for analysis of problems, looking at solutions and planning for action. Resource maps have been used to generate discussions among the participants about natural resources, their entitlement and utilization, problems related to deforestation and soil erosion etc. The focus gradually shifts from the identification and prioritization of problems related to the natural resources, to planning for intervention.

Key Questions for Resource Map

- What resources are abundant?
- What resources are scarce?
- Does everyone have equal access to land?
- Do women have access to land?

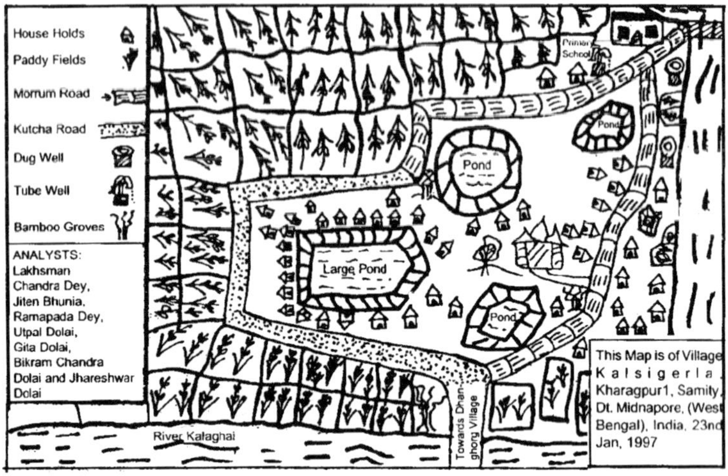

Fig. 4.34: Resource Map.
Source: Neela Mukherjee: *Participatory Rural Appraisal Methodology and Application* (Concept, New Delhi), 1997.

- Do the poor have access to land?
- Who makes decision on land allocation?
- Where do people go to collect water?
- Who collects water?
- Where do people go to collect firewood?
- Who collects firewood?
- Where do people go to graze livestock?
- What kind of development activities do you carry out as a whole community? Where?
- Which resource do you have the most problem with?

Steps in Resource Mapping

- Fix the location. Ensure that the location/venue has enough room to accommodate the expected number of people. See if it is in a central place in the village and accessible to all. Be sure that it is convenient and comfortable for everyone in the community/village. There should be enough shade for the participants. In case you decide to have the map drawn on the ground, make sure the surface fairly smooth for the exercise.

- Avoid the venue for mapping being in a religious place as there could be sensitivities involved.
- Fix a time for the exercise in consultation with the local people.
- Invite them for the mapping exercise.
- Reconsider where you will facilitate the Social Map: On the floor/ground or on Chart Paper. Both have their advantages and limitations.
- If the Map is facilitated on Chart Papers, ensure that more than one chart paper is joined together so that the people are not constrained by space to draw the map.
- Ensure you have the required material for mapping (apart from local material) like *Rangoli* powder, chalks, chart papers, marker pens, flash cards etc. in adequate quantity.
- Once at the venue, clearly explain the purpose of Resource Mapping to the people at the start of the process.
- Leave it to the people to use whatever materials they choose, including the ones you have brought along.
- "Hand over the Stick" or better still "Hand over the Pen" to the people. Empower them and let the people have total control and initiative in the mapping exercise.
- Suggest to the people to begin by marking the directions as they deem fit. Deviating from conventional mapping they may indicate the side from which sun rises as the East and mark it as such in the paper/ground.
- Facilitate so that people may start by drawing the prominent natural features of the area/village such as the main tank/ pond, or the river, if there is one or a Old Big Tree or whatever, even the main road. Most of the time people start by drawing a landmark (or water mark) and then move on to add other details. The fields and forest start appearing later.
- Watch who all are actively involved, and who all are being left out. Take proactive steps to involve the left out group in the process.
- Once the mapping is over, ask some people present there to identify their fields in the map.
- Request the participants them to depict the field and other details that are particularly necessary for the planning: like the crops that are grown in the fields; women headed households owning the fields; the kinds of trees in the village

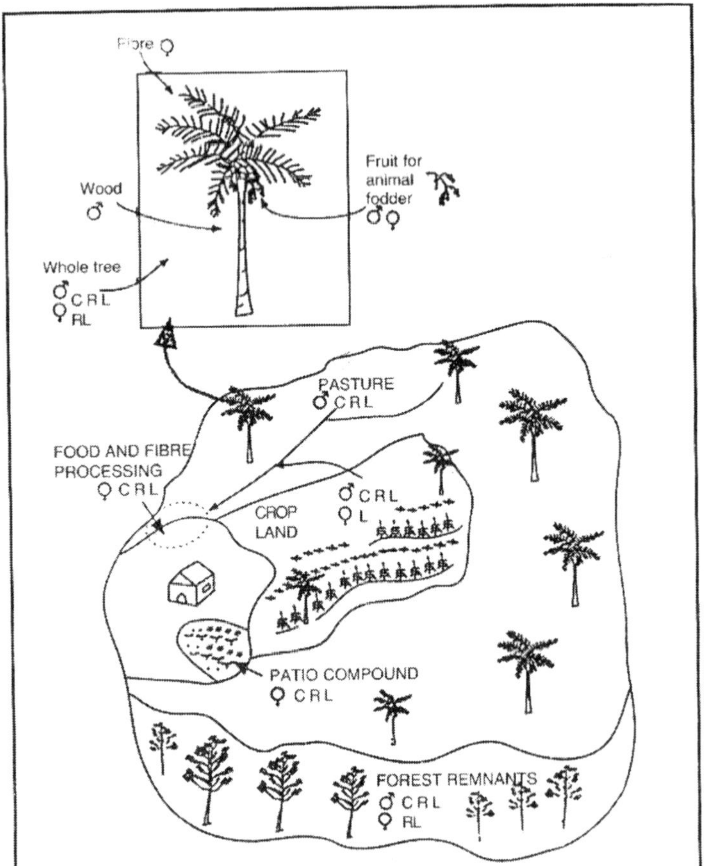

Multi-purpose use of land and trees in Pananao (La Sierra, Dominican Republic). Both men and women are present in this household. R = responsibility to provide a product thereof to the household, L = labour for the establishment, maintenance or harvest, and C = control of resource or process.

Fig. 4.35: Multi-purpose use of Land and trees in Pananao.

Source: *Power Process and Participation*, Intermediate Technology Press, London, 1996.

and the adjoining forests if there are any; common property resources like grazing land, fish ponds, natural sources of drinking water and irrigation water, tanks and so on.

Note: If the facilitator has something to add or clarify, he/she must wait for the right moment and not disrupt the process.

- Have the map copied on to chart paper(s) if the map was drawn on the floor or the ground. Ensure accuracy in copying!
- Triangulate the information generated with others in the locality.
- Display the Map at a prominent place where all people have free access so that if any errors have crept in those can be pointed out.
- Facilitate corrections of the errors in the map should any be found.
- Interview the map with open ended questions and the seven helpers. Clarify those aspects which are not clearly shown and request for more information, if necessary. Remember there is no second chance!

The outsiders' role is limited to facilitation and they should intervene only when necessary, like when the process is not progressing well or some people are left out.

A Resource Map can be painted permanently on walls or, on the floor, particularly where a watershed development programme is contemplated. Maps are made in public with the involvement of villagers.

They discuss various issues related to natural resources—present status, their felt needs and future plans—and finalize details of the location of the structures and activities, budget and time-frame. The maps prove handy for monitoring the progress. Use of the maps for discussions helps to increase awareness among the villagers, thereby improving transparency. Painted at a public place, such maps are available to the people at any point in time.

Advantages and Disadvantages

Advantages

Resource map is a popular PRA method with certain inherent strengths. The local people enjoy doing a resource map. The use of local material provides them with the scope to do the map in a creative way. Everyone understands what is happening. It is quite effective in planning for natural resources management. Local materials and mapping on the ground work in favour of the poor and marginalized who are generally left out in other processes.

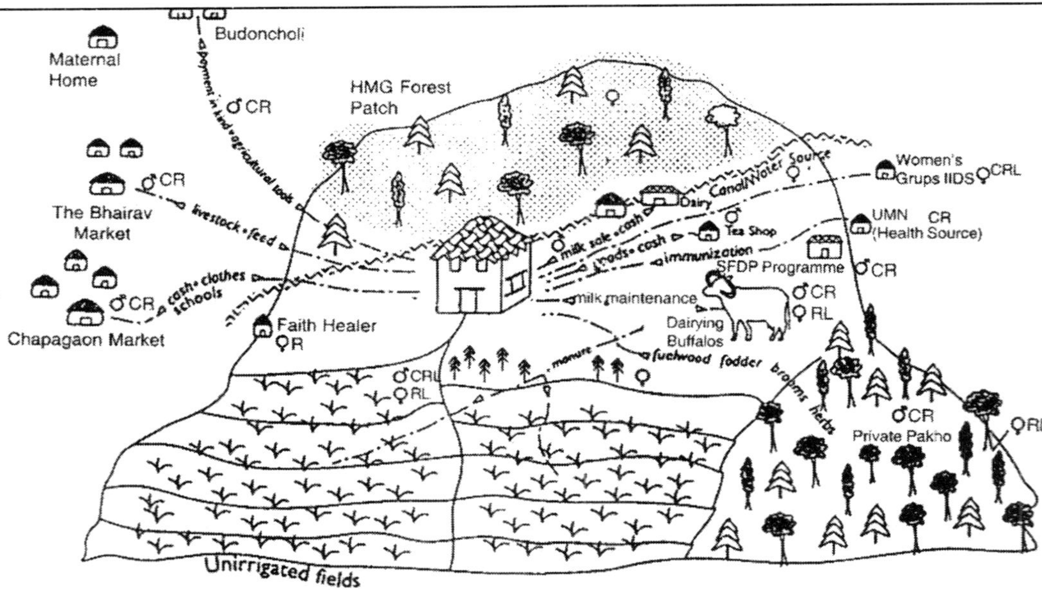

Pakho: Informal management system in which village households plant species suitable for fuelwood and fodder on government 'wasteland' (once forested, now barren), thereby converting that land to private property. Access to Pakho land varies widely by class, caste, and ethnicity.

UMN : United Mission to Nepal
SFDP : Small Farmer Development Programme
HMG : His Majesty's Government

C = Control of site/plants/products/relationship
R = Responsibility to provide products from the site
L = Labour input on site/actual use

Fig. 4.36: Pakho: Informal Management System.

Source: Power, Process and Participation, Intermediate Technology Press, London, 1996.

Limitations

There is a common tendency to over-emphasize the product and neglect the process as well as the discussions, which are equally important. In communities where issues like land holding and land tenure are sensitive to talk about, resource mapping is a difficult exercise. Many facilitators, particularly those who are not very experienced, find resource maps difficult to initiate. But once they start taking shape, the mapping goes ahead rather smoothly. Thus resource mapping is a powerful PRA method that is particularly useful in the area of natural resources management.

14. FORCE FIELD ANALYSIS

Definition

Force-field analysis is an influential development in the field of social science. It provides a framework for looking at the factors (*forces*) that influence a situation, especially social situations. It looks at forces that are either driving movement toward achieving a goal or a desired state (helping forces or positive forces) or blocking movement towards a goal or a desired state (hindering forces or negative forces).[1]

Let us start with a simple science experiment (this really is relevant, so stay with me for a moment please). You will need to sit down for this one. You are sitting? Good. Now, what's keeping you in the chair? Well, there are two answers really. One is gravity which is pushing you down into the chair. A driving force, if you like. The other is the chair itself, which provides an opposing force, pushing up against gravity, and stopping you falling to the ground. So, it would seem that while you are sitting you're in an equilibrium of sorts. Two forces keep you there. Gravity pushes down, keeping you in the chair, and the chair resists this, stopping you from falling to the ground. Two equal forces, a driving force and a resisting or restraining force, working to keep the equilibrium or *status quo*. Figure 4.37 summarizes the above situation.

Key Components of a Force Field Analysis

Use of Force Field Analysis

Force Field Analysis is a general tool for systematically analyzing

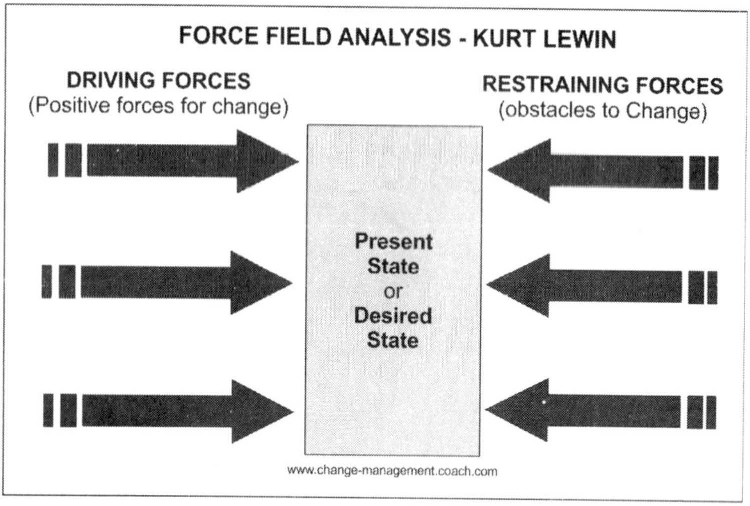

Fig. 4.37: Force Field Analysis—Kurt Lewin.

the factors found in complex problems. It frames problems in terms of forces or factors or pressures that support the *status quo* (hindering forces or negative forces) and those forces or factors or pressures that support change in the desired direction (helping forces or positive forces). A factor can be people, resources, attitudes, traditions, regulations, values, needs, desires etc.

As a tool for managing development, Force Field Analysis helps identify those helping forces or positive forces as also the (hindering forces or negative forces) that must be addressed and monitored if development is to succeed.

Key Questions for Force Field Analysis

- What development benefit will the change deliver?
- Who supports the change? Who is against it? Why?
- How easy will it be to make the change? Do you have enough time and resources to make it work?
- What costs are involved?
- What other business processes will be affected by the change?
- What are the risks?

Steps in Force Field Analysis

- Fix the location. Ensure that the location/venue has enough room to accommodate the expected number of people. See if it is in a central place in the village and accessible to all. Be sure that it is convenient and comfortable for everyone in the community/village. There should be enough shade for the participants. In case you decide to have the map drawn on the ground, make sure the surface fairly smooth for the exercise.
- Avoid the venue for mapping being in a religious place as there could be sensitivities involved.
- Fix a time for the exercise in consultation with the local people.
- Invite them for the mapping exercise.
- Reconsider where you will facilitate the Social Map: on the floor/ground or on Chart Paper. Both have their advantages and limitations.
- If the Map is facilitated on Charts Papers, ensure that more than one chart paper is joined together so that the people are not constrained by space to draw the map.
- Ensure you have the required material for mapping (apart from local material) like *Rangoli* powder, chalks, chart papers, marker pens, flash cards etc. in adequate quantity.
- Leave it to the people to use whatever materials they choose, including the ones you have brought along.
- Once at the venue, clearly explain the purpose of Force Field Analysis to the people at the start of the process.
- "Handover the Stick" or better still "Handover the Pen" to the people. Empower them and let the people have total control and initiative in the mapping exercise.
- Define the change you want to see. Write down the goal or vision of a future desired state. Or you might prefer to understand the present *status* quo or equilibrium.
- Brainstorm or Mind Map the Driving Forces—those that are favourable to change. Record these on a force field diagram.
- Brainstorm or Mind Map the Restraining Forces—those that are unfavourable to, or oppose change. Record these on the force field diagram.

- Evaluate the Driving and Restraining forces. You can do this by rating each force, from 1 (weak) to 5 (strong), and total each side. Or you can leave the numbers out completely and focus holistically on thc impact each has.
- Review the forces. Decide which of the forces have some flexibility for change or which can be influenced.
- Strategize! Create a strategy to strengthen the driving forces or weaken the restraining forces, or both. If You have rated each force how can you raise the scores of the Driving Forces or lower the scores of the Restraining Forces, or both?
- Prioritise action steps. What action steps can you take that will achieve the greatest impact? Identify the resources you will need and decide how to implement the action steps. *Hint:* Sometimes, it is easier to reduce the impact of restraining forces than it is to strengthen driving forces.

The force field analysis is backed by the Lewin change management model and has, over time, developed credibility as a professional change management tool.

Advantages and Disadvantages

Advantages

Limitations: Criticism of the force field analysis usually focuses on the subjectivity of attributing scores to the driving or restraining forces.

Some writers suggest the model applies within limited settings and that there are situations outside of these settings in which Lewin's theory may be less applicable.

At the end of the day this model of analysis is a tool that may or may not be useful in your situation. You can decide this or allow others to make a decision.

NOTE

1. The principle was first developed by Kurt Lewin, and is a significant contribution to the fields of social science, psychology, social psychology, community psychology, organizational development, process management, and change management.

5

Training for Gram Panchayat Development Planning

Introduction

This Book deals with the application of Micro-Gram Panchayat Development Planning interventions. Gram Panchayat Development Planning cannot be either facilitated or developed by people who are not properly trained in the skills required to prepare and facilitate Gram Panchayat Development Plan. Capacity-building of all functionaries involved directly in Gram Panchayat Development Planning and in facilitating such planning is of utmost important. There are several treatises on the subject but most are either too detailed to be used at only the Gram Panchayat Level or are not directly related to Gram Panchayat Development Planning *per se* or deal with only one aspect of the Gram Panchayat Plans. This Chapter is, thus, an indicative way of imparting a set of functional skills to the participants to facilitate **Gram Panchayat Development Planning** as is necessary for initiating community development through praxis.

This chapter is designed to train people and sensitize them to the philosophy of the people-centred development and stakeholder participation in the **Gram Panchayat Development Planning.** The seeds of the future involvement of stakeholders are sown at the planning stage. The chapter thus attempts to build the Capability Spectrum in terms of knowledge, skills and attitudes that the **Gram Panchayat Development Planning Team** must necessarily possess for facilitating the process of people-centred **Gram Panchayat Development Planning** in their communities.

Table 5.1: The Content Flow for training in Gram Panchayat Development Planning will be as under

Sl. No.	*Contents*
1.	Detailed Content Flow
2.	Note to Facilitators for using
3.	Session 1: People Centered Attitudes and Behaviour
4.	Session 2: My Dream Village
5.	Session 3: Context Analysis for Micro-Level Planning for Convergence for Convergence
6.	Session 4: Problem Identification and Prioritization
7.	Session 5: Solution Identification and Prioritization
8.	Session 6: Action Planning for Micro-Level Planning

Training Objectives

The training objectives of this Module are stated as follows:

- To enable the participants to comprehend the process of people's participation in planning for village development.
- To equip the participants with the functional skills required for engaging in planning for economic development and social justice at the micro-level.

Session 1—Their Training Objectives and Expected Learning Outcomes

The Section has five sessions on Micro-Level Planning for Convergence. The first five sessions are geared to satisfy the two stated objectives. For each session, the Expected Learning Outcomes at the end of the session that demonstrate the fulfillment of the two training objectives, at the levels of both the individual participants and group have been identified.

Session No. 1

This is a crucial session. For any participatory exercise, there are four pillars: tools and methods, process, attitudes and behaviour and sharing. All four are interdependent. But often facilitators miss out on attitudes and behaviour. This session is to emphasize the need for people-centric attitudes and behaviour and to provide set of attitudes

Table 5.2: The Session-wise Training Objectives and Expected Learning Outcomes are given in the following table:

Session No.	*Session Description*	*Training Objectives*	*Expected Learning Outcomes*
0.	People Centered Attitudes and Behaviour	The participants are conscientise about the desired pro-people and pro-poor behaviours and attitudes that are expected for a facilitator of participatory processes and learn to emulate them.	The participants will be enabled to comprehend the different kinds of people centred behaviours and attitudes and reflect on their own behaviour.
1.	The Dream Village	(a) To enable the participants to comprehend the process of stakeholder participation in planning for village developments. (b) To equip the participants with the functional skills required for engaging in and facilitating Micro-Level Planning for Convergence.	(a) The participants visualize their dream village and articulate their vision for village development. (b) They acquire functional skills for PLA methods in developing a perspective for village development.
2.	Context Analysis for Action Planning	Same as above	(a) The participants are able to contextualize their dream map to the realities existing at the village level. (b) They acquire functional skills for using PLA methods in analysing the existing condition in the village.
3.	Problem Identification and Prioritization	Same as above	(a) The Participants acquire functional skills for using PLA methods in identifying the problems confronting the village development. (b) They can adopt a problem solving approach for prioritizing.
4.	Solution Identification and Prioritization	Same as above	(a) The Participants acquire functional skills for using PLA methods in finding solutions to problems identified in the previous session. (b) They can adopt a problem solving approach for prioritizing solutions for development problems.
5.	Action Planning	Same as above	(a) They Participants acquire functional skills for using PLA methods in planning for village development. (b) They have hands on understanding of how to develop an Action Plan from a Tactical Plan.

and bahaviour that are considered which the facilitator should have to facilitate a Micro-Level Planning for Convergence exercise.

Session No. 2

In this session, the participants are encouraged to prepare a map of their dream village as a first step towards **Gram Panchayat Development Planning**. This session seeks to explore and expand the development vision of the participants and help them articulate their perspective of Gram Panchayat Development Plan. It is imperative for Facilitators to possess the essential ability to envision village development in its entirety. They have first to understand what village development is all-about. This session, therefore, attempts to develop the participants' vision-based upon their own development perspectives.

Session No. 3

In this session, participatory methods are used to conduct the context analysis for preparing the village development plan. This analysis is done based upon village level realities and with reference to four areas.

- Analysis of space, which includes analysis of resources available, infrastructure social condition etc.
- Analysis of time which includes evolution of the village, seasonality of income, food availability, employment, opportunities, credit needs etc.
- Analysis of relationships which includes an analysis of the importance of different institutions and their utility etc. to the community and their inter-relationships between the institutions, with which the community has interface.
- Analysis of preferences and priorities, which includes preferences for crops, trees, food, livelihood, seasons, institutions etc.

Session No. 4

This session involves the participants in acquiring the skills required to facilitate the community in identification and prioritization of village level development problems and needs which have to be addressed by the Gram Panchayat Development Plan. The problem identification is done by involving different groups in the process, especially women and other socially excluded groups. It may also be emphasized that there may be need to carry out the exercise of problem identification for **Gram Panchayat Development Planning** with different groups: men, women, aged and old, children, people with disabilities etc.

Session No. 5

In this session, the skills to help communities identify or range of solutions or suitable development activities for **Gram Panchayat Development Planning** and match them with the needs voiced by the people in the previous session. A method/technique for prioritization of the solution is then affected for arriving at an optimal set of development interventions. Perspectives related gender and social justice are also explored and included in the set of activities that are listed.

Session No. 6

In the last session, the **Gram Panchayat Development Plan** prepared by the process adopted in the last four sessions is transformed into a Tactical Plan by:

- Fitting it within a definite time-frame by specifying the time horizons for the proposed development activities.
- Specifying the financial allocations available from different funding sources for each of these activities.
- Ascertaining the appropriateness of the plan for marginalized groups.

Planning for the Rural Production Sector

The sequence of steps and the planning process outlined in the sessions Nos. 1 to 6 can be followed for the rural production sector whereby the participants prepare a participatory village plan for the development and strengthening of on-farm and/or off-farm livelihoods. The facilitator must ensure that the focus is on rural production sector. An indicative list of the possible activities is given below for guidance:

Rural on-Farm Productive Activities

1. Agriculture,
2. Agricultural Extension,
3. Land improvement,
4. Implementation of agrarian reforms,
5. Soil conservation,
6. Management of water resources,
7. Watershed development, and
8. Regulation of manure pits in public places.

Rural off-Farm Productive Activities

1. Animal Husbandry,
2. Dairying,
3. Poultry,
4. Fisheries,
5. Collection of minor forest produce,
6. Tiny, village and cottage industries, and
7. Traditional Rural Artisanship.

Planning for Rural Social Infrastructure

Similarly, the sequence of steps outlined in the five sessions 1-6 may be used for planning for rural social infrastructure. The focus of micro-level planning here will be on social infrastructure. The facilitator should impress upon the participants that one of the basic tenets of the people-centred **Gram Panchayat Development Planning** is that the agency of the individual/group/community has to be fostered by increasing the level of human well-being in terms of the social development indicators like literacy, health, access to drinking water, sanitation etc. This is particularly important for gender and other vulnerable groups. Poverty is a multi-dimensional phenomenon and not simply restricted to income poverty. Therefore, it is equally important to address the social, economic and political dimensions of deprivation. It is only then that Gram Panchayat Development Plan and its implementation will lead to social change, which is the ultimate development goal of **Gram Panchayat Development Planning**. Hence, special attention has to be given during planning for the creation of social infrastructure which enhances the quality of human capital in Gram Panchayat. A suggested list for assisting the facilitator in facilitating the **Gram Panchayat Development Planning** process is given below:

Productive Activities for Creating/Strengthening the Village Level Human Capital

(a) Education with special reference to the education of girl child, including primary and secondary schools.
(b) Adult and non-formal education.
(c) Markets and fairs.
(d) Family welfare, health, sanitation, primary health centres and dispensaries.
(e) Women and child development.
(f) Social development of socially marginalized as also physically and mentally challenged persons.
(g) Public distribution system for making food available to the indigent people.
(h) Relief and rehabilitation of disaster affected persons.
(i) Maintenance of the record of village level social development indicators.

Productive Action for Social Infrastructure/Physical Capital

(a) Social forestry and farm forestry.
(b) Management of common property resources.
(c) Rural housing.
(d) Drinking water.
(e) Fuel and fodder.
(f) Roads, culverts, bridges, and other means of transportation.
(g) Non-conventional energy sources.
(h) Maintenance of community assets.
(i) Construction and maintenance of public shelter for travellers and pilgrims and similar institutions.
(j) Construction and maintenance of cattle sheds, goat sheds, horse stand and cart stand.
(k) Construction and maintenance of slaughter houses.

(l) Maintenance of public parks, playgrounds etc.
(m) Removal of encroachments on public properties.
(n) Organizing voluntary labour and contribution for community works.

Training Methodology

The roles played by the Participatory Learning and Action Methods in this Section are two-fold. First, as a training methodology it is versatile. It suggested in this Chapter. Second the participants are prepared for fieldwork where they can draw up a **Gram Panchayat Development Plan** based on PLA tools and methods.

Table: 5.3: Module of Role Orientation

Module-1	*Role Orientation*
Session Theme	People-centred Behaviours and Attitudes
Duration	
Venue	Classroom without fixed furniture.
Seating	Sit or stand on the floor forming a circle; move around the room for the role play and group work. Participants may also sit on the chairs if they like to.
Session Objectives	To enable the participants to comprehend the different kinds of people centered behaviours and attitudes.

Expected Learning Outcomes

The participants are conscientisise about the desired pro-people and pro-poor behaviours and attitudes that are expected for a facilitator and learn to emulate them.

1. Game: "As Facilitator I mainly…."

In Step 1, play the game as a Facilitator, ***I mainly…*** This is a game for reflecting on one's own behaviour and how we seen by others. Follow these steps:

1.1. Facilitate a brainstorming exercise to complete the sentence "As a facilitator I mainly …" make a short list of behaviours like listen, think, argue, lecture, dominate, lead, facilitate and of roles, listener, thinker, debater, leader, facilitator etc. Ask participants to record each idea or similar idea on a flash card.

Table 5.4: Content flow and Training methodology

Sl. No.	*Content*	*Training Methodology*	*Training Aids*	*Duration (in minutes)*
1.	(a) How does a facilitator/ development functionary usually behave?	Step 1 Game as a facilitator "I **mainly....**".	Flash cards marker pens, flip charts, slides, etc	45
	(b) What are the appropriate behaviours for a member/ functionary	Step 2 Brainstorming		30
2.	Non- verbal behaviour	Step-3 Game: Non-verbal circles	Chairs, sticks to improvise	25
3.	Role of Facilitator	Step-4 Role play/ Drama	As may be necessary	30
4.	Game for enhancing group dynamics	Step-5 Chairs	Chairs	30
5.	Modelling of People Centred attitude	Step-6 Johari's window Step-7 Slide show	Slides, sketches	30
6.	Synthesis of learning points	Step-8 Visual method	Flip charts, marker pens	15

1.2. The next step is to join others who are similar. Post the words in different parts of room and ask the participants to move quickly to the word each thinks represents him/her best. Encourage the participants to move fast at this stage of the game. If any participants can not choose the word, they can form their own group.

1.3. The groups formed under each word then discuss their roles or behaviours and decide:

- What is helpful about it?
- What is unhelpful about it?
- How do others see me?
- Do I want to make any changes?
- How does it affect my role as Facilitator or development functionary?
- Does it meet the needs of people-centred development? If not why?
- Any other reactions.

1.4. The groups discuss their insight with the other groups. These discussions can help the participants recognize the value of all kinds of behaviours and roles and identity which of these are congruent with the philosophy of people-centred development.

2. Brainstorming for the Appropriate Behaviours of a Member or Functionary/Team Member

In step 2, based upon the previous discussion, brainstorm with the participants about the appropriate behaviour for a member or a functionary. Use slides and posters of pictures, wherever possible. Some behaviours suggested below:

- *Avoid Dominance*: Dominant behaviour is characterized by the inability to listen to others and appreciate the fact "that they know"; the tendency to ignore/override the development interests of others, impose one's own views and beliefs upon others etc.
- *Avoid biases*: There are eight kinds of biases to be avoided:
  - (a) Gender bias-ignoring men or women.
  - (b) People bias—Talking to vocal people, clean people, people with clean homes etc.
  - (c) Road side bias—Visiting places near the road only.
  - (d) Project bias—Look at pet projects where nothing has gone wrong.
  - (e) Professional bias—Looking at the development problems and solutions from the narrow respective of one profession.
  - (f) Seasonal bias—Carrying out fieldwork, important sessions etc. when it is most inconvenient for the people.
  - (g) Time bias—Carrying out fieldwork, important meetings, Village Assembly etc. when it is not convenient to the people.
  - (h) Diplomacy Bias—Not expressing opinions or view in order not to offend others or when people say what they think "outsiders" want to hear.
- Eschew arrogance like not listening to others' views; acting as "Mr./Mrs. know all"; being disrespectful towards the views of socially excluded sections or local culture, custom, usage etc.; being very conscious of one's own status as a facilitator etc.

- Do not lecture since this is against the principle of participation. People know their problems and solutions. Facilitator needs to help community bring them to the table.
- Do not seek 'blueprint' since development interventions have to be specific to community/stakeholder needs and hence cannot confirm to one fixed pattern.
- Seek and respect diversity since there are diverse perspectives and diverse needs of development stakeholders and "*their varied reality*" counts.
- Be self-critical and be self-aware. do not be judgemental. Encourage others to express themselves freely and listen to them. Be self-introspective and realize your strength and weaknesses.
- Be culturally sensitive by recognizing the tradition, usages dress culture, language and religion, customs etc. of the different sections of society and communities and respecting them.
- Respect others and their point of view by listening to others and encouraging debates.
- 'Deal with people': Do not avoid them or cut them out if they are 'difficult' or if they do not agree with you'. Difficult people are:
  - Dominant people,
  - Mr./Mrs. Know all, the "trappers",
  - The "arrogant people", the "destroyers",
  - The "thick skinned" and broad people,
  - The shy people,
  - The people with limited vocabulary, and
  - The procrastinators.

Such people may include government functionaries who do not wish to share information and power or community members who ask many questions in the meetings to disturb the proceedings only.

3. Game to Sensitize the Participants to Non-verbal Behaviour

In step 3, *Non-verbal circles*, an energizing game has been suggested with the objective of sensitizing the participants to how non-verbal behaviour can indicate dominance, submissiveness and friendliness. Follow the steps given below:

3.1 Form two sub-groups of the participants. The two sub-groups sit in two circles, facing inwards

3.2 One person in each sub-group is elected scorer, who also takes part in the game.

3.3 The first competition for each sub-group is to show and perform non-verbal action that demonstrates dominance.

3.4 One person continues until one of the two run-out of ideas.

3.5 Quickly ask the scorers, and invite each sub-group to choose its best non-verbal action.

3.6 Repeat the submissiveness.

3.7 Repeat for being 'nice to people'.

3.8 Repeat for different kinds of behaviour which have been identified in the previous steps.

3.9 Now, discuss about the importance of non-verbal behaviour. Analyse how much we communicate with our words and how much through non-verbal behaviour especially in exhibiting the behaviours which have been either recommended or discouraged in the previous step.

3.10 Discuss the importance of paralinguistic and facial expression. Indicate that current thinking on the subject maintain that in a training session we communicate only 7 per cent of what we communicate by words, 38 per cent by paralinguistic (tone, voice inflexion etc.) and 55 per cent by facial expression.

4. Role Play or Drama to Illustrate the Role of a Facilitator

In step 4 highlight the role of a village Local Leader using Role Play/ Drama staged jointly by the participants and facilitators. The script can narrate case studies if so desired. Several role models may be portrayed by the script like:

- Facilitator of participatory development and governance at the grassroots.
- Promoter of gender and social justice at the grassroots with special reference to the management of conflict and conflict resolution.
- Facilitator of the process of social and economic change.
- Proactive agent of community development.

- Regulator of the units of self-government at the village level.
- Custodian of public property at the village level.

5. Game for Enhancing Group Dynamics

In step 5 the participants play a game of chairs for enhancing their group dynamics, even further. The steps to be followed are given below:

5.1 Prepare three kinds of instructions on slips of paper, an example of which is given below:

- A: Put all the chairs in a circle within 15 minutes.
- B: Put all the chairs near the door within 15 minutes.
- C: Put all the chairs near the window within 15 minutes.

5.2 Explain to the participants the objectives of the game which are:

- To illustrate how to manage conflict by turning it into co-operation.
- To help them focus on the possible differences in the interpretation of instructions.
- To make the participants aware of the cultural and gender differences in handling conflicts.

5.3 Give each participant one kind of instruction (either A, B or C), distributing equal numbers of the three instructions. Ask them to keep the instructions given to them a secret.

5.4 Tell the participants to start the game following the instructions they have been given.

5.5 The focus of the exercise is on co-operation and conflict resolution by non-aggression. The three sub-groups cannot carry out their given tasks unless they cooperate. Several mutual solutions are possible, like:

- Putting all the chairs in a circle between the doors and the window.
- Putting first all the chairs in a circle, then near the door and next near the window.
- Putting one third chairs in a circle, one third near the door and one-third near the window.

5.6 The group will be seen to be using force and carrying their chairs desperately away or sitting on them near the door or window to avoid the chairs being displaced. Some participants will be seen trying to find a co-operative solution, while others will continue collecting and defending their chairs. The latter will frustrate the good intention of the former who then join the argument.

5.7 Analyse the experience with the participants exploring how they felt with about their chairs, the others who tried to take their chairs away and about the participants who were trying to co-operate. Ask them whether would play the game differently a second time. Also explore how they related the game to real life situations, say the dynamics they experienced in a Village Meeting or a meeting of the Village Leaders.

6. Use Johari's Window to Model People-centred Attitude

In Step 6, use the **Johari's Window** (See Figure 5.1) to focus attention on the fact that it is important to believe that people know (their problems and are capable of suggesting solutions). Also, that the realities of the poor people count most: People's analysis, People's criterion, People's monitoring, People's, evaluation, People's view and People's knowledge count and not ours. Discuss how these principles have underpinned the entire training programme where the facilitator has given more emphasis to the realities and knowledge of the participants than their own. The whole training process itself has been one of both behaviour and attitude modelling by the facilitator. The facilitator should discuss how the participants could use the training methods in their communities to elicit popular participation.

7. Use Slides to Model People-centred Attitude

In Step 7 use slides with pictures/sketches to model a spectrum of people-centred attitude with a particular reference to the following attitude:

- "They Know". It is important for a facilitator to appreciate the knowledge of the people since this is the first step towards facilitating their developments through participation and understand that their knowledge, their technology, their priorities, their preferences, their planning, their monitoring and their evaluation count.

- "Embrace Error": Everyone makes mistakes and there is no one correct way of doing things. So, if someone makes a mistake in trying a new way of doing things, or even otherwise, it is human and natural. Accept it. This ability also denotes humility and non-dominant behaviour and leads to efficient developments choices and decisions. This helps to inculcate the attitude of learning from mistakes and moving ahead.
- "Fail Forward", i.e. learn from your mistakes, improve and move forward, but do not either repeat mistakes or get demoralize with failure.
- Positive Person: "Yes I have an Idea". It indicates that the facilitator has enthusiasm. This is the essential quality of a facilitator as who has a vision and motivates others. If the facilitator is not enthusiastic, how can the people be expected to be enthusiastic.
- "I will not talk the talk, unless I walk the talk". The facilitators have to be a role model for his/her community and must exhibit the behaviours which she expects others to emulate. "Practice what you preach" as the old cliché says.
- Improvise, innovate and adapt: The quality of Village development depends upon the creativity and flexibility of the Village Leaders. The Facilitators must, therefore, constantly improvise, innovate and adopt existing ways of doing things.
- Listening, Observing and Learning. This attitude is significant because the Facilitator is prepared to listen to people. She/he cannot learn if she/he and if she/he is not Listening and Observing. And if she/he is not in the state of continuous learning, she/he cannot innovate and adapt for the development needs of their community. Additionally, learning from the people is critical for making informed development decisions which conforms to people's priorities, their needs, their preferences. To learn, it is imperative to listen, observe and learn.
- Communicate well, so that others can understand and participate. Communication is critical to make the process of development interactive.
- We are facilitators. They do it. People are the actors, not us. We are there to only facilitate the process so that people can

analyze, plan, implement, act, monitor and evaluate. This attitude underlies non-dominant behaviour and is important for initiating stakeholder participation in development.

8. Visual Method for Synthesizing What we have Learnt from the Session

In Step 8 the synthesis of the learning points is done by the facilitator with the help from the participants. To introduce good humour, do the synthesis by asking the participants to act out some of the desired and undesired behaviours and attitude for a facilitator.

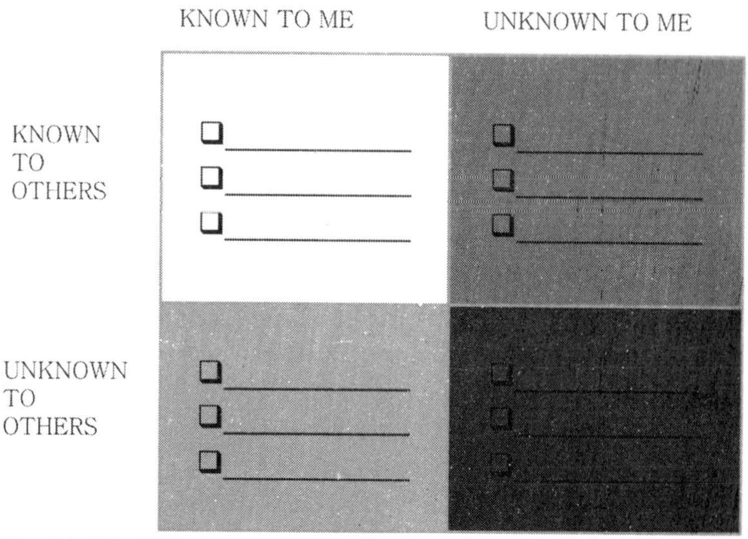

Fig. 5.1: Johari Window.

Session 2—Micro-Level Planning for Convergence

Session Theme—Community Perspective
Duration—150 minutes
Venue—Room without any fixed furniture

Seating: Sit and/or stand on the floor forming a circle; move about for a game and group work; Participants should be free to sit on chair if they so desire.

Session Objectives

- To enable the participants to comprehend the process of peoples participation in planning for village development and develop a perspective for development of the village.
- To impart the functional skills required for engaging in micro-level planning to the participants.

Expected Learning Outcomes

- The participants visualize their dream village and articulate their vision for village development. This provides a perspective for micro-level plan.
- They acquire functional skills for using PLA methods in micro-level planning for village development.

Table 5.5: Content Flow and Training Methodology

Sl. No.	*Content*	*Training Methodology*	*Training Aids*	*Duration (in minutes)*
1.	Energizing and Group Formation	Step 1: Card Game	Flip charts, marker pens, boards.	15 minutes
2.	Game for improving listening and observation	Step 2: Matches	3-6 match sticks or coins for each participants	15 minutes
3.	Creating/articulating the development vision or building the community's perspective	Step 3: Dream Mapping	Flash cards, flip charts, marker pens, posters, slides and other aids as desired by the participants	45 minutes
4	Setting the perspective for village development planning: The dream map provides the perspective	Step 4: Visual method for the presentation and analysis of the dream map and identification of key elements	Same as above	60 minutes
5.	Synthesis by facilitator/participants	Step 5: Visual Method	Slides, aforesaid materials	15 minutes

The Methodological Steps for Session 1

1. Play an Energizing and Group Forming Game

In Step 1, the card game is played with the objective to energize the group and form sub-groups of the participants for the group exercises that are an integral part of this session. The steps for playing the game are:

1.1 Make the participants stand in a circle.
1.2 Take a pack of playing cards and keep cards of the four houses, *viz.* Clubs, diamonds, hearts and spade with their faces down in the middle of the circle. The total number of cards should be equal to the middle of the circle. The total number of cards should be equal to the number of participants. Equal number of cards of each house should be kept if it desired to form sub-groups of equal size.
1.3 Ask the participants to run in a circle and pick up a card each while keep on running. The participants are the divided into four sub-groups, depending on the card they have picked up, *viz.*, clubs, hearts, diamonds and spades.

2. Play a Game for Improving Listening and Observation

Step 2, A game for improving listening and observation is given below:

2. The objectives of the game are to make each participant aware of the value of their contribution and encourage a listening attitude in the subsequent group work.
   2.1 Give each participant the same number of tokens like match sticks or coins depending upon the time available for playing the game. Say each participant has five coins or match stick.
   2.2 Ask them to sit in circles in the sub-groups formed, *viz.*, clubs, hearts, diamonds and spades.
   2.3 Every time a participant speaks in her sub-group, she has to put one of her tokens in the centre of the circle.
   2.4 If a participant has no token left, she cannot speak.
   2.5 A participant realizes that every remark is valuable and therefore, evaluates her remark before speaking.

Knowing that every speaker has made the evaluation, the other participants also listen.

2.6 The participants who have/have token(s) left are the winners.

3. Dream Mapping for Creating and Articulating the Development Vision

Step 3 For the **Dream Mapping,** the participants work in the four sub-groups. Each sub-group holds discussions about what their dream village would look like and how they visualize village development over a given period of time, say 5 or 10 years. The participants together can choose to present their dream village through pictures, drawings, maps or text highlighting the features it would possess. The facilitator should enlist the support of a co-facilitator and jointly facilitate the group work. Provide whatever stationary the sub-groups may desire such as coloured papers, coloured cards, pens, markers, scissors, gums and glues, tapes etc. and encourage them to be creative. At the end of this exercise, it is expected that each sub-group would have either depicted its dream village pictorially and or prepared a presentation about the same on chart paper etc.

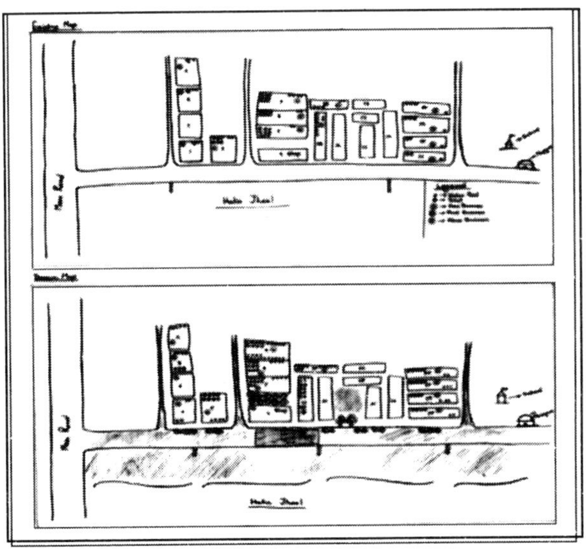

Fig. 5.2: Dream Map.

4. Presentation and Analysis of Dream Maps for Setting the Perspective for Village Development Planning

In Step 4, each of the four sub-groups uses the Visual Method for making a presentation about its dream village, followed by the facilitator facilitating an analysis of the key elements of each dream map. These elements are either noted down on flip charts pasted around the room or on flash cards. After all four groups have made their presentations, the key elements of the dream maps analysed. The dream map would show the fields will look how the houses will look, how the forest would change, how the state of health and literacy would vary or how much industrialization will advance over chosen time-frame. These key elements are then discussed further and the overall perspective for micro-level planning for each village development is outlined by the participants.

5. Visual Method for Synthesizing what we have Learnt from this Session

In Step 5, the synthesis of the learning points is done by the facilitator with the help of participants. The facilitator should focus on the fact that the key elements of the dream maps prepared by the participants will form the perspective of the whole planning exercise in the next sessions. The village development plan which will thus be eventually prepared, would, therefore, be *People Micro-level Plan* in the true sense of the term.

Session 3—Micro-Level Planning for Convergence

Session Theme: Context Analysis for Micro-Level Planning.
Duration: 4 half days or at the discretion of the facilitator.
Venue: Flat space or room large enough to hold at least 50 people.

Seating: Sit and/or stand on the floor forming a circle; move about for the game and group work.

Session Objectives: To enable the participants to acquire skills for analyzing the present situation of the village to inform micro-level planning to the participants.

Expected Learning Outcomes

- The participants are able to contextualize their dream map to the realities existing at the village level.
- They acquire skills in using PLA methods in analyzing the present conditions of their village for micro-level planning for economic development and social justice in their village.

THE METHODOLOGICAL STEPS FOR PRACTICAL EXERCISES IN SESSION 3

1. Analysis of Space: Take a Joint Walk or a Geographical Transect in the Village

In Step 1, let the participants take a joint walk with the villagers and discuss the changing face of the village, the natural resources and the other features of the village during the walk. The usual method for Geographical transact is to go to the highest point in the village and walk along with villagers, down to the lowest point. If the highest point has to be at the centre of the village, then there could be two

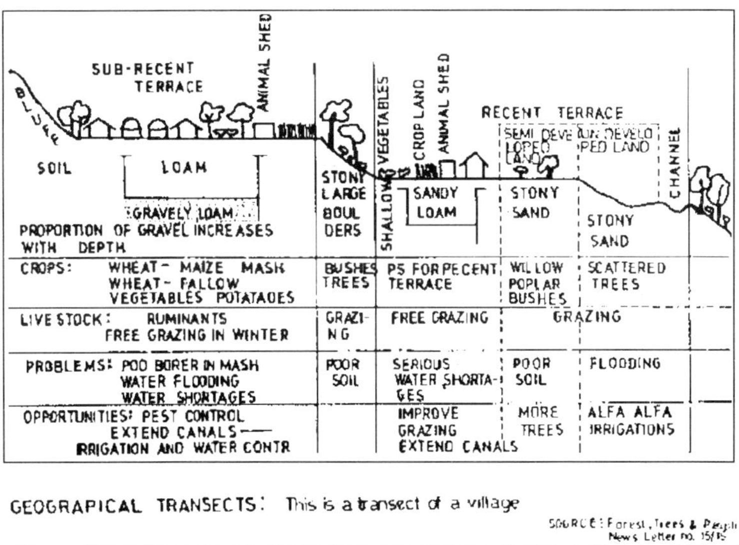

Fig. 5.3: Geograpical Transects.

Source: Forest, Trees and People, *Newsletter*, Number 15/16.

Table 5.6: Content Flow and Training Methodology

Sl. No.	*Content*	*Training Methodology*	*Training Aids*	*Duration (in minutes)*
1.	Context Analysis of Village Development Analysis of Space	Step 1: Joint Walk or Geographical Transect Step 2: Social Mapping or Modelling	White paper, marker pens, flash cards, chalks, stones	45 minutes 30 minutes 45 minutes 25 Total: 145
2.	Energizing Game	Step 3: Breakthrough	None	15 minutes
3.	Context Analysis: Analysis of Time	Step 4: Historical Transect OR Time Line OR Oral History Step 5: Seasonality Analysis	White paper, marker pens, flash cards, chalks, stones	45 minutes 45 minutes 45 Total: 135
4.	Context Analysis: Analysis of Relationships and institutions	Step 8: Venn Diagramming Step 10: Card Matching Game	White paper, marker pens, flash cards, scissors, glue, seeds of different varieties or pebbles	45 minutes 45 minutes
5.	Context Analysis: Analysis of Priorities	Step 11: Scoring, ranking, and Matrix Ranking Step 12: Force field Analysis	White paper, marker pens, different coloured cards, scissors, glue	45 minutes 45 minutes Total: 90
6.	Synthesis by Trainer/Participants.	Step 13: Visual Method	Slides, posters, maps and charts prepared by the participants during the session	15 minutes

joint walks one or either direction. During the walk record all "elements" (trees, houses, fields, bushes, crops etc.) seen on the surface as you walk along. Discuss with the villagers detail of the soil types, uses, problem etc. Record these. An example of a Geographical Transect is at Fig. 5.3.

2. Analysis of Space: Draw a Social Map of the Village

In step 2 involve the participants and some villagers in drawing a social map. A social map depicts the social aspects of a locality like household, their social categories, literate/illiterate HH, schools, roads, hospitals etc. The participants prepare the map, complete with all the HH-wise details examples caste compositions, school aged children etc. The HH on the map are also numbered. The procedure for facilitating a mapping exercise is at chapter 4. The facilitator then leads a discussion about the features of the map by asking probing questions, like:

- What is the condition of the houses?
- What is the state of the health of the villagers?
- How many people are literate?
- Is the social infrastructure in the village enough and in good shape?
- For each aspect and HH shown on the map, the problems and opportunities along with the role of the village in that context are discussed. Ask the participants to discuss the role of the Village Level Institutions, elected or traditional with regard to each item shown on the map. Some of these could be:
  - Housing,
  - Literacy,
  - Primary Education,
  - Health,
  - Immunization,
  - Maintenance of natural resources, and
  - Maintenance of roads.

Example of social map is shown in Figure 5.4 below:

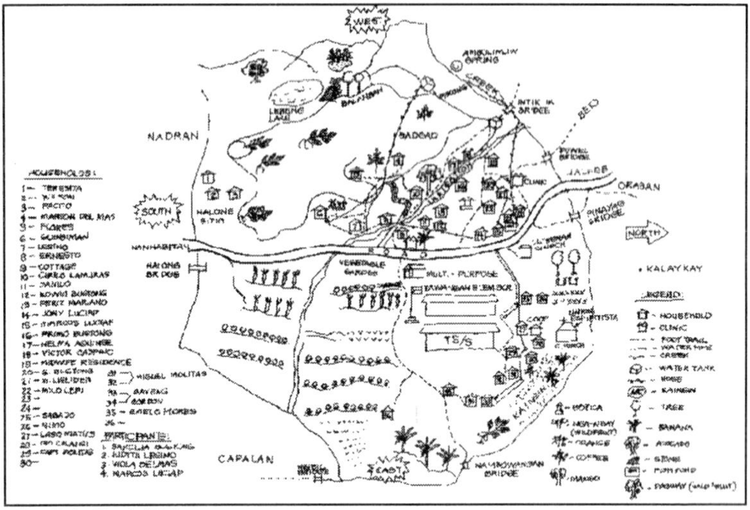

Fig. 5.4: Social Map.

3. Play Breakthrough and Energizing Game

In step 3, play the Breakthrough Game with the participants as follows:

3.1 This game may be used to energize the participants and also illustrate the importance of co-ordination and communication.

3.2 Divide the participants into two groups (Group A and Group B) of equal size and have them stand in two lines facing each other, about two meters apart.

3.3 Group A is asked to breakthrough Group B. No one is allowed to talk.

3.4 When the breakthrough occurs the one group I told they have five to ten minutes to plan a second breakthrough the other group is told that they have the same amount of time to organize a defence.

3.5 Repeat the attempt.

3.6 Ask the participants to reflect upon the differences between the two breakthroughs. The first breakthrough usually occurs early. The second is more difficult. Ask the participants to reflect upon the importance of coordination and communication, and what may be achieved as a group than as a set of individuals. Hint that for Group B, defending their group was easier because they coordinated their efforts. Group A similarly found organizing the breakthrough easier, though they may not have succeeded.

4. Analysis of Time: Draw a timeline to trace the development of the area being planned for

In Step 4, involve the participants in drawing a timeline. The steps in doing the timeline are described below:

4.1 Identify an elderly person and request her to talk about the history of her village and initiate a discussion about the village. This can be done with a group of villagers also.

4.2 Some suggested key questions could be as under:

- When was`the village established?
- What are the important events in the History of the villagc?
- What major changes took place?
- What are the reasons for these changes?
- How have these changes affected the community?

4.3 Ask one of the participants to note down the major events briefly on cards in bold letters as the group or the participants narrate the events occurrences. If the participants are unable to do so, one of the facilitators can help.

4.4 Once the participants feel that the list of events is more or less complete, ask them to keep the cards in chronological order—the earlier events on the top or the later events lower down. Request them to read out the events and ask them whether they are happy with the order or if they would like to modify it. Also ask the participants to add events etc. if they wished too.

4.5 Now, request the participants to associate years/dates etc. with the events.

4.6 Add years to the left side of the events. Failure of memory and not using their system of calendar may hinder the process of the participants getting the exact years. Use best judgement to arrive at the years.

4.7 Now, initiate a discussion on the timeline to help the participant analyse and reflect on it. Interview the timeline by asking open ended questions to clarify doubts and to get an in-depth understanding about the evaluation of the village and any aspect of the village.

5. Analysis of Time Continued: Listen to the Oral History of the Village

In Step 5 participants listen to the "local people describe the trends in local conditions from a historical perspective. Such local trends are more or broad overview of selected issues comparing two periods, an old period and the current period". While the term seasonality or season is used the analysis could be in terms of seasons (winter, summer etc.) or months (in local parlance etc.) or in terms of weeks. A reflection on oral history may help the participants to analyse the factors that helped or hindered the development of the village and put the subsequent steps into perspective.

6. Analysis of Time (Continued): Do the Seasonality Analysis for the Village

In Step 6, the participants engage in drawing seasonal diagrams to show seasonal variations in availability of food, of employment, of income, of livelihood and problems. "Each season has a specific problem and local people have different strategies for "sourcing" their livelihood". While the term seasonality or the seasonal is used the analysis could be in terms of seasons (winter, summer) or months in local parlance) or in terms of weeks. The suggested steps for seasonal diagram are:

6.1 Explain the objective of the exercise to the participants.

6.2 Start discussions about the present season and the work they have been doing during the season with the villagers. Move to the present month and ask what other months are there facilitate so that participants/community write name of months on the cards in bold letters.

6.3 Ask them to identify a unique thing about each month one by one, which would remind them of the month. It can be a symbol or drawing. Encourage them to do it themselves. Facilitate so that the participants write or redraw the unique things on cards to represent season, months or weeks. This can be fun and adds to their involvement, even of the illiterate meaningfully. Mark cards bearing the unique things pertaining to different months or season or weeks on the end with names of the respective month or season or week respectively written.

6.4 Facilitate so that participants can draw a grid with chalk on the floor or on the ground. Use the pens and several flip charts joined together can also be made. In the grid ensure that participants have columns—one column for each month or season or week and one additional column for the items to be studied and as many as rows as the items you want to study. Keep the cards with names of the month or season or week and the corresponding visuals or symbols horizontally as the first row or the column heads.

6.5 Now, on the first column encourage participants to take the items whose seasonal variations they intend exploring. Ask the participants to show the condition, amount or state of the item, in month or season or week, when the aspect or activity is on. As them to represent the magnitude of the activity using different number of leaves, seeds or sticks of different sizes or lines. For instance one may be interested, say, in the availability of wage labour during various months. Seeds can be used to indicate the number of days of employment in different months. Different kind of seeds may be used to show the availability of employment for men and women separately. Similarly, sticks of different sizes can be used to indicate the quantity of rainfall during each of the months. After completing one aspect or activity move to another, until all of them are similarly covered.

6.6 Give the participants the opportunity to think on whether they would like to take up any other aspect or activity or make any modifications to the diagram. If they wish to facilitate changes.

6.7 Interview the diagram, i.e. ask them question on aspects you are not clear. Use the six helps—why, what, where, when, whom and how to interview the seasonality diagram.

6.8 Facilitate a discussion and analysis among the participants and others present. The points of discussion could include:

- Major findings and learning.
- Implications of the findings.
- Recommendations and action points.

6.9 Copy the diagram on a flip chart with legends and detail of the participants, facilitators, locality, date etc. if it is drawn on the ground or floor.

6.10 Triangulate the findings of the seasonality diagram with other key informants or groups or key performants. Examples of seasonality diagrams are at figures 5.5(a) and 5.5(b).

Items	Jan-Feb	Mar-Apr	May-Jun	Jul-Aug	Sep-Oct	Nov-Dec
Light meals	■■■	■	-	-	-	■
Begging	■■■	■	-	-	-	■
Migration	■■■ ■■■	■■	■■	■	-	-
Unemployment	■■■ ■■■	■	-	■■	■■	■
Income	-	-	■■■	■■■	■■■ ■■■	■■■■ ■
Disease	-	■■■	■■■ ■	■■■	■	-
Rainfall	-	■■■ ■	-	-	■■	■■■

Fig. 5.5(a): Seasonality Diagrams.

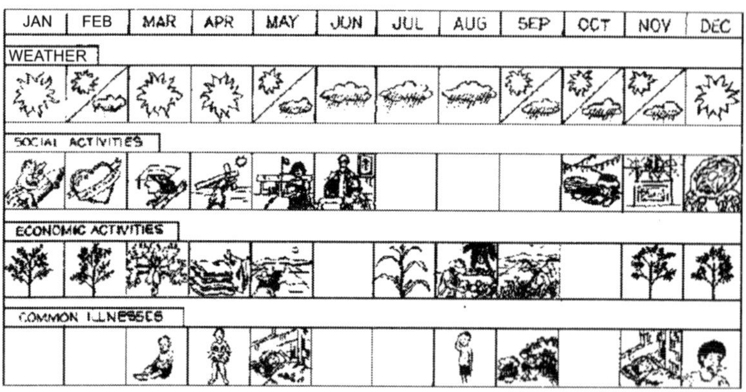

Fig. 5.5(b): Seasonality Diagrams.

7. Analysis of Relationship: Do the Venn Diagramming for Depicting the Relationship with Different Institutions/Individuals Interfacing with the Village

In Step 7 the participants draw a Venn diagram also called "Chapatti Diagram" for studying the relationship of the village with the institutions/individuals with which interfaces. The suggested steps in the process of doing the diagram are as follows:

7.1 Explain the purpose of the carrying out Venn Diagramming to the participants. It is the diagram depicting two variables (relationships) between the village on the one part and the institutions and individuals on the other part.

7.2 Encourage participants to list various institutions or individuals which the village interacts with, such as the Police Station, Block Development Officer etc.

7.3 Participants are facilitated to write and/or depict each institutions or individuals on small cards. Visual depiction with the help of symbols or pictures becomes necessary if there are non-literate participants.

7.4 Facilitate a process when the participants place the cards in a descending order according to the perceived importance of the individuals or institutions from the point of view of the village. It is wise to help participants arrive at a common understanding of what they mean by importance. Once the cards are arranged in an ascending or descending order of importance, ask the participants whether they agree or would like to make changes in order of importance. Encourage them to think and make changes, if they consider changes are required.

7.5 The participants may then assign stones, leaves or even paper circles of different sizes to the institutions or individuals in such a way that bigger the stone, leaf or paper circle, the greater is the importance of the institution or individual for the village. Write or depict the individuals or institutions on the paper circle and in case of stones or leaves, name of the institution or individual is written on slips of the paper and keep beneath the stone or leave which represent it. Make sure the name of the institution is visible. Thus, the size of the stone, leaf or paper circle denotes the importance of the institutions or individuals to the village. Two institutions or individuals could be of same importance. In such a case stones, leaves or paper circles of same size could represent them.

7.6 Ask the participants to make a small circle on the middle of a chart paper or on the ground, or on the floor representing the village. The participants now place the stones or leaves or paper circles in such a way on the chart paper or on the ground or on the floor around the Village so that those institutions or individuals which are more accessible to the village are kept close, while those which are less accessible are kept further away from the circles representing the village. Thus, the distance of a paper circle or stone or leaf (representing an institution/individual) from the central circle (the village) denotes its degree of accessibility to the village. Greater the distance lower is the accessibility. There is an inverse relationship shown between distance and accessibility.

7.7 Once all the stones, leaves or paper circles of different sizes are placed around the small circle representing the village, discuss the placement and if the participants want to make any changes either of the size of the stone, leaves or paper circles or of the distance at which they are kept from the village, encourage them to do so.

7.8 Remind the participants that the distance in a Venn diagram is not geographical distancc. It is thc mcntal or social distance.

7.9 In case, certain institutions or individual are equally accessible to the village or efficient or efficacious, they could be placed at the equal distance from the village.

7.10. It may be reiterated that the participants can use the distance of the stones, leave or the paper circles representing the institutions from the central circle (the village) to denote the efficiency, usefulness, honesty or whatever attributes they wish to or are necessary for the analysis.

7.11 Discuss why they have assigned different sizes to different institutions and why they have placed the cards at different distances from the circle denoting the Village in such a manner.

7.12 Interview the Venn Diagram using the six helper: why, what, where, whom, when and how.

8. Analysis of Relationships: Draw the Relational Matrices for the different institutions/individuals interfacing with the village

In Step 9 the participants draw the Relational Matrices for the different institutions/individuals interfacing the village. An example of Relational Matrices is given in Figure 5.9 as on pages 246-247.

The steps for the exercise are:

8.1 The participants are encouraged to write the names of the different institutions/individuals interfacing with the Village on flash cards, ensuring that only one name is written on one flash card. Then these cards are arranged and as items in the first columns of a matrix.

8.2 Tell the participants that they are encouraged to write all the different kinds of relationship that individuals/institutions can have with the village. These relationships could be like technical support, finance, maintenance of peace etc. These cards bearing the name of relationships are placed at the first row of matrix.

8.3 Now encourage the participants to ask whether there is direct or an indirect connection between the institution/individual at serial number 1 and its/her/his relationship with all the different relationships. It is possible that there exist no relationship.

8.4 If there is a direct connection between the two, write 'D' in the square common to them and if there is an indirect connection, write 'I' and if there is no connection put a cross.

8.5 Repeat the process for all the institutions/individuals occurring in column 1 in relation to all the relationships occurring in row 1.

8.6 Repeat the process for all the institutions/individuals in relation to the relationship 2.

8.7 Repeat the process for all the institutions/individuals have been pitted against all the relationships.

8.8 Remember always to ask the question whether particular institutions/individuals have a direct or indirect or no relation with the relationship. Never do it other way around.

8.9 Now, ask the participants to count the number of direct or indirect connection that each institution/individual has with the relationships.

8.10 Ask the participants to record each count at the end of the each row.

8.11 One may give the score of two for each direct connection, a score of 1 for each indirect connection and 0 for no connection. Then work out a total score for each institution/individual.

8.12 The institutions/individuals are now ranked according to the number of direct/indirect connections or the scores obtained.

8.13 Interview the institutional diagram with the six helpers—Why, what, when, whom, where and how.

9. Analysis of Institutions: Do the Venn Diagramming for depicting the different institutions/individuals interfacing with the village.

In Step 9, the participants draw a modified Venn diagram as in Step 7 earlier, for studying the institutional linkages of different institutions/ individuals with the village.

9.1 In studying relationship, like in Step 7, the participants assign again stones or leaves, paper circles of different sizes to different institutions.

9.2 Those institutions which are closely related to each other are to be placed near each other.

9.3 These institutions which are overlapping interest are represented by stones, leaves or paper circles, kept overlapping each other.

9.4 Encourage participants to make any change they want to make either about the size of circles or of their positions.

9.5 Interview the modified Venn diagram using the six helpers—why, what, when, whom, where and how.

9.6 Discuss with the participants the implications of the relationships. For instance, if the intuitions have considerable overlap, then there is congruity of interest, objectives, mission, vision and values of the institutions, which in-turn show cohesion.

10. Analysis of Institutions (Continued): Do the Force Field Analysis for Institutions

In Step 10, the rationale for conducting the force field analysis (FFA) is to ascertain the institutions which impart positive and negative forces on the development of the village respectively. The steps for doing the FFA have been described earlier in session 6 and are reproduced below:

10.1 Explain the objectives of the exercise to the participants, *viz.*, of finding institutions which impart positive and negative forces on the village.

10.2 Please clarify that force is an energy which acting on a body is capable of or trends to change its position. Example of force could be the gravitational force, which pulls down objects to the earth. Also, distinguish between positive and negative forces.

10.3 Keep a large sheet of paper or a flip chart with the present state of the village written or depicted on it, in front of the participants and ask them to concentrate on the same. A horizontal live across the flip chart or floor could depict the present condition. The present condition of the village may also be depicted on the floor or ground with chalk/coloured powder etc. Ask the participants to visualize the village in a state of temporary equilibrium by two sets of institutions releasing opposing forces, one favour in improvement (positive forces) and the other inhibiting them (negative forces). Ask participants to list one set of institutions first followed by other.

10.4 Facilitate that participants write down or depict the institutions identified on flash cards in bold letters. Clarify that if an institution seems to be made of multiple elements, each element should be listed separately as institutions. Different colour cards can be used for positive and negative forces, if the facilitators so desires.

10.5 Spread the cards with institutions releasing negative forces below the line and those releasing positive forces above the line.

10.6 Ask them to take a look at the cards and see if they would like to make any change in their position.

10.7 Next the participants may be facilitated to assign weights to each of the institution denoting the strength of the forces released. This can be done in two ways. One, the participants can use onc of the scoring methods or keep each force card at varying distance from the "present status line" in such a way that the distance denote the strength of the force imparted by the institutions. Greater the distance, higher is the perceived strength of the force of the problem.

10.8 Check with the participants whether they are satisfied with the diagram and relative strength of the forces as depicted or would they like to make any modifications.

10.9 Once they are satisfied with the diagram, ask them to discuss on how they can bring changes in the situation. Which of the institutions releasing positive force reinforced and which institutions releasing negative forces can be reformed, abolished or neutralized.

10.10 Interview the force field analysis using the six helpers: why, what, where, whom, when and how.

10.11 An example of a Force Field Analysis is at Figure 5.6.

11. Visual Method for Synthesizing What We have Learnt from this Session

In step 11, the synthesis of the learning points is done by the facilitator with the help of participants. The facilitator should focus on the key elements of the session and help the participants to recall the inputs.

Session 4—Micro-Level Planning

In Session 4 several tools for problem identification have been discussed. This Session is like a "tools box". The Facilitator while facilitating a Gram Panchayat Development Plan need not use all the tools to identify problems and must exercise her/his best judgement in selecting the appropriate tools. Remember the more tools are used, more resources, especially communities' time, will be required.

Session Theme: Problem Identification and Prioritization.
Duration: One half day or at the discretion of the facilitator.
Venue: Village Locale.

Session Objective:

1. To enable the participants to comprehend and prioritize the Problems of the village in Gram Panchayat Development Planning for Convergence for Village Development.
2. To impart the functional skills required for engaging in micro-level planning to the participants to overcome the problem.

Expected Learning Outcomes

- The participants acquire functional skills for using PLA methods of identification of problems of village development.
- They learn about prioritizing development problems using the acquired skills.

Table 5.7: Content Flow and Training Methodology

Sl. No.	*Content*	*Training Methodology*	*Training Aids*	*Duration (in minutes)*
(1)	(2)	(3)	(4)	(5)
1.	Energizing Game	Step 1: Dragon	None	15 minutes
2.	Problem Identification	Step 2: Semi-Structured Interviews Step 3: Key Informant Interviews Step 4: Delphi Method	White paper, flash cards, marker pens, chart paper	45 minutes 45 minutes 45 minutes

(*Contd.*)

(1)	(2)	(3)	(4)	(5)
3.	Problem Identification	Step 5: Scoring and Ranking Step 6: Matrix Scoring	White paper, seeds, marker pens	45 minutes 45 minutes
4.	Synthesis by Trainer/ Participant(s)	Step 7: Visual Method	Notes, charts and matrices created by the participants	15 minutes

THE METHODOLOGICAL STEPS FOR PRACTICAL EXERCISES IN SESSION 4

1. Play an Energizing Game

In step 1 all the participants play "Dragon" an active game as follows:

1.1 The objective of the game is to energize the group before they begin the next phase of micro-level planning.

1.2 Find an open space outside and everyone to stand there.

1.3 Ask the group to form a line or a dragon and ask participants to run and concurrently ask the front of the line to catch its tail. Then stop the dragon, turn the participants to face the other direction, and have the tail then catch head.

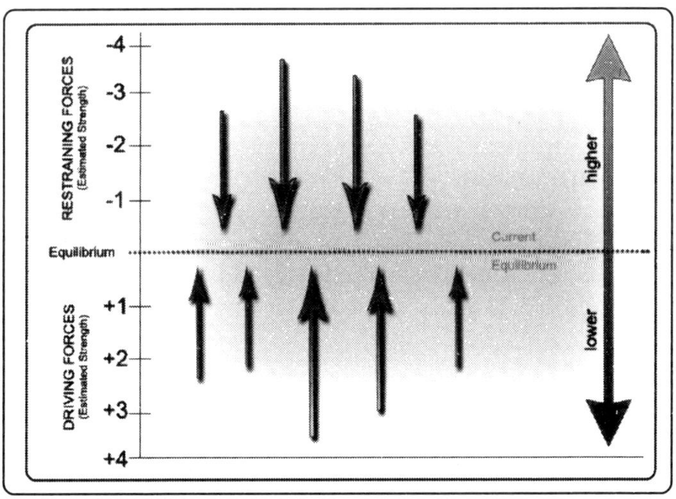

Fig. 5.6: Force Field Analysis.

1.4 This will result in a lot of smiling and laughing. This provides only a brief and energizing break for the participants during the training. This fact should be told to the participants otherwise they would be expecting an underlying moral theme from the whole exercise.

2. Hold Semi-Structured Interviews of Some Villagers

In Step 2, the facilitator facilitates the participants in holding, Semi-Structured Interviews of some of the villagers. The facilitator should take care to include all sections from the village community. A series of interviews involving different groups of respondents may be held. These interviews may be conducted by different sub-groups from among the participants. The focus of the interview is to explore the development problems faced by the villagers, their sources and impact, the coping strategies, restraints and opportunities. There can be pre-determined set of questions for this kind of interview. The questions asked are open ended, probing and flexible. "For the local community semi-structured interview is conducted in an informal manner in a relaxed setting where queries emerge according to the responses received. It is a combination of outsiders initiating the interview followed by discussion by the local people on the topic concerned".

2.1 The semi-structured interviews are to be conducted in the context of the Analysis discussed in session 15. That is, the semi-structured interviews are to be conducted to identify the problems based on analysis of space, of time, of institution, of relationship and of priorities/preferences.

2.2 The problem identified are then recorded on cards, one problem is on one card.

2.3 Semi-structured interviews are to be held using open ended questions. Never use leading questions or directive questions or closed ended questions. Examples of open ended, leading questions, directive questions and closed ended questions are given below:

> Open ended question: *What is the prospect of harvest this year?*
>
> Closed ended question: *The prospects of harvest are this year is bad. Yes/No?*
>
> Directive questions: *Should you not say that the prospect of harvest is very good this Year?*

Leading questions: *The prospect of a good harvest this year is very good. Isn't so?*

2.4 The facilitator and the participants have to listen carefully to all the discussions being held and take notes about the problems being faced by the villagers and other relevant details.

2.5 While recording the outcomes of a semi-structured interview, the participants should distinguish between what are facts, what are opinions, what are rumours and what is hearsay.

3. Hold Interviews of Key Informants

In Step 3, the facilitator facilitates the participants to identify some key informants from among the villagers and then interviewing them. These key informants may include the Village Level Leader, the Self-Help Group leader, some extension workers etc. The focus of the interview is the same as in step 2; the interviewers take the notes of all that is discussed.

3.1 The Steps followed in step 2 has also to be followed in step 3.

3.2 If the findings of Semi-structured interview with key informants generate new issues, as distinct from findings generated through semi-structured interview with group(s), the difference has to be reconciled and/or reasons for the difference probed.

4. Use the Delphi Method to Form Problem Clusters

After the interviews are over, then in Step 4, the facilitator and the sub-groups of the participants can each make a brief presentation about the development problem faced by the villagers and compare their notes. The problems are made into clusters depending upon their affinity using the Delphi method.

4.1 Use the information from the interviews to generate a set of village-level development problems.

4.2 Request volunteers to write each problem on a card (one on one card).

4.3 The cards/papers then placed upon the ground or pinned upon the wall and groups according to concept areas. One some or all the participants can do either of these exercises. Cards showing the same problems are removed or bunched together.

4.4 The participants must agree on the criteria for grouping or clustering, since this provides the theme areas.

4.5 Now, discuss each theme with participants.

5. Now, Score and Rank the Problem Clusters

In Step 5 use the Scoring and Ranking Methods to prioritize the problem clusters. The steps are given below:

5.1 Ask the participants to write down each problem clusters on a flash card, recording only one problem on one card so that participants arrange the cards in one column.

5.2 Facilitate participants to identify the most important problem, based upon their discussions with village community.

5.3 If you are using free scoring ask the participants to place a large volume seeds opposite the most important problem.

5.4 Then ask the participants to identify the next important problem. Encourage the participants to place some seeds against this problem, but lesser in quantity than placed against the most important problem.

5.5 Proceed in this fashion, placing lesser and lesser quantities of seeds against the other problems according to the gravity of the problem diminishes, until all the problems have been scored.

5.6 Now request the participants to rank the problem. The problem which secured the largest quantity of seeds is the problem with the highest rank. The problem which gets the smallest quantity of seeds against it is the lowest in rank. (See Figures 5.7 and 5.8 of Scoring and Ranking).

6. Use the Matrix Scoring Method is Prioritize the Problem Clusters

In Step 6 we use the Matrix Scoring Method to compare the different kinds of development problems that have been scored and ranked in the previous step. The essential steps are reproduced below:

6.1 Explain clearly the purpose of the exercise to the participants, namely, of finding out their priorities and the criteria against which they have expressed their priorities.

6.2 Initiate a discussion about the clusters of the development problems that have been scored and ranked in the previous step.

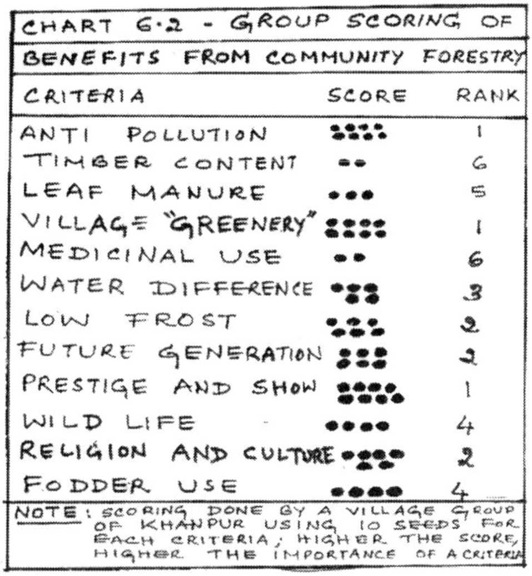

Fig. 5.7: Group Scoring of Benefits from Community Forestry.

6.3 The next step is to facilitate a process which helps the participants to arrive at the criteria which have been used in the scoring and ranking process. Some practitioners find that one of the simplest way to determine the criteria is to do a quick comparison between the pairs of problems discussed in the previous step. Arrive at the reasons why the participants find that a particular problem is more serious than the other. These reasons are actually nothing but the criteria. Alternatively a straight forward education of the criteria against which priorities have been expressed can also lead to good results.

6.4 Ensure that the criteria are all positive and precise. Use of positive and negative criteria in the same exercise can be confusing. Write one criteria on one card.

6.5 Draw up a matrix with the problems appearing as the first column and criteria appearing as the first row. One can do it the other way round also. However, keep in mind that the comparisons are made criterion-wise and not problem-wise. It means you take up a criterion and then do scoring for all the problems against that criterion. Once one criterion is over, move to the next, do the scoring for all the problems and record them until all criterion are covered for each of the problems.

Ranking of Institutions by Village Group, Karambeli, Penn Taluka, District Raigad

Serial Number	Name of the Institution	Stone Placed	Rank
1	Local NGO	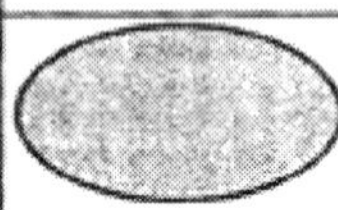	I
2	Zilla Parishad Office	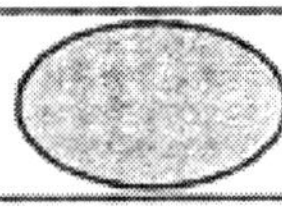	II
3	Panchayat Office		III
4	Gram Panchayat		V
5	Talati Office		IV
6	Tribal Welfare Office (Adibasi Office)		VII
7	Tahsildar's Office (Local Revenue Office)		VI
8	Samaj Kalyan (Social Welfare) Office		X
9	Jangal Samiti (Forest Society)		XI
10	Police Station		VIII
11	Credit Cooperative Society		IX

Notes: Village Analysts: Maruti Pawar, Ram, Pai Ram Pawar, Sonoo Pawar, Rama Wadmore of village Karambelli, on 13-2-2001. Facilitated by Amitava Mukherjee.

Fig. 5.8: Ranking of Institutions by Village Group.

6.6 Now interview the matrix scoring using six helpers. Why, what, when, where, whom and how.

7. Visual Method for Synthesizing what we have Learnt from this Session

In Step 7, the synthesis of the learning points is done by the facilitator with the help of the participants. The facilitator should focus the synthesis on the prioritized problems and the fact this prioritization can be achieved through the use of participatory methods.

In Session 3 several tools for problem identification have been discussed. This Session is like a "tools box". The Facilitator while facilitating a Micro-Level Plan need not use all the tools to identify problems and must exercise her/his best judgement in selecting the appropriate tools. Remember the more tools are used, more resources, especially communities' time, will be required.

Session 5—Gram Panchayat Development Plan—Planning for Convergence

Session Theme: *Solution Identification and Prioritization.*
Duration: One half day or at the discretion of the facilitator.
Venue: *Village Locale.*

Session Objective

1. To enable the finding solutions to the problems of the village
2. To impart the functional skills required for finding solutions and prioritizing them, in micro-level planning to the participants.

Expected Learning Outcomes

- The participants acquire functional skills for using PLA methods in finding solutions to problems for micro-level planning development.
- They can adopt a problem-solving approach for identifying solutions for development problems using the acquired skills.

THE METHODOLOGICAL STEPS FOR PRACTICAL EXERCISES IN SESSION 5

1. Use the Method for the Reversal of the Problem

In Step 1:

1.1 The problems identified are all written down by the participants are on flash cards and placed on the floor/ground as one column. The problems are all in the form of negative statements.

1.2 Now, encourage the participants to write on card the opposite of the problem. For instance if the problem identified and prioritized by the community is "Lack of Education Facilities for the Girl Children" then the opposite of the problem will be providing facilities for Girl Children.

1.3 Once all the opposites of the problems are worked out and written on cards they (opposites) are placed alongside the "problem cards". Once the process is completed there will be two columns. One of the problems and the second of the "opposites", on separate cards. These cards are placed alongside the respective "opposites". Now, there will be three columns. The column specifying the "opposite" is the column of solutions. The following Table 5.8 illustrates the point.

1.4 Now, if there is more than one problem and there is more than one solution, we may need to prioritize the same. The facilitator should encourage the people to rank or score the problems and/or the solutions using the method of discussed earlier.

1.5 The participants now have a list of prioritized solutions of problems.

2. Hold Semi-structured Interviews of Some Villagers

In Step 2 the facilitator can alternatively facilitate the participants in holding Semi-structured interviews of some of the villagers. The facilitator should once again take care to include all sections of village community. A series of interviews involving different groups of respondents are conducted by different sub-groups amongst the participants. The focus of the semi-structured interviews to explore the solutions or development interventions to the development problems which have been identified in the previous session.

Table 5.8: Content Flow and Training Methodology

Sl. No.	*Content*	*Training Methodology*	*Training Aids*	*Duration (in minutes)*
1.	Finding the Objectives: Reversal of the Problem	Step 1: Locating the objectives	Posters, flip charts, markers etc.	15 minutes
2.	Finding Solutions or Development Interventions	Step 2: Semi-Structured Step 3: Group Discussions Step 4: Delphi Method	White paper, pens, flash cards, marker pens	45 minutes 45 minutes 45 minutes **Total: 150**
3.	Prioritization of Solutions or Development Interventions	Step 5: Listing Step 6: Problem-Activity Matrix	White paper, marker pens	15 minutes 45 minutes **Total: 60**
4.	Setting up Activities: The Prioritized Solutions provide the Activities	Step 7: Reorienting Activity and Aggregating Wherever necessary	Do	45 minutes
5.	Injecting Gender Equity & Social Justice	Step 8: Delphi Method Step 9: Relational Matrix		45 minutes
6.	Synthesis by Trainer/ Participants.	Step 9: Visual Method	Notes, charts and matrices created by the participants	15 minutes

2.1 The facilitator and the participants have to listen carefully to all the discussions being held and take notes about the solutions or development interventions for the problems suggested by the villagers and other relevant details.

2.2 See section 2.1 to 2.5 of session 16 follow the same steps.

2.3 The same set of activities can also be done in focused group discussion.

3. Use the Delphi Method to Cluster the Solutions for Development Interventions

After the interviews are over, then in step 3, the facilitator and the sub-group of the participants can each make a brief presentation about the solutions or development interventions suggested by the villagers and compare their notes. The solutions are clustered depending upon their affinity using the Delphi Method. The steps are:

3.1 Use the information from the interview to generate the solutions to the development problems.

3.2 Request volunteers to write each solution on a card or a piece of paper (one solution in one paper/card).

3.3 The card or a piece of paper then placed upon the ground or pinned on the wall and grouped according to concept areas.

3.4 The participants must agree on the criteria for grouping or clustering, since this provides the theme areas.

3.5 Now, discuss each theme area with the participants.

4. Now, List the Solutions or the Development Interventions

In Step 4, list the main solutions that flow from the previous step.

5. Use the Problem Activity Matrix Method to Determine the Relationship between the Solutions and the Problems

In step 5, we use the Problem Activity Matrix to determine the relationship which the different solutions or development interventions have with the problems that have been identified, scored and ranked in the previous session. The following steps are suggested for this exercise:

5.1 Ask the participants to write the different identified problems on Flash Cards. Place the flash cards as items in the first column of a Matrix.

5.2 Ask the participants to write the planned development interventions on flash cards place this set of flash cards as items in the first row of the matrix.

Table 5.9: Solutions or the Development Intervenations

Problem	*Opposites*	*Solutions*
Unemployment	Employment for all	(i) Providing employment for all. (ii) Creating off-farm employment. (iii) Making credit available.
Illiteracy amongst girls	Literacy amongst girls	Providing education for girls.
Lack of drinking water in the village	Drinking water available in village	(i) Providing drinking water by digging wells, (ii) Ensuring water supply by running water trains, and (iii) Fitting a diesel pump in a river.

5.3 Now, encourage the participants to ask whether there is a direct or an indirect connection between problem number 1 and development intervention number 1. It is possible that there is no connection between the intervention and the problem.

5.4 If there is a direct connection between the two, write D in the square common to them, if there is an indirect connection, write "I" and if there is no connection, put a cross.

5.5 Repeat the process for all the development activities in relation to problem no. 1.

5.6 Repeat the process for all the development activities in relation to problem no. 2.

5.7 Repeat the process for till all the planned activities have been pitted against all the identified problems.

5.8 Remember to always ask the question whether a particular activity has a direct or indirect or no relationship with the problems. Never do it the other way around.

5.9 Now, ask the participants to count the number of direct and indirect connection that each activity has with the problems.

5.10 Ask the participants to record each count at the bottom of each column.

5.11 One may give a score of 2 for each direct connection, a score of 1 for each indirect connection and zero for no connection. Then work out a total score for each activity.

5.12 The activities are now ranked according to the number of direct/indirect connections or the scores obtained. This ranked set of activities now become action points.

An example of a set of Relational Matrices is in Figure 5.9 below:

Matrix I: Problem Matrix

Problem Code	*1*	*2*	*3*	*4*	*5*	*6*	*7*
1	—	✓	✓	✓	✓	✓	✓
2	✓	—	✓	✓	✓	✓	X
3	✓	✓	—	✓	X	X	X
4	✓	✓	—	—	X		X
5	✓	✓	X	X	—	✓	✓
6	✓	X	X	X	✓	—	X
7	✓	X	X	X	✓	X	—
Number of Inter-Connections	6	5	3	3	4	4	2

Problem are indicated by their problem code.

Source: Based on Ralph Diaz, Relational Matrix Technique (Nagoya: UN Centre for Regional Development, 1978 modified).

Matrix II : Cause-Effect Problem Matrix

Problem Code	*1*	*2*	*3*	*4*	*5*	*6*	*7*	*Cause Connections*
1	—	CE	E	CE	C	C	C	5
2	CE	—	E	E	E	C	C	2
3	C	C	—	C	0	0	0	3
4	CE	C	E	—	0	C	0	3
5	E	C	0	0	—	E	E	1
6	E	E	0	0	C	—	0	1
7	E	0	0	0	C	0	—	1
Effect Connections	5	2	3	2	1	1	1	

Source: Same as Matrix –I.

Projects	*Project Code*
Off-season Employment	A
Supply of HYV seeds, fertilizers etc.	B
Agricultural Extension Service	C
Lift Irrigation	D
Vegetable Cultivation	E
Toilet Construction	F
Drinking Water	G
Health Education	H

Matrix III: Problem – Project Matrix Problem Code

Project Code	*1*	*2*	*3*	*4*	*5*	*6*	*7*
A	D	—	—	—	I	I	—
B	I	D	—	D	I	I	—
C	I	D	—	D	I	I	—
D	I	I	D	I	I	I	—
E	D	—	—	—	I	D	I
F	—	—	—	—	I	—	D
G	—	—	—	—	I	I	D
H	I	—	—	—	I	D	D

Matrix IV: Project-Matrix

Project	*A*	*B*	*C*	*D*	*E*	*F*	*G*	*H*
A	—	—	—	X	—	X	—	—
B	—	—	X	X	—	—	—	—
C	—	X	—	X	—	—	—	—
D	X	X	X	—	—	—	—	—
E	—	—	X	—	—	—	—	X
F	X	—	—	—	—	—	—	X
G	—	—	—	—	—	—	—	X
H	—	—	—	—	X	X	X	—

Fig. 5.9: Matrix I–IV.

6. Draw a Relational Matrix of the Issues Regarding Gender and the Prioritized Activities

In Step 6 the participants draw the relational matrices for the different gender issues and the activities. The step for the exercise are:

6.1 Ask the participants to write the issues on gender equity and social justice on flash cards and place them as item in the first column of the matrix.

6.2 Ask the participants to write the activities prioritized in step 6 as item in the first row.

6.3 Now encourage the participants to ask whether there is a direct or an indirect connection between the gender issue on gender equity and social justice number 1 and the activity 1 or there is no connection.

6.4 If there is a direct connection between the two write “D” in the square common to them; if there is an indirect connection write “I” and if there is no connection put a cross.

6.5 Repeat the process for the gender issues in relation to activity number 1.

6.6 Repeat the process for the gender issues in relation to activity number 2.

6.7 Repeat the process till all the gender issues have been pitted against all the activities.

6.8 Remember to always ask the question whether activity planned has a direct or indirect or no relationship with issue cluster. Never do it the other way around.

6.9 Now ask the participants to count the number of direct and indirect connections that each gender issue has with the activity.

6.10 Ask the participants to record each count at the bottom of each column.

6.11 If the activities addressed the activities, than the activities planned would meet the requirements for insuring gender equity.

6.12 In case issues are not repeated addressed by the activities, than additional step has to be taken to ensure that activities are generated to address the issue. For so doing all the steps for planning have to be repeated with specific focus on gender equity.

6.13 Repeat step 6 for issues relating to social justice.

7. Visual Method for Synthesizing What We have Learnt from the Session

In Step 7 the synthesis of learning points done by the facilitator with the help of participants Facilitator should refer to the visual created repeatedly.

Session 6—Gram Panchayat Development Planning

Session Theme: *Action Planning for the Micro-Level Planning*
Duration Flexible.
Venue: *Village Locale.*

Session Objective

1. To enable the participants to comprehend the process of stakeholder participation inaction planning for the village development.
2. To impart the functional skills required for engaging in action planning for the participants.

Expected Learning Outcomes

- The participants acquire functional skills for using PLA methods in action planning for village development.
- They have hands on understanding of how to develop an action plan from a tactical plan.

Table 5.10: Content Flow and Training Methodology

Sl. No.	*Content*	*Training Methodology*	*Training Aids*	*Duration (in minutes)*
1.	Injecting the time Element	Step 1	Flash cards, flip charts, marker, pens	60 minutes
2.	Determining the Allocations for projects	Step 2	Do	60 minutes
3.	Budgeting	Step 3		60 minutes
4.	Synthesis by Trainer/ Participants.	Step 4 Visual Method	Notes, charts and matrices created by the participants	15 minutes

The Methodological Steps for Session 5

1. Use the Methods for Determining Allocation of Projects

1.1 In Step 1 all the activities or development interventions are all written down by the participants on flash cards.

1.2 First, the participants identify the activities or development interventions which people themselves can execute without any external help, are classified as people's sector.

1.3 Second, the participants classify the activities or developmental interventions which can be executed with credit, like a flour mill or an oil mill. These are classified as the bank sector.

1.4 Third, participants then identify the activities and development interventions which can be carried out, by the funds from the government only, like building bridges or constructing roads. These activities are clubbed under another sector called the government sector.

1.5 Fourth, identify activities which can be carried out by mobilizing funds from the donor agencies like UNICEF or International non-government funding agencies like CARE, OXFEM and Ford Foundation. Such activities can be child immunization or supplementary nutrition; these activities may be classified as donor sector activities.

1.6 Fifth, now, let the participants identify activities which require contribution and combined effort of all, namely the people's bank, donor and government. These activities are clustered under the combined sector.

1.7 Finally, facilitate so that the participants identify the activities which cannot be executed by any of the above sectors. That is called residual sector.

1.8 Develop a table such as Figure 5.10 called activity sector classification matrix:

People Sector	*Bank Sector*	*Government Sector*	*Donor Sector*	*PRI Sector*	*Combined Sector*	*Residual Sector*
Activity-1p	Activity-1b	Activity-1g	Activity-1d	Activity-1pi	Activity-1c	Activity-1r
Activity-2p	Activity-2b	Activity-2g	Activity-2d	Activity-2pi	Activity-2c	Activity-2r
Activity-3p	Activity-3b	Activity-3g	Activity-3d	Activity-3pi	Activity-3c	Activity-3r
Activity-4p	Activity-4b	Activity-4g	Activity-4d	Activity-4pi	Activity-4c	Activity-4r
Activity-5p	Activity-5b	Activity-5g	Activity-5d	Activity-5pi	Activity-5c	Activity-5r
Activity-6p	Activity-6b	Activity- 6g	Activity-6d	Activity-6pi	Activity-6c	Activity-6r

Fig. 5.10: Sector Classification.

1.9 The participants attention should now be drawn to the importance of this activity sector matrix the locating sources of financing.

2. Converging

2.1 Draw the attention of the participants to different schemes of the Government.

2.2 Ask them to list all the Schemes that are currently operational.

2.3 Facilitate so that the Activities in column 3 of Figure 5.10 are written as first column of a Matrix.

2.4 Facilitate so that all the Schemes/programmes of the Government as listed in step 2.2 are written as first row of a Matrix.

2.5 Now, ask the participants to put a tick mark against an activity in the government sector which is covered by a Government Scheme/ Programme as in Figure 5.11.

Schemes/ → Programmes	*Pradhan Mantri Gram Sadak Yojana*	*Indira Aawas Yojana*	*MGNREGA*	*National Social Assistance Programme*	*Atal Pension Yojana*	*Deen Dayal Upadhyay Gram Jyoti Yojana*	*Pradhan Mantri Suraksha Bima Yojana*	*Swach Bharat Abhiyan*
Activities ↓								
Seasonal Employment			X					
Homes for Homeless		X						
Road Connectivity	X							
Old Age Assistance					X			
Insurance to needy							X	
Rural Electrification						X		
Toilets at households								X
etc.								
etc.								

Fig. 5.11: Government Schemes/Programmes.

2.6. This exercise will help find resources for different activities planned and ensure that relevant Government Schemes/Programmes are utilized and dovetailed.

2.7 A similar exercise could be carried out for the Bank Sector and the NGO Sector.

3. Methods for using Time Element

3.1 In Step 3 take a table as Figure 5.10 (The activity sector classification).

3.2 Facilitate so that the participants are able to identify activities in People's sector which "Must be done". Let the participants write **'M'** against these activities. The participants then locate the activities which "Should be done" and write **'S'** on cards showing these activities. Finally, the participants should identify the activities which "Could be done" and write **'C'** on cards bearing names of these activities.

3.3 The participants repeat the same process for the Bank Sector, Donor Sector, Combined Sector and Residual Sector Activities.

3.4 The participants generate the MSC Analysis Matrix as Figure 5.12.

3.5 The facilitator is to draw attention of the participants to the fact that "Must Do" activities are mandatory without which the interventions will collapse "Should activities" enhance the quality of the intervention and "Could Do" activities embellishes the interventions.

4. Rough Budgeting

In Step 4 budgets are prepared

4.1 For people sector, the costs of activities are estimated by the people themselves. The participants may facilitate the process.

4.2 For the bank sector budget the costs of interventions are calculated by the participants according to unit cost norm of the Bank.

4.3 For the Government sector, costs of activities are to be estimated by the participants according to norm specified by the Government. If the community feels that the costs are "under-estimated" a "difference of cost" charge may be prepared.

4.4 In case of activities covered by donor sector it may be necessary to arrive at cost estimated from different sources, People's

		First Year	Second Year	Third Year	Fourth Year	Fifth Year
People's Sector Activities	Must Do	Activity-1p	Activity-2p	Activity-3p	Activity-4p	Activity-5p
	Should Do	Activity-1p	Activity-2p	Activity-3p	Activity-4p	Activity-5p
	Could Do	Activity-1p	Activity-2p	Activity-3p	Activity-4p	Activity-5p
Bank Sector Activities	Must Do	Activity-1b	Activity-2b	Activity-3b	Activity-4b	Activity-5b
	Should Do	Activity-1b	Activity-2b	Activity-3b	Activity-4b	Activity-5b
	Could Do	Activity-1b	Activity-2b	Activity-3b	Activity-4b	Activity-5b
Government Sector Activities	Must Do	Activity-1g	Activity-2g	Activity-3g	Activity-4g	Activity-5g
	Should Do	Activity-1g	Activity-2g	Activity-3g	Activity-4g	Activity-5g
	Could Do	Activity-1g	Activity-2g	Activity-3g	Activity-4g	Activity-5g
Donor Sector Activities	Must Do	Activity-1d	Activity-2d	Activity-3d	Activity-4d	Activity-5d
	Should Do	Activity-1d	Activity-2d	Activity-3d	Activity-4d	Activity-5d
	Could Do	Activity-1d	Activity-2d	Activity-3d	Activity-4d	Activity-5d
PRI Sector Activities	Must Do	Activity-1pi	Activity-2pi	Activity-3pi	Activity-4pi	Activity-5pi
	Should Do	Activity-1pi	Activity-2pi	Activity-3pi	Activity-4pi	Activity-5pi
	Could Do	Activity-1pi	Activity-2pi	Activity-3pi	Activity-4pi	Activity-5pi
Combined Sector Activities	Must Do	Activity-1c	Activity-2c	Activity-3c	Activity-4c	Activity-5c
	Should Do	Activity-1c	Activity-2c	Activity-3c	Activity-4c	Activity-5c
	Could Do	Activity-1c	Activity-2c	Activity-3c	Activity-4c	Activity-5c
Residual Sector Activities	Must Do	Activity-1r	Activity-2r	Activity-3r	Activity-4r	Activity-5r
	Should Do	Activity-1r	Activity-2r	Activity-3r	Activity-4r	Activity-5r
	Could Do	Activity-1r	Activity-2r	Activity-3r	Activity-4r	Activity-5r
		1st Year	2nd Year	3rd Year	4th Year	5th Year
Total	Total Must*					
	Total Should**					
	Total Could***					
	Grand Total#					

Fig. 5.12: MSC Analysis Matrix.

estimate, Bank NABARD's unit costs/Government prescribed cost because Donors often do not have fixed costs.

4.5 Cost estimates for combined sector may also be arrived at following the clues provided in 4.4

4.6 The sub-totals are then added to arrive at the total.

4.7 Fig. 5.13 is a format for developing a rough budget estimate.

	Quantity Required	*Equipment*	*Infrastructure Required*	*Information Required*	*Person hours of labour required*	*Money required*	*Risks Involved*
Activity 1p							
Activity 2p							
Activity 3p							
Activity 4p							
Activity 5p							
Activity 6p							
Activity....							
Activity N-1p							
Activity Np							
Grand Total for the year							

Fig. 5.13: Simple Format for Rough Budget Estimate.

Note: 'P' stands for People sector. For other sectors, p will be substituted by 'g' or 'b' for government and bank sector respectively or whatever as the case may be.

5. Synthesis

In Step 5 the facilitator synthesizes micro-planning for convergence process through a visual or visuals. She/he may like to use Figs. 5.11, 5.12 and 5.13 to synthesize the learning on micro-planning for convergence.

Bibliogrpahy

Aabdul Aziz: "Democratic decentralization: experience of Karnataka". *Economic and Political Weekly*, XXXV(39): 3521-6, 2000

ADB: *Emerging Asia - changes and challenges*, Manila: Asian Development Bank, 1997.

Alok Tiwari: *Micro-Level Planning: for Socio-Economic Development*, Riga, VDM Verlag Dr. Müller, 2011.

Amitava Mukherjee (ed.): *Participatory rural appraisal methods and applications in rural planning*, New Delhi: Vikas Pub. House Pvt. Ltd., 1995.

Amitava Mukherjee, B.N.Yugandhar, D. Bandyopadhyay: "Convergence of Programmes by Empowering SHGs and Panchayati Raj Institutions", *Economic and Political Weekly*, Vol. 37, Issue No. 26, 29 June, (2002).

Amitava Mukherjee: *Participatory Rural Appraisal: Methods and Applications in Rural Planning (Essays in Honour of Robert Chambers)* 2nd Revised Edition, 2004.

Amrtha Kasturi Rangan, Sabita Kaushal and Swati Bansal: "'Blue' print for a model village", *India Water Portal*, 2014.https://www.indiawaterportal.org/articles/blue-print-model-village

Arnab Chatterjee: "Old Wine, New Bottles: Panchayats Planning in West Bengal", *Economic and Political Weekly*, 38(39), 2003

Baldev Singh: *Decentralisation, Panchayati Raj and District Planning*, New Delhi: Atlantic Publishers and Distributors Pvt. Ltd., 1996

Bernd Seiffert and Joseph Kodamanchaly: *Guidelines for Participatory Village Planning, for the National Programme, for Food Security and Poverty Reduction*, FAO, Cambodia (2005).

Bibek Debroy and P.D. Kaushik. (eds.): *Emerging Rural Development through Panchayats*. New Delhi: Academic Foundation, 2004.

D. Narayana: "Participation of the poor and excluded in local governance: The Indian decentralisation experience" in Vaidyanathan, A. & Krishna, K.L (Ed.), *Institutions and Markets in India's Development: Essays for K.N. Raj*, (pp. 360-393). New Delhi: Oxford University Press, 2007.

Down to Earth: "Promoting integrated village planning", *Down to Earth*, New Delhi: 2019 https://www.downtoearth.org.in/classroom/promoting-integrated-village-planning-31848.

Economic and Political Weekly, 37(19): 1850-51.

Gary Paul Green: *Handbook of Rural Development, University of Wisconsin-Madison,* Glasgow: Edward Edgar, 2013.

Government of Andhra Pradesh: *Smart Cities, Smart Wards*, Hyderabad: NRHM, 2015.

Government of India : *Report of the Task Force on Devolution of Powers & Functions Upon Panchayati Raj Institutions,* New Delhi, Ministry of Rural Development and Panchayati Raj Development, 2001.

Government of Haryana: *Guidelines for the preparation of Gram Panchayat Development Plan, HAMARI YOJANA – HAMARA VIKAS*, Development and Panchayats Department, Government of Haryana, Chandigarh (undated).

Government of India: *Guidelines for Preparation of Gram Panchayat Development Plans*, New Delhi: Ministry of Panchayai Raj, 2011.

Government of India: *Governance in GPs, Active Panchayat, Book-III,* New Delhi: Ministry of Panchayati Raj, 2014.

Government of India: *The State of Panchayats*: *2007-08*, Vol. 1, New Delhi: Ministry of Panchayati Raj. pp. 135-163, 2008.

Government of India: *Annual Report 2005–2006,* New Delhi: Ministry of Panchayati Raj, 2006.

Government of India: *Constitution (Seventy Third) Amendment Act*, New Delhi: Government of India, 1992.

Government of India: *Planning at the Grassroots Level : An Action Programme for the Eleventh Five-Year Plan,* New Delhi: Planning Commission, 2007.

Government of India: *Manual for Integrated District Planning,* New Delhi: Planning Commission, 2008.

Government of India: *National Capability Building, Framework*, New Delhi: Ministry of Panchayati Raj, Government of India, 2014.

Government of India: *Guidelines for Saansad Adarsh Gram Yojana*, New Delhi: Ministry of Rural Development, 2014.

Government of India: *National Human Development Report*, New Delhi: Planning Commission, 2002.

Government of India: *Report of Committee on plan projects: study team.* (Chairman: Balwantrai, G. Mehta). New Delhi, Planning Commission, Government of India, 1957.

Government of India: *Report of the Committee on Panchayati Raj Institutions*, New Delhi, (Asoka Mehta Committee)

Government of India: *Report of the NITI Aayog to Restructure the Existing Scheme of the Ministry of Panchayati Raj as Rashtriya Gram Swaraj Abhiyan,* New Delhi: Ministry of Panchayati Raj, 2017.

Government of India: *Report of the Team for the Study of Community Projects and, National Extension Service* (Balwantrai Mehta Committee), 1959.

Government of India: *Report of the Working Group on Block Level Planning,* New Delhi: Planning Commission.

H. Hegde: "Local self-government in Karnataka: planning from below", in Malcolm Adiseshiah *et al.*, *Decentralized Planning and Panchayati Raj*. New Delhi, Institute of Social Science and Concept Pub. Company. 2000.

H.R. Jadav: *Village Development Planning*, New Delhi: Concept Publishing Company Private Limited, 2009.

Hari Prasad Chetri: *Panchayati Raj System and Development Planning: The Case of Sikkim*, New Delhi: R.K. Books, 2008.

I. Mohamad: *Panchayati Raj: System and Rural Development*, New Delhi: D.P.S. Publications, 2011.

IIED: *A trainers guide for participatory inquiry*. London: Sustainable Agriculture Programme, International Institute for Environment and Development, 1994.

IIED: *Participatory Learning and Action: A Trainers Guide* London: Sustainable Agriculture Programme, International Institute for Environment and Development 1995.

Institute of Rural Management: *Status of Panchayats Report—An Independent Assessment*, Anand: IRMA, 2008.

Iyer, K.G. Land as the vital resource with the panchayats. In Amitava Mukherjee, ed. *Decentralization, Panchayats in the Nineties*, pp. 108-127. New Delhi, Vikas 1994.

J. Chathukulam *et. al.*: "Five years of participatory planning in Kerala: Rhetoric and Reality" *Economic and Political Weekly*, 37 (49): 4917-4926, 2002

Jaysri Ray Choudhury: *Development and Regional Planning,* Sangam Books Ltd.

Jean Dreze and Amartya Sen. *India: Development and Participation*, New Delhi: Oxford University Press, 2002.

Jos C. Raphael: *Decentralised Planning In India*, 2000.

K. Rajesh: *Institutions and practices: A study of the People's Planning Campaign and the Kerala Development Programme,* PhD thesis submitted to the Institute of Development Studies, University of Mysore, Bangalore:

Kang, S.S. "Decentralization and tourism development: The Kerala experience". In, report of the International Colloquium on Regional Governance and Sustainable Development in Tourism-driven Economies, pp. 101-116. Quintana Roo, Mexico, 20-22 February 2002.

K. Sivachithappa: *Micro Level Planning for Regional Development : Indian Experience,* Adhyayan Publishers, 2011.

Kuldip Mathur: *Panchayati Raj: Oxford India Short Introductions,* New Delhi; Oxford, 2013.

L.C. Jain: *Decentralisation and Local Governance*, Hyderabad: Orient Longman Private Limited, 2005.

LBSNA & FAO. 1995. District planning: Lessons from India–Planning guide, training materials for agricultural planning, Mussoorie: Lal Bahadur Shastri National Academy of Administration, and Rome: FAO, Agricultural Policy

T.T.M. Issac & Harilal, K.N. : "Planning for empowerment: people's campaign for decentralized planning in Kerala". *Economic and Political Weekly*, XXXII (1&2): 4-11, 1997.

Tharakan, P.K.M.: "When the Kerala model of development is historicised: A chronological perspective", Kochi: Centre for Socio-Economic and Environment Studies, *Working Paper No. 19,* 2008.

UNDP*: Manual, Integrated Village Planning and Development, Lessons from Hiware Bazar, Gangadevapalli, Ramachandrapuram and Piplantri Gram Panchayats,* New Delhi: Ministry of Panchayati Raj, undated.

United Nations Asia Pacific Development Institute: *Local Level Planning and Rural Development: Alternative Strategies*, New Delhi: Concept Publishing Co., 2006.

V. Annamalai: *Role of gram panchayats in managing common property resources for the benefit of rural poor: a study in Karnataka and Haryana.* Case Studies Series 10, Hyderabad, India, National Institute of Rural Development, 2000.

Victoria A. Beard, Faranak Miraftab, Christopher Silver (eds.): *Planning and Decentralization, Contested Spaces for Public Action in the Global South,* London: Routledge.

Y.K. Alagh: *Panchayati Raj and Planning in India: Participatory Institutions and Rural Roads*, Mimeo, 2005.

Index